DATE DUE

NO 1 '63	MAY 1 8 1978		
DE 20 '63	NOV 2 1983		
JUL 10			
OC 23 '64			
AP 25 '67			
OC 20 '67			
FE 2 '68			
AG 8 '69			
NO 11 '69			
NO 25 '69			
AP 7 '70			
OC 19 '71			
NO 16 '71			
DE 7 '71			
FE 12 '74			
MY 20 '75			
NOV 11 1975			

Katherine H. Read

SCHOOL OF HOME ECONOMICS, OREGON STATE COLLEGE

W. B. Saunders Company

PHILADELPHIA AND LONDON

The Nursery School

A Human Relationships Laboratory

THIRD EDITION

To Greg and Jay

*as they start on their
Nursery School adventures*

Preface to the Third Edition

Interest in nursery education is growing steadily. The last decade has seen a greater public acceptance of nursery schools. In the nursery school itself there is more flexibility and imagination in program planning, more appreciation of the needs of individuals, especially of children with handicaps, more consideration of the problems of parents.

In spite of this progress, much remains to be accomplished. Nursery schools, good ones, will not be available for many children until there is much more public support for them than at present, with more adequate salaries for nursery school teachers and better training opportunities. Lack of support reflects the lack of real understanding of the function and the value of the nursery school for children.

The need for more knowledge is pressing, but we are not yet making use of all the knowledge we have. Those who have been students in a laboratory school or those who have had children in a nursery school will need to be active in giving support as citizens in their communities. They will be aware of what good nursery schools and day care centers can offer to families.

In this revision I am again indebted to Mary Alice Russell for the perceptive pictures she has taken in nursery school settings. I also wish to express my appreciation to Gertrude Chittenden for her helpful suggestions for revision. I continue to be grateful to the children, the parents and the college students who have shared experiences in learning with me.

Katherine H. Read

Preface to the Third Edition

Preface to the First Edition

The real need we all have to understand human behavior is perhaps more pressing today than ever before. This book has grown out of the experience of some years of teaching college students, using the nursery school as a laboratory. As I have worked with students, I have found them eagerly seeking to understand behavior—the behavior of children, of other adults, and their own behavior. In the nursery school they usually discover more meaning in what the child does than they had been aware of previously. They begin to see new meanings in the behavior of the adults around them and—a more difficult perception—in their own behavior.

Throughout this book I have used the word "she" in referring to students because at present most of the students in the nursery school laboratory are women. We may hope that someday this will no longer be true. There should be as many men as women using the nursery school as a laboratory to learn about people and to prepare for that most important profession, parenthood.

A student recently remarked, "I'm glad that the nursery school course is required for I would never have taken it otherwise." I confess to misgivings myself when the course became a "required" one for us. It is much pleasanter to teach an "elective." But there may be advantages for a teacher in being faced with the challenge of helping all students discover something of the meaning which lies back of overt behavior, not just helping those students who have already recognized its importance. In facing and trying to understand resistances, the teacher grows in insight and in ability to accept differences herself. I have learned as much from my students as they have from me, I am sure.

I have learned as much, too, from the parents of the children whom I have known. If anyone of them thinks that he or she can recognize himself or his child in these pages, it is because there is so much in common in the behavior of all children and all parents. The same problems face us all and many of us find the same kinds of solutions. There is a universality about being a parent which makes it easy to identify with others. Who hasn't known a resistant child, an angry child, a tired child, a frightened child or an unhappy child? We have all tried to help children like these. We have met all this behavior in the same child!

The names used in this book are not the real names of the children except in cases where credit is given for literary achievements. Details have been changed to avoid identification. But they are real children and they have been my best teachers. I am grateful to them for what they have taught me.

One of the satisfactions in any profession comes from contacts with other interested professional people. I have been fortunate in my colleagues and have gained immeasurably from work with them. Each has opened up new avenues of growth for me—Ethel Kawin, Harriet O'Shea, Catherine Landreth, Herbert Conrad, Sara Prentiss, Miriam Wiggenhorn, Jean Haskell, and many others—some of whom I have met only through their writings.

Time spent in the nursery school is, of course, not enough to ensure learning. There must be constant interpretation and evaluation, so that the learning which takes place will be sound—not just repetition of error or strengthening of misconception. The nursery school laboratory of necessity makes heavy demands on its staff and on the people or the institution that supports it. It serves significant purposes and yields a rich return in understanding when its demands are adequately met.

KATHERINE H. READ

Contents

III

Understanding Feelings in Areas Where Feelings Are Strong

IV

Observing Individual Growth and Guiding It

I

Getting Acquainted
with the Laboratory

1

Introducing
the People

THE NURSERY SCHOOL IS A HUMAN RELATIONSHIPS LABORATORY

The nursery school is a place where young children learn as they play with materials and share experiences with other children and with teachers. It is also a place where adults can learn as they observe children and participate with them. It is a laboratory for the study of human relations. As students we can use the nursery school laboratory for learning about people.

We need to understand people, including ourselves, if we are to be successful as parents or teachers, or in whatever profession we may follow. Relationships with people are important to all of us. They are so important that we need to use laboratories such as the nursery school to learn all we can about what people are like and how they live together.

Fig. 1. They enjoy each other as they play.

What is the nursery school laboratory like? What kind of people will we meet there? What kinds of relationships will we observe? How will we learn from observing or participating? What do we really want to learn about people which will help us in our own living?

As we ask questions such as these, we are aware that most of us are not familiar with this kind of laboratory. Few people have had much opportunity to learn about children as people as they work with them, or to learn about their own responses to children.

How Will Students Feel in This Laboratory?

We might start out by looking at how a student will feel as she starts working in the nursery school laboratory. An understanding of our own feelings will give us a better understanding of the children and their feelings.

In going into a nursery school laboratory, students are going into a new situation. They will be expected to do some things when they are not certain of how to do them. They may not be sure of just what is expected, even if they have been in other nursery schools. They do not know these children or these teachers. They are not sure of what happens there. They do not know simple things such as where the paints are stored or where a mop is kept. Even though they are given directions and instructions and someone has showed them through the school, they are sure to find that they have forgotten or were not told something they really need to know.

Unexpected things keep happening, things no one prepared them for. Often what a student tries does not work out in the way she intended it. She may greet a child cheerfully and the child's response is, "Go away." She may follow the example of the teacher, using the same words in approaching a group, "It's time to put things away now," but she gets a different response. "We are not going to," the children say.

In addition, the student is not at all sure of what she is expected to do. Should she interfere when one child hits another? What is she supposed to do? Should she just watch? Should she ask a teacher? Should she try anything that occurs to her? The student is almost certain to feel uncomfortable and inadequate. Because she feels unsure of herself, she may become critical of all that she sees. She decides she would never let children behave like that! She may feel she dislikes the children or the teachers or the whole situation. She may, on the other hand, feel very discouraged with herself.

Students Can Expect to Feel Inadequate at First

All these responses are natural. In a new situation everyone has feelings of inadequacy. The important thing is to realize how we feel and something about why we feel as we do.

First of all, students can expect to feel inadequate when they begin their first experience in the nursery school and probably for some time after that. They cannot possibly be prepared for all that may happen. No one can give them instructions which will cover everything and certainly not in the time they may have had in preparation. Of course they will not feel sure of what is expected of them or what they are supposed to do. The teacher herself is not sure of that for she does not know them or what is possible for them.

What we can do about the feeling of being inadequate at this point is to feel comfortable about having it. We will be inadequate when we start, if we have something to learn, and we might as well accept this as a reality. It is all right to be inadequate when one begins a learning experience. No one should expect to know in the beginning what we hope will be learned in time. We do not need to expect it of ourselves.

There is a lot to learn and we hope to learn something. The more we have to learn, the more inadequate we really may be in the present situation. There is no need to fight against feeling inadequate or to deny the feeling. It is part of the experience. We might as well try to live as comfortably as we can with the feeling and enjoy our successes as we begin to have them.

Our Own Experience Here Helps Us
Understand the Experiences of Others

But we can learn something about people from these experiences. We know, because of recognizing our own feelings, that people who are unsure of themselves in a situation are likely to be critical, to pass rather harsh judgments, to be defensive or resist or maybe withdraw. Perhaps we will recognize and be more understanding of these reactions in others.

We can be sure that the children who are entering nursery school are meeting a situation which is new for them. They will feel uncertain and often defensive. If we remember these things, we will understand their resistances, their withdrawals or their attacks. "Go away, I don't like you," may be an expression of great insecurity. We are likely to respond differently when we understand.

Our own experience will give us more insight into the responses of others, both children and adults. We will be capable of more empathy or feeling with others as we identify our own feelings. In doing this we have already begun to use the nursery school as a laboratory.

In doing this we may also be able to help children in learning to understand themselves and others. We can interpret to them the meaning of behavior as we come to understand it ourselves. Someone has pointed out that ". . . we should begin to teach psychology in the first year in school. . . . Children at that age can learn a great deal of sound psychology. For instance, psychology taught to small children, in terms of: What makes people mad? Why do people

throw temper tantrums? Why do people behave in this way or that?
might be very valuable."*

We Will Learn Most from the Children

Let us look at the children we may meet there.

The children form the core of our study. They are the people from
whom we will probably learn the most, not just because they are the
most active and the likeliest to be heard when one walks into a
school, but because they will show us most clearly how they feel.
They are people who have had only a limited number of experiences.
Their responses to situations are relatively simple and direct. They
act as they feel. When a child is thwarted in carrying out a purpose,
for example, he is likely to cry or kick or throw something. One child
may be more likely to cry and another to throw something in similar
circumstances, for patterns of behaving are already established. But

* Chisholm, Brock: Prescription for Survival, New York. Columbia University
Press, 1957, p. 81.

Fig. 2.   Cooperative effort in pulling a block of wood by the
rope into the boat.

these patterns are less influenced than those of the adult by such factors as fear of consequences. They express feeling more directly. The child has neither the capacity nor the inclination of the adult to modify his responses. When he is angry, he may yell at his mother or his teacher, "I don't like you. You go away." It isn't hard to identify the feeling back of these words!

We can learn from children for another reason. Their behavior changes rapidly. In a different environment or under different methods of handling, they may blossom forth with quite different ways of behaving. We have some check on what our handling is accomplishing by watching the children. How does one help a person feel more secure? How does one help a person gain social skills? We can test our attempts to find answers to important questions like these by the changes which take place in the behavior of children as we handle them in different ways or change their situation. The "proof of the pudding" lies in what the child does.

Watching children, we will see that they are surprisingly different in spite of their limited experience. Let's introduce some children so that we may feel acquainted and better able to recognize what may lie behind the behavior of other children with other names whom we will find in the nursery schools where we are working.

Jean, Who Has Lived under Favorable Conditions

Jean is a small, sturdy looking child. She is one of the younger children in the group, but she is independent and resourceful and plays with all the children. She entered the group several months after school had begun but she was soon acquainted with everyone and everything. Being the youngest in a family of four children may have helped her.

Jean appears to like people and trust them. She approaches other children easily and is not defensive in her responses to their approaches. If they reject her, she turns to something else. She is seldom rejected, however, for when she joins a group it is with a purpose in mind. She brings an idea or a new material. She learns quickly. She is primarily interested in activity and joins groups of active children where projects are going on.

At first certain boys were likely to hit her. When this happened, she cried loudly and went to the teacher for comforting. Then she returned to carry on with the same group. Soon she began to be sought after as a companion. The boys who had hit her in the beginning vied for her attention. She is matter-of-fact and impartial in playing with them. Her sympathy is apparent and intelligently given. For example, she took a child with a scratch to the first aid cabinet.

Jean has many interests. She loves music and although she is a vigorous, active child, she occasionally spends as much as half an hour listening to music. She paints, uses clay, builds with big blocks and is often busy in the housekeeping corner. She stands up for herself and will hit another child who tries to take from her. Her social skills are excellent and seem to reflect a very realistic appraisal of what other children are like. She solves her problems well, both with materials and people.

An interesting example of how she fitted herself into a new experience occurred on the second day she had lunch at school. She was not clear about what was expected at the table but she followed the teacher's directions and seemed to enjoy the experience very much. She took several additional servings of everything, including dessert. The dessert consisted of fruit and cookies. The children had helped make the cookies earlier in the morning. When Jean asked for another cookie, the teacher at her table replied, "You can go to the kitchen and ask Mrs. M for another cookie. I'm sure she has more there." The teacher was unaware that plans had been made to let each child take a cookie home after lunch. The teacher watched Jean go in the direction of the kitchen as she had indicated to the child. When the teacher glanced up two or three minutes later, she saw Jean going in the direction of the kitchen again but this time she had her coat on. For a moment the teacher was startled and then she realized what must have happened. The cook, when asked for a cookie, had told Jean, "You may have one when you have your coat on ready to go home." So Jean had trotted to the coat room, put on her coat and was returning. Adults make such queer requests! She was given her cookie and with it in her hand she went back to the coat room, removed her coat and returned to her place at the table and happily ate her cookie.

Jean could adjust even to demands as unusual as this one! She kept her purposes in mind and left other matters up to those who might be expected to know. She accepted things as they happened.

Fig. 3. They explore as they play. (H. Armstrong Roberts.)

Jean's confidence spills over to others. She takes care of herself, faces problems and feels comfortable. Others are more comfortable and confident and purposeful because of her presence. Her interest in music, for example, brought her in contact with another child, Keith, who was very passive and withdrawn. For this child listening to music seemed more like a retreat. He seemed afraid of experience and limited himself to music and stories. The teacher had not found a way to help him, but through his contacts with Jean he changed. He began to follow her, began to do what she did and even asserted himself. For example, he and Jean had been playing together one morning when Jean started to climb up the slide. Another boy followed her up saying to Keith, "Go away. You can't come up." Keith answered very loudly, "You can't go up. You'll have to go home." The child insisted, "You can't come up, Keith." Keith kept right on climbing and said in a determined way, "Yes, I can." When he was hit, he hit right back. The staff could hardly believe this was the timid child they had known earlier. Without actively leading, Jean is a strong force in the group.

Charles, Who Is Fighting to Find His Place

Charles is a rosy-cheeked, brown-eyed boy of three and a half. He comes running into the nursery school in the morning, greeting the teachers and the children with enthusiasm and plunging into activity. Everything catches his attention, a new book on the table, a bird's nest brought by one of the children, the pin on the teacher's dress, the garage of blocks that the children are building. Observed over one fifty-minute period, he engaged in more than thirty activities with a show of whole-hearted interest.

He is eager to join other children in whatever they are doing and makes many attempts to get others to join him. He directs any play that he is in with a flow of excellent language and a vigor and enthusiasm that overwhelm opposition. But the other children drift away from him or reject his advances, perhaps because he cannot brook opposition. He hits or bites when blocked or even when there is no apparent provocation. He is impulsive and quick so that it is difficult for the teachers to keep him from attacking others. He is constantly taking things from other children. If he sees someone using a tricycle, he immediately wants it. If he sees someone swinging, he wants to use the swing himself.

He has picked up many adult verbalizations which he understands only partially but he knows that words are often used to justify acts. "I want to swing," he cries as he sees Jill in the swing. "Why?" asks Jill reflectively. "Because I have to learn how," he answers her. He quickly gets on the tricycle that Bruce has left for a minute. When Bruce cries, "I want it," his answer is, "When people get off trikes, I have to get on and ride around." Usually he does not wait until people get off. When he is absent with one of his rare colds, Mary's comment is, "I'm glad. Now he won't bite me today."

His behavior often surprises the teachers as well as the children. One morning as he started to pour a drink, he said to the teacher cheerfully, "Do you know what I'm going to do?" To her negative reply, he answered, "I'm going to pour this water on the floor." He did just that before her startled eyes and immediately mopped it up willingly, becoming absorbed in watching the way it ran down the corridor, exclaiming, "The water doesn't wait for me."

His observations and his attack on problems reveal a superior intelligence. He loves books and listens to reading with sustained attention. He accepts adult suggestions readily and is quick to see their point. One gets the impression that he can see the value of constructive ways of managing people, but that his own feelings get in his way and are often more than he can manage. Eager for social contacts but carried away by his impulses, he appears genuinely sorry when he hurts another child.

Typical of Charles' behavior is the following incident. As he came on to the playground one morning he saw Bill on a tricycle. He ran to him, grasping the handle bars firmly and saying in a persuasive voice, "Give me your trike, Bill. I want to pull you." Bill made no move to give up the tricycle and Charles repeated the request several times in the same persuasive tone. Then still talking, he pushed Bill off and rode away, calling back, "I'll be right back, Billy. I'm only going to take a little ride." But Bill ran after him and grabbed for the tricycle. Charles hit him and the teacher had to intervene and help Bill recover his tricycle. Deprived of the tricycle, Charles threw himself on the ground, crying loudly. Suddenly he jumped up and ran to the shed where the toys were kept, calling to Bill to wait for him. He came out with another tricycle and rode off after Bill, trying vainly to get Bill to play with him.

The demands for adjustment have been heavy for Charles in his home. The family has moved many times. They have expected adult-like behavior from this little boy. He has been spanked, threatened, made to sit on a chair and reasoned with. His parents think he is a difficult child to manage. They appear to have little understanding about what a load their expectations have been for him or how often he has been confused about what is expected. A new baby at home has complicated the situation further. Again, his parents have not recognized what the coming of the baby has meant to Charles. They have succeeded in making him hide his feelings to such an extent that they report that "he adores his baby sister and is very sweet to her." His biting at nursery school is probably related to this situation at home.

Anxious to conform to adult standards and be accepted, eager for friendships with children but often meeting rejection here as with adults, with strong drives and confused feelings which are more than he can cope with constructively, Charles is very much in need of guidance and quite able to profit from it. He needs to be with people who will reduce the difficulties he has to face, who will give him suggestions for solving his problems acceptably, and who will interpret the needs of others to him. Bound to be a force in any group because of his intellectual capacity, his strong drives and physical vigor, he will be a damaging influence or an inspiring one, depending on the guidance he is given. With the qualities of a leader, he may go in either direction.

THE ADULTS

Jean and Charles are like some of the children whom we will meet in the nursery school. Now what about the adults who will be there? What are they like? How are they different from the children?

Adults are people with the same kinds of feelings as the children but they are likely to express their feelings less directly and less openly. Their patterns of response are modified by many experiences which have taught them to control and often to conceal their feelings even from themselves. An adult who is angry seldom hits or throws, but he or she may do the next job poorly or may criticize someone for no apparent reason or just do nothing. Many times the adult's responses are as inappropriate and unacceptable as the child's but they are usually harder to relate to their cause. Perhaps in part because they are patterns which have been in use a long time, they do not change as quickly.

But there is one difference between the child and the adult that gives the adult a real advantage. The adult has the capacity to be objective—to study and analyze his own feelings and behavior. Because of this capacity to be objective he can modify responses to make them more appropriate as he understands them. He can do this himself, using such sources of help as experiences in a nursery school or conferences with a trained counselor. In various ways he can gain insight into what his responses mean and how they may serve his purposes more effectively.

We Need to Understand Ourselves

Probably the most important adult each of us will meet in the nursery school is ourself. We all need to understand ourselves better. It is important for us to understand ourselves if we are to understand others because every one of us is alike in many respects. It is important because our feelings will influence the relationships we maintain with other people.

What are we all like? What do we know about ourselves and others?

All of Us Were Children Once

In the first place all of us were children once and we can never escape that fact. What happened to us then still influences what we are like now. Some of us may wish that the things that happened to us in childhood had been different. Others may feel grateful on the whole for the experiences that were theirs. But whatever happened still matters tremendously. That's why we can understand ourselves and other adults better by trying to understand what children are like and watching the effect on them of the things that happen. That's why we are interested in learning something about behavior, so that we may act with a degree of wisdom when we ourselves may be responsible for what happens to infants and young children.

For one thing, we are probably still being influenced by the fact that we started out tiny and helpless, dependent on the adults around us. The way our needs were met during this period of dependency is still affecting what we do. If we lived with people on whom it was good to be dependent because of the warmth and abundance of their giving, if we were fed when we felt hungry, played with and loved when we wanted attention, we were *satisfied* during this period of dependency. If the adults around us were themselves satisfied people who did not try to prolong needlessly our dependence, we were free to become independent when we were ready. Growing up under conditions like these, we are now neither fighting against being dependent nor seeking reassurance by demanding more protection than we need.

People who have had this kind of background are likely to find it easier to be loving and giving when they are grown. Their response to children is likely to be warm and spontaneous, for they are free of the need to be babied themselves and they can accept the dependency of children without fostering it. They will not be disturbed by the necessity of depending on more experienced people for direction in a new situation like the nursery school. They are independent but they do not distrust dependency.

Others of us may have lived with people on whom being dependent was not such a pleasant experience. We were denied food when we felt hungry, and left to "cry it out" when we felt helpless and alone. There may have been many reasons for such handling by parents, such as ignorance of the real needs of infants, poor health, too many responsibilities, or the influence of the parents' own childhood experiences. Under this handling, however, we may have fought against being dependent, finding it hard later to accept the necessity of being dependent under any circumstances. Or we may have continued to seek to have our "dependency needs" met by trying to be more dependent than we needed to be, as though to make up for what we didn't have earlier.

For most of us the pattern was not all one way or the other. We had some poor handling along with the good, or some good handling along with the poor. There are still times when we resent having to be dependent and times when we want to be dependent. Only the ratio of frequency in which these feelings appear differs for us.

All of Us Were Members of Families

Another factor influencing our behavior is the position each one of us held in our families. Some of us were only children; others were oldest or youngest or any number of middle positions. The position meant different things in different families. Families are likely to be

Fig. 4. They enjoy group experiences.

competitive places. Children want attention and compete for it—from their parents or from each other. Some are more successful, others less successful, in getting it. The rivalries and hostilities that people have experienced in the family situation influence them in group relationships later. In school, one person may only feel comfortable when she is getting the major share of attention in class, another may envy and resent the attention others receive but do nothing more than blame the teacher and retreat from competing just as she did in her family. A person with a more favorable family situation may feel free to claim attention when she wants it but not to be disturbed by the conflicting demands of others. In the nursery school, for example, a student who happens to be the youngest in her family may identify herself with the baby in the school and resent seeing her teased. She will want to see the aggressor punished just as she wanted to see punishment given to those who teased her in her childhood. Under the guise of wanting to be "fair" she may try to impose a "justice" that really belongs to a situation from her own past from which she has not yet succeeded in untangling herself. Recognizing patterns of past feelings which still exist gives a person a better chance to handle her own reaction intelligently.

All of Us Met Frustration in the Growing-up Process

Let us take one more example of the way our childhood patterns enter into how we feel and behave in the nursery school or anywhere else. As a result of the frustrations that are an inevitable part of the growing-up process, we all have feelings of resentment and hostility which we will handle better if we can recognize them. It is needless, and may be damaging, to try to deny these feelings. We all have them because we were babies once. The baby is subject to many limitations. He can't reach the toy he dropped; he trips and falls when he tries to walk; he isn't allowed to touch many interesting objects. He may be subjected to toilet training which interferes with his play and restricts his activity. There are many necessary and perhaps many unnecessary limitations in the child's world. Frustration rouses resentful, often hostile, feelings. How much hostility a child feels depends somewhat on whether the adults in his world help to minimize the inevitable frustrations or aggravate and increase them by a mistaken idea of "disciplining" him. If the necessary limitations are imposed with gentleness by a comfortable, confident, loving person, they will not rouse much resentment, but if they are imposed by someone who is cross and confused and struggling with his or her own feelings of hostility, they will rouse a great deal of negative feeling in the child. He will want to fight and hurt in return and these feelings will spill out in many situations, against anyone who interferes with him.

A child finds it easier to accept restriction and meet frustration if he feels warmth and love in the person limiting him. Few of us, however, have been fortunate enough to have been handled all the time by people who have tried to decrease the feelings of hostility and aggressiveness which are part of the growing-up process. Growth demands some aggressiveness, but most of us feel too much resentment and our feelings spill out in inappropriate ways in too many situations. When these negative feelings spill out inappropriately, they may make us feel guilty and afraid without knowing what's wrong. They may keep us from learning things which we may really want to learn.

All of Us Tend to Resist Changing

A characteristic which we all have in common is that of resistance to change. In spite of ourselves we find all kinds of reasons for avoiding real change in our thinking and in our behavior. New ways of behaving, no matter what their merit, are rejected until we manage to handle our resistances. The more insecure we are, the less likely we are to feel that we can afford to change, for change involves uncertainties. Even a too-ready acceptance of a new point of view may mean only a superficial acceptance, in itself a defense against any real change. It is important for us to be aware of this universal tendency to resist the new, the different, so that it will not block us when we try to profit from the thinking of others. We must assert our right to use experience, whether it is a morning in the nursery school, a discussion period, or the reading of a book, to reach sounder conclusions that we held before the experience. We must try not to be dominated by mere resistance to change.

We All Have Feelings That Need Draining Off

A child often expresses negative feelings by hitting or biting or being mean to animals. He probably also finds some outlet for them when he plays in mud, bangs, pounds or makes a lot of noise. It's good for him to have opportunities to drain off such feelings in harmless ways—for they will come out somehow. We all need to find avenues for draining off destructive feelings through vigorous activity or through some satisfying expression in art or music or in spilling things out to a friend or in participating in something in which we feel adequate. When we have such avenues, we keep our negative feelings down to manageable proportions.

Identifying Our Negative Feelings Is Important

If negative feelings are not drained off, they may come out later in ways that are difficult to identify. Feeling very strongly about a thing, for example, is an indication that it's serving as an outlet for extra emotion—especially if most people do not seem to feel as strongly about the same thing. It may be a good thing to stop and ask oneself, "Why do I feel so strongly about this thing?" We can direct strong feeling more safely if we understand why we feel as we do, and the likelihood of our meeting the needs of the child is increased if we understand our own needs and feelings.

For example, a student finds herself feeling very indignant that a child is allowed to play with his food at the table and even leave some of it uneaten. She may feel this way because she was not allowed to play with her food when she was a child. Now that she has accepted adult patterns, identified herself with the adults in this situation, all the resentment that she felt at being denied the delightful experience of playing with food as well as tasting it is turned into her feeling about seeing a child permitted to do what she was not allowed to do, what she was forced to consider "bad." It is not easy to take on values, and we often pay a heavy emotional price when they are forced on us too early. We can't bear to see others getting by cheaply!

We won't discuss here whether a child should be allowed to play with food or not. We are only pointing out that it is important to be able to decide this on the basis of its meaning for the child and whether it's a good thing for him, instead of on the basis of our own emotional conflicts. In other words, it's important to be able to identify the emotional forces which lie behind our reasoning.

We Need to Accept All Kinds of Feelings

It is essential for all of us in the nursery school laboratory not to be ashamed or guilty about the feelings which we have. We've been taught so often that we must be "good" that we may be afraid to face the negative feelings that exist in us. They go unrecognized and interfere with our thinking more than they would if we had accepted them.

As adults we can afford to look at our feelings because we have more capacity for managing them than we had as children. As children, we felt strongly and our feelings overwhelmed us. Anger turned into a violent temper tantrum, perhaps. We may have felt guilty and afraid, and we may not have had much help from the adults around us at this point. What we needed were adults who acted calmly and firmly and who helped us keep our behavior within limits but who were not shocked by our behavior and did not act aggressively toward us, frightening us further. Instead of being calmly reassuring, the adults around us may have become emotional themselves. They may have punished us and made us afraid and guilty about our behavior. As children we could not face our own feelings without the safety of supporting, accepting adults. Now that we are grown, we have less need to feel so afraid. We are not so helpless as we were as children. We have more ability to handle feelings when we know that they exist.

It is also essential to be aware of the ambivalence of our feelings. Feelings are usually mixed. Feeling comfortable or uncomfortable, enjoying and not enjoying, loving and hating are all mixed together although we may be aware of only the feeling which is strongest at the moment. We may be surprised at sudden changes in feeling because we have not been aware that other feelings were present all the time. We may want to learn more about people and yet resist learning. For example, we may like and dislike the same person and he in turn may have some of both kinds of feelings about us. We seldom feel all one way or all the other way about a person or an experience.

It is not for us to say whether people ought or ought not to feel and act as they do. We make very little progress when we blame or praise them or ourselves for the way they or we feel and act. We make progress when we try to understand why we behave as we do.

Getting angry or discouraged with ourselves or anyone else is usually unprofitable. It is tremendously profitable to recognize that we can do something to change our ways of feeling and acting if we are willing to try. Sometimes resistance is the result of childhood experiences which occurred repeatedly. Recognizing the source of her resistance, a student can handle it more appropriately, saying to herself, "I don't have to feel and behave as I did when my mother—or my big sister—or my father—was bossing me. I'm no longer a child. I'm grown up, and I'm free to use a suggestion if I think it's a good one or to reject it if I think it's a poor one." She can free herself from the control which old childhood patterns may still be exerting over her in adult life.

Everyone Has Problems to Face

There are certain problems which the members of each group of adults in the nursery school have in common. *Students,* as they start using the nursery school as a laboratory for learning about human behavior, have the problem of facing and accepting the almost inevitable feelings of inadequacy which a new situation brings. In later chapters we will suggest possible ways of handling these feelings after they have been accepted, but they will exist to some extent for everyone in the beginning of the experience. *Teachers* have the common problem of making the skills and understanding they have achieved available to students while maintaining a favorable situation for the children in the school. Their professional growth includes deepening their understanding of ways of meeting the needs of students as well as of children. *Parents* whose children are in nursery school face the problem of being able to leave the child free to take the step toward greater independence which going to school represents. Their confidence in what they themselves are as parents, the degree of security which past experience has brought them, and the way they have handled the resistance which we all feel toward change, will play a part in the ease or difficulty they feel in becoming parents. *Other adults* in the school also have problems in facing and adjusting their own needs to the needs of the school. The cook must find satisfaction in what she is accomplishing and in sharing in the goals of the school. The janitor must be able to understand and accept the needs of the children if he is to see his job as one of making the school a good place for children instead of merely a good place for a janitor.

We Can Learn from All the People in a Nursery School

The whole school is thus full of human beings who must understand and accept their own feelings and those of the members of
other groups if the situation is to be a constructive one for children.
From all these people we can learn things which will help us understand human relationships better. Using our experience in the
nursery school laboratory, we may become better parents or teachers
or people ourselves because we have grown in understanding human
beings.

Some of the things that we will learn about ourselves and others
will be confusing and disturbing. Human behavior is complex and
difficult to understand. It will be important to talk things over with
someone. Certain questions may be brought up for discussion in the
group where other people may be helped to clarify these same feelings in themselves. Some less clear or more personal matters may be
talked over with a teacher whose longer experience has added to
her understanding of behavior.

PROJECTS

1. In your first observation periods in the nursery school, learn the
   names of the children, and note as much as you can that will help
   you identify them such as anything unusual about their behavior
   or appearance. Obtain information about the length of time each
   one has attended nursery school and something about their family experiences such as whether they are the oldest or youngest,
   whether they have moved from one house or town to another,
   and so on. Learn the names of the staff members also.
2. As you observe the children in the group, see how many patterns
   of behavior you can identify. For example, are there:
   (a) Children who seem to trust adults?
   (b) Children who have many interests and engage in a variety
       of activities through a morning?
       Children who seem to limit their activities and interests?
       (Distinguish here between a long period of sustained inter-
       est in one activity vs. continued play in one activity which
       seems more automatic than purposeful, more like a retreat
       than an absorbing interest.)
   (c) Children who combine materials in unusual ways, engage

freely in dramatic play, enjoy creative, often messy materials?

Children who are conventional in their use of materials, seldom or never engage in messy play, or seldom use more creative types of materials or carry on much dramatic play?

(d) Children who seem quite dependent on others, who follow a teacher around, or frequently ask for help, or follow another child almost constantly?

Children who appear very independent, going to a teacher for help only when it is really needed, playing alone as well as with others?

(e) Children who seem to like many children and approach them freely?

Children who seem to avoid approaching children?

3. Make a list of the things which children do which you dislike— the things which children do which make you want to step in and do something about their behavior immediately. Then make a list of the things which children do which you approve of or which you enjoy seeing them do. Keep both of these lists to look over later.

REFERENCES

1. Biber, Barbara: Teacher Education in Mental Health. Orthopsychiatry and the School. Edited by Morris Krugman, New York, American Orthopsychiatric Association, Inc., 1958, pp. 169-173.
2. Black, Irma S.: The People in Nursery School. Child Study, Winter 1949-1950.
3. Brody, Sylvia: Theory and Research in Child Development: Implications for Nursery School Teachers. Journal of Nursery Education, Winter 1959, Vol. 14, No. 2, pp. 3-13.
4. Childhood Education, May 1954 issue on Understanding Ourselves and Others.
5. Chisholm, Brock: Can People Learn to Learn to Know Each Other? New York, Harper & Bros., 1958.
6. Feldwon, Yonata: What Is the Real Meaning of "Acceptance"? Child Study, Spring 1958, Vol. 35, No. 2, pp. 20-23.
7. Fraiberg, Selma: The Magic Years, New York, Scribners, 1959.
8. Hymes, James L.: Teachers Listen, the Children Speak. New York, State Society for Mental Health, Rev. 1954.
9. Menninger, William C.: Self-Understanding—a First Step in Understanding Children. Chicago, Science Research Associates, 1951.
10. Rasey, Marie, and Menge, J. W.: What We Learn from Children. New York, Harper & Bros., 1956, Ch. 5.
11. Stone, Dena: Children and Their Teachers. Tales told out of Kindergarten. New York, Twayne Publishing Co., 1957.

2

Describing the
Nursery School

We expect to use the nursery school as a laboratory for learning about human behavior so that we may be more understanding in our relationships with people. If we are to see meaning in the experiences that human beings may have there, we must know something about the nursery school itself.

What is a nursery school? Who are the children and what is the program offered there? Why are there nursery schools? How did they develop and what is their place in the world today?

For our purpose it will be sufficient to give a very brief definition of what we mean by a nursery school. Many excellent references exist describing the organization and equipment of nursery schools in detail. They can be used by those who are concerned with establishing and maintaining a school. Our concern is understanding human behavior with the nursery school as our laboratory. We need only a background for the purposes of our discussion.

What Is a Nursery School?

The nursery school as we will define it is a school serving the needs of two-, three- and four-year-old children by offering them experiences adapted to what is now known about the growth needs at these age levels. It shares with parents the responsibility for promoting sound growth in a period when growth is rapid and important, just as the elementary school shares this responsibility with parents of the elementary school age child.

MANY FACTORS ARE CONSIDERED IN A GOOD NURSERY SCHOOL PROGRAM

The kind of experience a child has in a nursery school depends on the number of children in the group, the teacher-pupil ratio, the age range within a group, the length of the school day, the training and experience of the staff, the physical setup, etc. The good nursery school will give careful attention to all these factors. We will consider them briefly because they are related to our concept of a nursery school.

The Number of Children in a Group

In a good nursery school the number of children in any group will not be large. Space arrangements, the ages of the children, the experience of the staff, will be among the factors determining the exact numbers. There will usually be less than twenty children in a group, for large groups create strains and reduce the contribution which the school can make to individuals. There will be at least one teacher to every eight or ten children. Every group, no matter how small, will have two adults present all the time. A well-staffed school may have three teachers with eighteen or twenty children, for example, while a school with a smaller number of children may be well staffed with one trained, experienced teacher and two less experienced assistants. Young children profit from group experience only if they can receive individual care when they need it. The school makes a significant contribution to parents and children only when it is adequately staffed.

Length of the School Day

The length of the nursery school day varies in different schools. The child gains most from school experience when it supplements his home experience. Three or four hours a day spent in school serve this purpose in the case of most nursery school age children. Some young children spend a longer period of the day in school because their mothers are working. In such cases the school must plan to provide more of the experiences which we would like to see children find in their own homes.

Rest and Eating

Naps or rest periods are individual rather than group affairs and can usually be managed better at home than at school. Eating, on the other hand, has its social aspects. Five meals a week, eaten with a group of other children, make an excellent experience for a child. It is often enough to overcome a host of problems which may have centered around eating at home. The noon meal should be part of the nursery school experience when possible. It has real values for a

Fig. 5. Ready for nursery school experience.

Fig. 6.   Lunch is a quiet time. (H. Armstrong Roberts.)

child. A former nursery school child was asked by an interested adult whether he liked nursery school, kindergarten or grade school best. He thought for a minute and then he replied, "Nursery school—because they fed me there."

Ages and Range in Age

The question of what the ages and the range in age of the children are in a good nursery school is a difficult one to answer because chronological age is not the only measure of maturity. Other things such as the variety of experience which a child has had affect his readiness to attend a nursery school. The best evidence that we have at present indicates that most children are ready for nursery school when they are around the age of three years. They seem to need three years in which to "live out" the period of dependency on parents, to achieve sufficient security in the home and with their parents to be ready to belong in a school group and to identify with adults outside the home. Taking this step too soon may distort growth just as much as failing to take it when the time is ripe.

Every mother will, of course, see in her child an eagerness to be with other children long before the child is three. This readiness can be met by informal experiences with children of the same age, by visiting or having a visitor for an hour or more. These informal experiences prepare the child for regular, sustained group experiences later. Few groups at present are planned to meet the needs of two-year-olds. The small size of the group into which a two-year-old can fit himself, the short day and the amount of individual care he needs, make the program an expensive one if it is to be a good one.

Some schools are providing group experiences for two-year-olds in small groups consisting of from four to six children who may meet together once or twice a week for an hour or two while their mothers remain with them. The real satisfaction the children feel in playing beside other children of the same age and the benefits of the experiences of physical contacts with others, sharing with them, and exploring a rich environment are great. It is likely that more schools will experiment with offering two-year-olds an experience adapted to their needs when possible as a step in preparation for more sustained group experiences.

In most nursery schools the age range within the group will be relatively limited so that the program can be more easily adapted to the needs of the children who make up the group. When children of widely different ages are together, the needs of one age level are likely to be sacrificed to the other although individual members may profit from occasional contacts with children of other ages. Even experienced teachers may find it easier to meet the needs of three-year-olds and four-year-olds if they are in separate groups with flexibility as to the age of "graduation" from groups. Development is so rapid during the preschool period that a difference of a few months makes a significant difference in maturity.

There is some evidence that a narrow age range in a group may increase competitiveness among the children and offer them less chance for learnings which come from being with children who are younger and older. Unless the situation is unusually favorable, however, that is with well-trained staff members and an adequate physical setup, it is probably wise to keep the age range within the limit of not more than a year and a half at most.

Somewhere between the ages of four and one half and five the nursery school child develops into the kindergarten child. His interests become more sustained and his capacity for group play increases. He is ready for kindergarten and the community needs to have a kindergarten ready for him to enter. Incidentally, a good kindergarten is also an excellent laboratory in which to study human behavior. Almost all our discussion might be applied as well to a kindergarten as to a nursery school.

The Program Is a Flexible One

With this definition of factors to be considered in a good nursery school, we will turn to the kind of program which a nursery school offers children. We will suggest here only the activities and the setting of the nursery school, leaving the discussion of the significance these have for the people in the school to later chapters.

Respect for individual difference is the basis for planning a nursery school program. Following this principle means a flexible program, with little activity in which everyone participates at the same time. Because the nursery school offers this kind of program, it gives us the chance to study individual behavior.

What Does a Typical Program Include?

For every child the morning starts with health inspection by the teacher or nurse. While the parent waits, the teacher or nurse will check the child's throat, his nose and the condition of his skin. She may ask the parent about what she observes and the parent will take this opportunity to pass on pertinent information about the child; for example, the fact that he went to bed late the night before and may be more tired than usual. If the teacher finds an inflamed throat or "runny" nose or other symptoms of illness, she will send the child home with the parent for further observation. Both parent and teacher are responsible for protecting the children against any possible exposure to infection. The morning health inspection is the occasion when they pool their opinions about the child's health, but the decision as to whether the child can remain at school is made by the teacher or nurse.

After the health inspection, which takes place before the child enters and comes in contact with other children, children may be offered a drink of water. Children need to drink plenty of liquids and they may be encouraged to do this if a pitcher and cups are ready as they enter.

When the children first arrive, they usually like to spend some time outdoors unless they are chilled or fatigued by a long trip to school. Children are fresh and full of energy in the first part of the morning. They are dressed for outdoor play when they arrive. Because the early morning is the least sunny part of the day, it may be important to make sure that this is not the only time the children spend outside. The amount of time that a child spends outdoors will, of course, depend in part on the weather. It will also depend on the child's vigor and activeness and perhaps on the way he is dressed. The more time a child can spend outdoors, the better the experience is for him. The teacher may encourage outdoor play by taking equipment outside, such as housekeeping materials, or by setting up an easel in a suitable spot out of the glare of the sun, or by bringing a record player out for some music. She may take small groups for a walk. Outdoor activities like raking leaves in the fall or digging in the spring are usually seized on eagerly when someone sets an example. Good outdoor equipment to make the play yard an interesting place encourages children to spend more time outside. Many

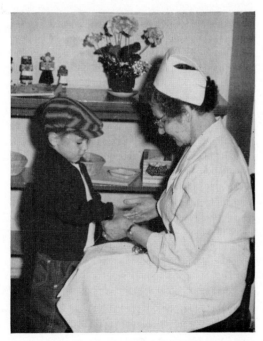

Fig. 7. Health inspection.

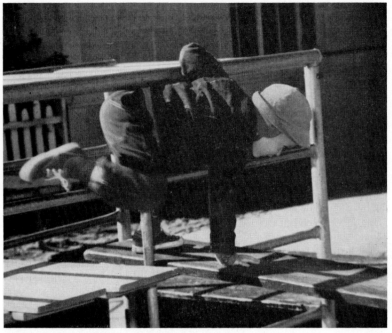

Fig. 8. Active play in individual ways.

children who are active and suitably clothed and whose interests at the moment are largely along motor lines, will play outdoors most of the time when the weather permits. They will gain from this if the outdoor environment is rich and stimulating.

In a good nursery school program each child will have the opportunity for quiet play as well as vigorous play. He will find art media available for self-expression and the chance for experiences with literature, music and science. Social experiences will, of course, be part of his other experiences. For each child the sequence of the day's events will differ. We will try to describe the pattern of events by following a hypothetical child through a day. His program might be something like this.

Let Us Follow a Hypothetical Child Through a Day's Program

Our hypothetical child arrives with his mother. After inspection and a drink he runs outdoors and plays for half an hour, riding a tricycle vigorously for awhile and then joining a group in hauling the building blocks to a corner of the playground to make a building. All the children on the playground share in working on this project for a time. A swing and a climb on the jungle gym complete the cycle of outdoor activity for our child.

He comes inside and takes off his outside wraps with very little help. Then he uses the toilet and runs into the playroom where he is accepted by two girls who are playing in the doll corner. He joins them and takes on the role of "father." He sweeps busily; he wheels the doll buggy around; he converses over the toy telephone about an evening engagement. Then the group has trouble over who is to use the iron, and he loses interest. He turns to painting at the easel and grows absorbed in his painting. He is a child who seems very sensitive to color. He paints large areas with vivid color, covering the paper. His painting on a second sheet of paper is quite similar to that on his first. In a businesslike way he removes his finished paintings and puts them away to dry. Relaxed and content, he leaves the easel and goes to the table for a cup of fruit juice which is served at the end of the first hour in school. He finishes his juice quickly and returns his cup to the tray. Then he joins a group who are

Fig. 9. Looking for worms.

Fig. 10. They play actively together.

marching to music which the teacher is playing on the piano. Our child tries the drum and then the bells as he marches. When the marching stops, he stays with a group around the piano who have begun to sing with the teacher.

Soon he notices that some children are outside and runs and gets his wraps, needing some help with his boots. The children outdoors are busily engaged in digging, each in his separate hole, some filling pans and some transferring the dirt to a big pile. They comment to each other as thoughts occur to them. They have occasional conflicts, most of which are settled without help from the teacher nearby, because they are all satisfied in their activity and are enjoying being together. Someone finds a worm and the teacher explains how the worm eats and digs. By the time the group begins to grow weary, it's almost noon. The teacher steers them inside to get cleaned up in time to hear a story before lunch.

When his wraps are off, our child uses the toilet again, spends some time enjoying washing his hands—and they really need washing! Then he joins the group who are just starting to listen to a story about fire engines. For nearly ten minutes they listen to stories and comment, sometimes relevantly and sometimes not, as the teacher listens, too, and then turns their attention back to the reading. By the time everyone has "toileted" and washed, it's time for fifteen minutes of rest on cots while the tables are being set for lunch. While the children are resting, they listen to victrola music. It's been a good morning and they are relaxed and comfortable.

Being active and vigorous our small boy enjoys most of his lunch. He dislikes squash but manages a bite on the teacher's suggestion and takes a second helping of everything else. He drinks more milk, too. As his interest in food wanes, he gets a little too sociable and tries for the attention of his quieter neighbor by poking him with a spoon. The teacher gives him her attention by asking him whether he finished digging his hole outdoors. He decides to do some more digging and finishes his meal quickly, runs to the coatroom and gets his wraps. He is outside digging when his father comes and he has to leave, a little reluctantly, to go home for his nap. The day at nursery school is over.

Other Children Follow Other Patterns

Another child's day might have been different. It might have included an excursion to the barns to see the new lambs on their wobbly legs or it might have included a walk down the street to watch the cement mixer and the men at work laying a new driveway. It might have included a trip to the fire station to see the shiny fire truck there and touch the carefully piled hoses and try on the fireman's hat.

Instead of painting at the easel as our hypothetical child did, another child might have rolled up his sleeves and plunged into finger paints, sweeping his arms across the paper or patting with his palms to music. Another child might have patted and squeezed the moist clay and rolled it into long "worms." His music experience might have consisted in playing on the piano himself while he turned the pages of his favorite song book or in listening to a visitor play a violin. His more vigorous play might have been done at the workbench, hammering an airplane into recognizable shape. For any of the children, the pattern of the day would have included a variety of experiences in living and exploring the world.

Let Us Follow a Hypothetical Teacher Through Her Day

We followed a hypothetical child through a morning. Now, let us follow a hypothetical teacher through her day.

Our teacher arrives early enough to meet her assistants and confer briefly with them about the schedule and special activities planned for the day. With their help she gets the school ready for the children. One of the assistant teachers mixes paint and sets up the easel ready for use. The other assistant goes outside to open the sandbox and the storage area so that the sand toys, wheel toys and blocks will be ready when the children arrive. Short handled shovels for digging stand near by with the bamboo rakes for raking the leaves which have begun to fall. Lengths of hose and rope hang on the storage shed wall along with two or three small ladders for the "fireman" play which has been going on during the last week or two.

Inside, the piano is open. Some books lie on the table in the reading corner. The housekeeping corner is in order and in the coat room there are clean towels and wash cloths on the hooks. The teacher is near the entrance when the first child comes in with his parent. She sits in a low chair near the entrance and on the table beside her is a small flashlight for inspecting throats, along with the roll book where she checks the children's names as they come. She has put a bowl with branches of bright colored fall foliage on the table. The child who has just arrived comes forward with mouth wide open for his throat inspection. The teacher looks inside, using her flashlight, notes his healthy skin color and listens to his story of how the family car almost didn't start this morning. She smiles at his father who says "good-by" to his small son and leaves on his way to the office. This first-comer announces he is going right outside to ride a tricycle and the teacher assures him that one of the other teachers is waiting for him there. Other children come, each meeting inspection in his characteristic way, many needing a minute to talk with the teacher or with other children before going on to an activity. Parents greet each other and chat as each waits for the teacher to check his or her child. One mother indicates that grandmother arrived last night and the extra excitement may show in her child's behavior. The children who wish to play inside pull off coats, caps and mittens and put them into their individual lockers. Mary pulls a chair close to the teacher. Mary has not been in school long and still feels safer when she is near the teacher, especially in the first few minutes after her mother has left. The teacher includes her in the conversation.

By the end of a half hour the children are all there except John who's on a trip with his parents and the twins whose mother telephoned earlier that she was keeping them at home since they seemed to have the first signs of a cold.

Now the doll corner is occupied. Two children are building an elaborate gas station with blocks. These two seem to like to build the first thing in the morning when it's usually quiet inside and they can be undisturbed. The teacher decides to go outside with Mary since more of the children are out there, leaving the assistant teacher to supervise inside and give help to the occasional child who comes in to use the toilet. Mary has taken a doll carriage out with her and they walk around together. The "gardeners" are busy with their shovels again in the digging area. Mary ends up joining a quieter group in the sandbox, filling cans and pans, and lining them up in rows on a board which serves as an oven. The assistant is watching closely the group who are digging since that area is crowded and the search for worms in the ground sometimes creates conflicts. It is the teacher who answers a request by a child in the swing, "Swing me." She sings as she pushes the child. Then she notices that Charles has been patiently puzzling over a pulley but can't get it to work. He needs help before his discouragement becomes greater than he can bear. The teacher helps him straighten it out. It works!

George wanders over to the teacher. He has grown tired of digging and may be feeling a need to escape from group pressures. The teacher suggests cleaning the rabbit hutch and getting fresh water and some rabbit pellets for "Mopsy." George likes the rabbit and undertakes the work with enthusiasm. The more active members of the group are now organizing a parade. Each one wants a wagon tied to a tricycle. There are not enough to go around. They need help with tying ropes and working out the dispute over the possession of the tricycles. The teacher is busy! Part of the settlement includes starting projects at the work bench for those who are without tricycles. Several "airplanes" are produced here and then most of the group turn into "painters." They paint the airplanes a variety of colors with newspapers underneath to catch the drips. They have caught the "painting" spirit and want to go on painting. The teacher brings out the big paint brushes and a pail of water. Most of the children respond by getting a small can, filling it from the pail, and starting out to brush water on the equipment or side of the shed with a big brush, working busily.

Soon it's mid-morning and juice time. The assistant goes in to get the juice. The quieter children are ready to go inside, for it is crisp and cool. They remove their coats before they have juice. The teacher reminds the others that it's "juice time" as they come to a good "stopping place" in activities. The more active children go in and have juice without removing their wraps and return immediately outside. Members of the group are now engaged in moving all the blocks, loading them on the wagons, dumping them at the end of the walk where three children are busily laying out roads. They are working near where some boxes and walking boards were placed the day before.

The other assistant comes out and our teacher goes inside. She notices that Bill has the drums on the floor and is beating each one in turn in a most professional manner. After she takes off her coat, the teacher goes to the piano and plays softly in time to his beating. Soon other children join in, using other instruments. Some begin to march with bracelets of bells on the wrists and a tambourine worn as a crown. After a time, the assistant puts clay out on the table and finally some of the marchers have changed to pounding and rolling the clay. Some add water to make a delightful, sticky mess, quite different to feel or to touch. A few children remain at the piano and the teacher plays and sings with them. Mary is there close by the teacher, but part of the group. When the teacher leaves to check with the cook and make out a lunch chart, these children move on to play in the housekeeping corner except for Susan who continues to play and sing by herself. The teacher returns and has a chance to sit quietly near the housekeeping corner and make notes of the activity and conversation. Finally she suggests to those few who have not yet been outdoors that it's time to go outside. She gives some help with coats and they go out for more active play.

Johnny has played more freely since he discovered water, so the teacher puts out a large pan half filled with water. She lays a bar of soap, a strainer, and some pans near by. Johnny is soon up to his elbows in the water. Seeing him, Jan gets a doll and starts bathing the baby. Several children have been painting. The assistant is reading to a small group. It has been a satisfying morning for everyone with a variety of activity, a free flowing yet ordered program.

Some days are more strenuous, especially when the weather makes it impossible to spend much time outdoors. A stormy day would require more plans for such activities as finger painting, cookie making, and perhaps more reading and music and science experiences inside.

On another day there might be a new child going through a difficult period of adjustment and in need of more individual help.

The time comes in this program to pick up and get ready for lunch. The assistant comes in with the children who have been playing outdoors and gives them any help they may need with their wraps. They have parked their tricycles and transported the blocks back to the storage area before coming in. They go to the toilet and wash while the group inside is putting blocks back on the shelf, clay back in the crock, babies to bed, etc. The teachers help quietly and encouragingly. As the children finish, they too go into the toilet room where one of the assistant teachers is ready to help.

Our teacher selects some books and arranges the story corner. She is ready to read as the children start coming out after toileting and washing. There is a good deal of conversation until the group is settled. Some of the younger children go to a smaller group where the other assistant tells them a story, showing pictures. The attention

Fig. 11. Water has many possibilities.

span of this group is short and they have little interest in any conversation except their own! It is a quiet period and the second assistant who has finished helping in the coatroom goes to the rest room to prepare it for the children. She is ready there to help them come in quietly and settle down for a rest when the story period is over. She may play a record while they rest.

During the rest period one assistant sets the table with the cook's help. Our teacher usually finds that she is needed in the rest room. Lunch itself is another busy period as children and adults share a meal together. Not only the food but the social situations are engrossing. After lunch the parents call for the children. The school day is over.

Our hypothetical teacher and her assistants check the school, cleaning paint jars, moistening the clay, straightening out the doll corner and the toy shelves, putting paintings away, etc. Then they sit down for a short staff meeting to discuss questions about situations which occurred during the morning, how the dispute over using the wagons might have been settled, what Mary needs to increase her confidence, the developing relationship between quiet Dave and Eric who is always ready to defy adult authority. The assistants leave and the teacher prepares for a conference with a parent who will be coming in soon.

Throughout the school day all the teachers have lived with the children, aware of what each child was doing, ready to step in quickly when necessary, making provision for rich play opportunities but not interfering in the play, taking notes whenever possible, keeping the needs of individuals in mind but aware of the movement of the whole group. They have given particular attention to the "transition points," the ending of play, changes from indoors to outdoors, changes from one routine to another.

If this kind of day seldom happens in reality, it is this structure which lies behind even those days when there are more interruptions and more problems to face. We will discuss the handling of problems in later chapters. Here we will only point out that planning like this enables the teachers to work together and to give the children a sense of sureness about what happens in a nursery school day.

Different Types of Schools Have Developed Serving Different Purposes

Nursery school programs such as we have described developed in our twentieth century world to meet needs of both children and parents.

Much of the early expansion in the nursery school field took place as the result of "emergencies." The depression of the thirties and the crisis of war in the forties led to the establishment of many nursery schools or child care centers. It is to be hoped that some day a sound program of education for young children will be supported, not to minimize the evils of a depression or to enable larger numbers of women to work outside their homes, but because it seems important to serve the physical, social, emotional and intellectual needs of children. A program based on a recognition of the needs of children themselves will have somewhat different emphases than the emergency programs of the past decades have had.

Some of the best nursery schools available to children at present are those maintained by colleges and universities as laboratories for their students. Most of the larger colleges and universities have nursery schools which students use as laboratories for learning about people and which may also be used for research in this field. These schools offer leadership, set good standards and add to the knowledge we have about young children. They are financed in large part by the institution itself and are an important part of nursery school development in the United States.

The number of private nursery schools has grown rapidly in the last few years. Because of their cost these schools offer nursery school experience only to children from wealthier families. When private schools are staffed by competent, trained people, they provide good care for a limited group of children. Very few states, however, set adequate standards or give educational supervision to private nursery schools. The result is that there is little assurance for parents and children that such schools are always good schools. Parents themselves must depend on becoming qualified to judge whether a school offers a constructive experience if they wish to protect their children.

There is little need to mention here the parking places for children which have developed solely as commercial ventures and which do not meet any educational standards. Parents who leave their children in such parking places must expect to have them suffer damage much as cars are likely to get bumped fenders by carelessness on parking lots.

In some communities parents have organized cooperative nursery schools and hired a trained teacher as a director while acting as her assistants in turn. The participation of parents as assistant teachers raises special questions about the effect this may have on the relationship between the parent and her own child. We will discuss these points later but we will point out here that, with good professional leadership and a seriously interested group of parents, sound programs have been developed which have been of real benefit to parents and children at somewhat less cost. Sometimes parents have arranged informal play group in neighborhoods, which run for a short time and meet the needs of the neighborhood group temporarily.

Churches may provide quarters for nursery schools during the week. Sometimes the church itself operates a nursery school with a trained staff as a service to young children and their parents.

Some nursery schools are also beginning to offer the opportunity for richer first-hand experiences to handicapped children. In many places a blind child may be enrolled in a group of sighted children. When the help of a visiting consultant for the preschool blind is available so that teachers, children and parents are prepared to handle the anxieties that they inevitably feel, the experience is a rewarding one for the group as well as for the handicapped child. Other nursery schools are especially designed to meet the needs of children with handicaps, such as cerebral palsy, or mental retardation or auditory as well as visual handicaps.

Day care centers which have children on an all-day basis because they cannot be cared for in their own homes are undertaking programs similar to those in nursery schools in many cases. They are planning for the child's social, emotional and intellectual development as well as his physical development. Standards of care for children in these centers should be an increasingly important concern to communities as more and more women work outside the home. It is estimated that the number of children needing care is already much greater than the number of centers available.

The question of making the nursery school part of the public school program deserves to be raised today. It should be a more and more important issue as nursery schools demonstrate what they have to offer children and as more well trained teachers are available. As the cost of crime, delinquency and psychiatric disability becomes more widely recognized, the nation may feel the need to spend more than it is now spending on prevention in order to avoid part of the heavy price which these social deficiencies exact from individuals as well as from the social group.

VALUES OF NURSERY SCHOOL INCLUDE EDUCATION FOR PARENTS

A very real value of the nursery school today is in the education it makes available for parents. Most fathers and mothers have had very limited experience with young children before becoming parents. They may have done some "baby sitting" but they often lack the experience of daily living with children. They are not likely to have had a chance to observe their own parents dealing with the problems of small children as people did who grew up when families of eight or ten were more common than today.

Most parents, too, have had very little training in school in the area of understanding children. They have not had chances to observe children at play and discuss what they see with someone who is qualified to interpret behavior to them. They have not had contact with the body of knowledge about children's development which we have today. Courses dealing with the subject are only infrequently offered. When offered, they may give students no first-hand experience. We hope that there may be an increasing number of schools which will offer students some adequate preparation for their important tasks as parents in the future. As Chisholm has pointed out, we have "learned quite a bit about how children develop from birth toward maturity. But very little of that knowledge is yet implemented."*

The nursery school offers parents as well as students a chance to learn about children. The parent who brings his child to nursery school can observe children, his own and others. He can discuss questions with the teacher, meet with other parents and learn from them. A nursery school can serve as a real educational center for parents at a time when their interest in learning about children is high. With nursery school making opportunities for learning available to parents, first children may have a better chance!

Nursery Schools Are of Value as a Supplement to Family Life

Nursery schools are of value, too, because they offer parents and

* Chisholm, Brock: Prescription for Survival. New York, Columbia University Press, 1957, p. 26.

children a chance to have some experiences apart from each other. There is a real need for some separation when families live in small homes or apartments without much outdoor space available.

Too close and constant contact with adults under unsuitable conditions increases the irritations which both child and adult feel. With a child literally "under foot" almost constantly, a mother is likely to find it harder to be loving and patient on the one hand or to keep from overwhelming him with anxious attention on the other hand. Resentments develop because of the interferences and limitations which both are likely to suffer. The child in the small family often carries a heavy burden in the anxiety and attention centered on him, undiluted and undivided. Nursery schools may offer opportunity to both parent and child to have some freedom from contacts which may be limiting because they are constant and close. Nursery schools may make it easier for a child to grow up with less resentment and with a healthy measure of independence.

Another reason why nursery schools are needed today lies in the limited number of first-hand experiences available to children in homes. We probably can hardly estimate how modern life limits the intellectual development of children by limiting their first-hand experience. Few of the activities related to the daily needs of the child are carried on at home. The results of research that seem to indicate that attendance at nursery school has an effect on the intelligence level of children may be a reflection of the advantages of the larger number of first-hand experiences that are offered at school over the number offered in the modern home.

Many Unmet Needs Remain

There is overwhelming evidence today that what we have been offering children is not good enough. Many children are not healthy according to the definition of health proposed by the World Health Organization. "Health is defined as a state of complete physical, mental and social well being, not merely the absence of disease or infirmity." While we have made tremendous strides in improving the physical health of children, we have given little attention to improving their mental and social well being. Little of the money spent in medical research goes into attacking problems of mental health, although it is estimated that more than half the patients visiting a doctor's office suffer from illnesses complicated to a large extent by emotional factors. Our resources for preventing mental and social ill health remain very limited.

We are not even applying the knowledge which we have. The extent of emotional as well as physical disability among the men and women examined for the armed services indicates the degree to which people are handicapped in their development. Many of these disabilities are preventable with the knowledge we now have. We can only conclude that the conditions under which children are growing up are not nearly good enough to ensure healthy adults.

The world today is a different place from what it was 100, 200 or 500 years ago. We can be glad of the many improvements in physical comforts, but the demands of life in the modern world have created new tensions, removed old safety valves and made the social and emotional development of individuals at once more difficult and more important. The conditions under which children are growing up today are probably not as good as they were a few generations ago in some respects. Nursery schools have developed in our twentieth century world as one answer to the problems created by these changed conditions.

REFERENCES

1. Barnouw, Elsa, and Swan, Arthur: Adventures with Children in Nursery School and Kindergarten. Thomas Y. Crowell Co., 1959.
2. Beyer, Evelyn: Nursery School Settings—Invitation to What? National Association for Nursery Education Bulletin, 1958.
3. Clark, Eileen: A Nursery School Procedure (Part 1). New York, The Dalton Schools, 1949.
4. Frank, Lawrence, and Frank, Mary: How to Help Your Child in School. New York, Viking Press, 1950, Ch. 3.
5. Gilkeson, Elizabeth, and Schecter, Estelle: New Concepts in Nursery Education. Bank Street Profile, edited and published by Bank St. College of Education, New York, 1957, pp. 28-36.
6. Gruenberg, Sidonie: Our Children Today (Ch. 6—The Beginning Education by James L. Hymes and Ch. 7—Nursery Education, Its Uses and Dangers by Anna Freud). New York, Viking Press, 1952.
7. Isaacs, Susan: Childhood and After. New York, International Universities Press, 1949, Ch. 5.
8. Jones, Betty: A Study of Age Grouping in a Summer Nursery School Experience. Journal of Nursery Education, Winter 1959, Vol. 14, No. 2, pp. 26-32.
9. Mead, Margaret: "The Impact of Cultural Change on the Family" in the Family and the Urban Community, Spring Lecture Series, Merrill-Palmer School, Detroit, 1953.

10. Omwake, Eveline: The Children Call It School, and So It Is. Journal of Nursery Education, Winter 1959, Vol. 14, No. 2, pp. 14-20, 42.
11. UNESCO: Publication No. 9—Problems in Education, Mental Hygiene in the Nursery School. 1953.
12. UNESCO: Publication No. 11—Problems in Education, Pre-school Education and Mental Health. 1955, pp. 57-81.
13. Winter, Frances B., and McFarland, Margaret: Developing Inner Strength. Journal of Nursery Education, Fall 1958, Vol. 14, No. 1, pp. 14-17.
14. Wolffheim, Nelly: Psychology in the Nursery School (Translated by Charles L. Hannam). New York, Philosophical Library, 1953, Ch. 7.

3

Equipment
and Curriculum

THE EQUIPMENT AND CURRICULUM
INFLUENCE HUMAN RELATIONSHIPS IN THE SCHOOL

The physical setup of a nursery school—the building and its equipment—is a factor in influencing the human relationships in the school. The many problems of planning and equipping a school are only solved properly in terms of the needs of the people who use it. We are interested in the way these problems may be solved because we are interested in the relationships of the children and the adults in the school. A well-planned building in which supervision is easy, for example, makes it possible for the teacher to give help when help is needed and lessens her fatigue, leaving more of her energy for work with the children. She is likely to do a better job when there are fewer frustrations due to handicaps in the physical setup. Suitable, adequate equipment means more satisfying group play for the children, too, and greater learning opportunities for them.

The planning which is done for the curriculum is also a factor in determining what satisfactions the children will find at nursery school and what kinds of growth are possible for them. As students of human relationships we are interested in curriculum as well as equipment. Because we are accustomed to thinking of a curriculum in terms of courses and credits, it may be difficult for us to recognize a curriculum in the form in which it appears in the nursery school. But the nursery school does have a planned program for learning even though these learning opportunities are not divided into "periods" which occur in regular succession. Its curriculum opens the door to new interests and enriches already existing ones.

Equipment

Let us look first at the nursery school equipment, and analyze briefly the part it plays in determining what experiences the children will have.

The Nursery School Building

The nursery school building itself is an important factor in determining the learning possibilities within a school. A good deal of thought should be given to its planning, for it may extend or limit the experiences the children have. There are references available which describe functionally designed schools. We will only suggest here some ways in which the building affects the behavior of the people in the school.

Many of the ways in which the building affects the people in it are obvious. For example, independence in the children is promoted by such things as low shelves where material is easily available, low hooks for wraps, low toilets and washbasins. These same things will save the staff members time and effort, leaving them free for other activities with children. Health conditions are influenced by adequate heating, freedom from drafts, a floor that can be easily cleaned. Safety is largely dependent on the absence of hazards in the buildings and the play areas. The amount of space and the relation of the indoor and outdoor play areas influence the kind of play which will take place. A free flow of play between indoors and outdoors enables children to have more contacts with each other and to satisfy a greater variety of play interests.

There are other less obvious ways in which the building affects the behavior of the people in it, as by an attractive, pleasing atmosphere in which the color and the space areas bring satisfaction. Sound-proofing, which reduces noise without the need of restricting children's activities, is another way in which the building can promote the goals of the school. Windows which have a south and west exposure and which are low enough for the children to use comfortably add to their experience in many ways.

Adapting the program to meet the needs of children is easier if the building is planned so that it offers the maximum in flexibility. Advances in structural design and materials make possible construction which permits greater flexibility than formerly. Movable partitions allow changes in the size and shape of spaces to fit the needs of a particular group. Since no one can be expected to foresee what future needs may be or what possible uses there may be for space, we should value planning which permits the maximum flexibility. Careful planning when building or remodeling is essential if the purposes of the nursery school are to be served effectively.

Fig. 12. Swing high, swing low.

Fig. 13. Climbing.

Selection and Arrangement of Equipment Is Important

The amount of equipment and its usefulness depend almost as much on the resourcefulness and imagination of the staff as on the amount of money available in the budget.

There are minimum essentials in equipment, of course, and these will be for the most part raw materials which the children can use in different ways at different stages of their development. A sandbox, for example, serves two-year-olds and five-year-olds equally well. It is used by both these age groups with pleasure, but in very different ways because of the creative possibilities it offers them. Other minimum essentials are blocks of different sizes and shapes, boards and boxes, barrels and perhaps a smaller ladder or two. Paints and easel space, clay, dolls and home-making equipment are included here as well as equipment that promotes large muscle activity. Tricycles, wagons, climbing equipment and swings come under this heading.

Indoor equipment which is in the minimum essential class includes a piano, a record player, drums and bells, books and manipulative materials for quieter play. These quiet play materials will include small autos, airplanes, trucks which may be used in connection with block building, trains, simple jigsaw puzzles, nested wooden blocks, paste and paper and scissors. There are many pieces of equipment such as blocks and housekeeping equipment which serve both inside and outside play needs.

Material which promotes dramatic play, both indoors and outdoors, is raw material. This material includes anything such as a square of cloth or a piece of hose which may be used to suggest the roles of people whom children observe in the world around them. With the simplest props, the roles of mother, father, grandparent or sibling are acted out as well as occupations such as fireman, delivery man, policeman. The professional role most frequently played is likely to be that of doctor. Materials for plenty of such dramatic play are among the minimum essentials for a nursery school.

Fig. 14. A first-hand experience.

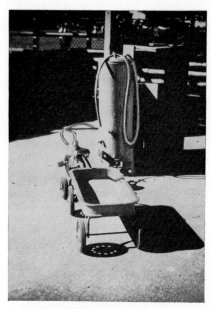

Fig. 15.   A gas station.

Provision for water play is too frequently overlooked. It is among the minimum essentials because of the great value of water play for young children. Small tubs, pails, shallow pans for dabbling in water, floating things, washing things, or for just enjoying water should be part of every school's inventory of equipment.

The minimum play essentials can be supplemented in many ways. One good place to find such supplements is the local second-hand store or junk shop where one may find wheels of many sizes, including old automobile steering wheels, parts such as old automobile magnets, inner tubes and tire pumps. These things enrich the children's play in unexpected ways. A tire pump is of interest to the mechanically minded children for experiments with air currents, and it can also be combined with short lengths of garden hose to equip a "gas station" or a "fire engine." Sometimes one can set up pulleys in ways that hold real learning possibilities for the children. At one school the children had fun with a pump fastened on a large barrel. They would pump and pump, watching the water run out of the spout and listening to it gurgle back into the barrel. They used it as a source of water for sand play. They learned about "priming" and developed their arm muscles, too, as they pumped. Another group had an old butter churn and liked to churn up a handful of soap flakes into mountains of suds. Old spoons, pans, strainers and gaily painted tin cans make desirable additions to the sandbox equipment. Variety in equipment supplied is one means of enriching the experiences of the children.

Arrangement of equipment is also of importance. Group play often depends on the way in which equipment is placed. An easel with room for two children provides for social as well as art experiences. Space in the doll corner encourages its use by more children and reduces the number of their conflicts. Two things of a kind such as two doll buggies or two telephones mean more social play. Storage space where the children themselves can get the equipment offers opportunity for them to be independent and self-sufficient. Even the use made of the wheel toys will depend in part on the amount and the type of hard surface space available. A broad walk which circles the playground will handle the traffic in a way that a solid block of hard surfacing at one end of the playground cannot do. These are all ways in which arrangement of and for equipment influences the children's behavior.

Fig. 16. A tunnel.

Fig. 17.   A trip to the creamery.

By providing materials which have been carefully selected and by offering adequate arrangements for their use, the nursery school helps ensure a rich environment for the children which stimulates intellectual development as well as social and emotional growth.

The Curriculum

A good nursery school curriculum is the result of careful planning. It offers children opportunities to learn when they show interest and readiness. It is based on the spontaneous interests of the children themselves and consists of first-hand experiences. A resourceful teacher will take advantage of the many chances the children offer her, and will see that their experiences are extended to include all the areas for learning in which they show an interest.

If young children are to learn, they must have first-hand experiences. They profit very little from experiences which are second-hand out of books or through being told about a thing. They must first form concepts from actual first-hand experiences of their own if their thinking is to be sound. Later, on the basis of what they know from experience, they can understand reports by others of related experiences or grasp generalizations. But they will avoid many errors in thinking if principles are preceded by actual experiences with phenomena. It is important that the nursery school build this background of first-hand experiences in preparation for the learning which will come later from books. The children in nursery school should have many "laboratory experiences."

When we stop to think how difficult it would be to understand generalizations about the behavior of children without having had actual experiences with them, we can better appreciate how necessary first-hand experiences are for children in all the many areas where they are learning. Even though we have had a great deal of experience with human behavior, we still profit from having the nursery school serve as a laboratory, so that our discussions may be based on actual, first-hand experience even at this point in our learning. For the children any curriculum that is to have value will be a curriculum full of first-hand experiences.

Let us take an example of learning at the nursery school level. In the field of science the children in a school may have some experiences which help them develop a broader concept of what the word "root" means. A group digging in the ground discovers roots from a nearby vine. They find these roots are too tough for their shovels to break. Then they discover smaller roots which they can pull up quite easily. Because the children seem interested in their find, the teacher helps them discover where these roots come from and explains why they are there. She encourages them to explore for more roots, and they come upon a potato left in the ground from the garden of the year before and tiny roots of weeds and grass. They pull up a carrot, too, and perhaps the teacher brings out some beans and helps the children plant them on a wet blotter or bit of cotton. They watch the beans sprouting in the next few days and see the development of roots taking place. Perhaps other experiences with roots are added to broaden the children's concept of roots. Learning like this is not likely to be forgotten and results in sound concepts.

The teacher plays an important part, as can be seen in this example. By the experiences that she makes possible for the children, by the equipment she supplies them, and by her interest and the explanations through which she brings these experiences within the measure of their understanding, she does her teaching. She helps them relate new experiences to what they already know, and broadens their areas of learning. If the teacher had not been present in

Fig. 18.   Touching.

the example just given, the group might have seen roots only as things which interfered with digging.

Let us turn now to the questions of what curriculum experiences are most desirable for children in nursery school.

Art and Music

We will discuss art, music and rhythm experiences in more detail in the chapter on Creative Expression. Here we will only remind ourselves that experiences with art and music should be part of the curriculum, available every day even though every child may not participate in them each time. Some art materials should always be ready for use. Others may be brought out on request or when variety is needed. An open piano invites playing, as does a shelf with instruments for making sound. Informal singing such as may accompany swinging, and group experiences with music of a more formal kind belong in the daily program of the school.

Literature

Experiences with books are also part of the daily program in a good nursery school. A variety of well-chosen books should always be available under conditions which will encourage their proper use.

Bookshelves or a rack for books with plenty of table space and chairs adjacent make it possible for a child to look at books comfortably. A heap of picture books piled on a small table can only lead to misuse of the books. Children cannot be expected to handle books carefully if the space is crowded; nor can they be expected to be interested in them for long if they are not comfortable as they use them.

A few colorful books laid out on a table near the bookshelf may serve to attract the children's attention to the books. Adding a new book or changing the selection available stimulates interest. Reading groups should be small, for the child likes to be close to the teacher and the book. He is easily distracted in a large group where he does not have this closeness. Reading need not be confined to one story period. Some children will want many opportunities to listen to

Fig. 19. Painting.

Fig. 20. Looking at books.

stories while others may not. Small informal groups formed when there is an interest meet these needs. In pleasant weather reading can be done outdoors in a shady spot, and the new location creates new interest.

Books Should Fit the Interests of the Children

Variety in the books selected for the nursery school library is important, for children differ in their interests just as we do. I remember one little boy who showed no interest in books. He had evidently had few experiences with books at home, or else his experiences had been with books that were not suited to his level of development. But he did like cars, and one day he found a small book about cars. He looked at it carefully for a long time and then asked the teacher to read it to him while he listened attentively. For days he carried this book around. Sometimes he would stop and find someone to read it to him again. Then he began enjoying other books and joining the group when they listened to stories. Through the one book which was related to his interest, he had begun to discover the world of books.

This case illustrates the importance of having books that are related to the children's individual interests. Each nursery school group will enjoy a somewhat different selection of books, depending on their particular environment and the experiences they have had. Books about trains will be popular in one place and books about boats in another. Everywhere, children will enjoy books about boys and girls and animal pets, for they are all familiar with these subjects. In selecting books we must remember that the function of books for the young child is not to present new information, but to re-create for him the world he knows and by re-creation to strengthen his understanding of it. New knowledge should come from first-hand experiences and not from the printed page. We will find many city children thinking of milk as coming from a bottle no matter how many stories they have had about the cow and her contribution to the bottle. Stories about cows have more meaning after a trip to the barn. Books like *Let's Go Outside* present information that can be used in connection with experiences in the garden. It's fun for the children to find the pictures of earthworms and read about them after having discovered worms in their digging, or to find the picture of tadpoles when there are some tadpoles swimming in the bowl at school. Whatever the children's experience, it can be broadened and enriched through books related to experiences.

Books Should Be Attractive and Interestingly Presented

Books which are desirable for the nursery school not only are about familiar, everyday subjects, but are short and written in simple, correct English with many clear illustrations in color. There are many books which are reputedly for young children but which fail to hold their interest because they are not attractive in appearance and their vocabulary is above the child's level. The child who has these books will be less likely to develop an interest in them. He will be handicapped, for there are advantages in liking books. Much of what we learn later in life will be through books.

When we present stories to children, we should avoid reading rapidly so that children have to strain in order to understand. Anyone who has tried to follow a conversation in a foreign language with which he is not too familiar will understand how difficult even the ordinary rate of speech may be for the child who is listening to reading. As we read, we need to remember that children are still in the process of learning the language. We must read slowly and with inflections that will clarify the meaning as well as add interest and variety. In telling stories one has the advantage of being able to keep closer to the audience. Telling as well as reading stories is an ability which every teacher should work to develop.

Effect of the Story on the Child Deserves to Be Considered.

We have mentioned realistic stories as suitable for nursery school. The suitability of "fairy tales" and imaginative tales in general may well be raised here. Folk and fairy tales formerly constituted almost the entire literary fare available to children along with the moralistic tale. If one has a chance to look at samples of early literature for children, one will realize how much change there has been in books for children in the last hundred years. John Newberry, the so-called "father of children's literature" who first took advantage of the market in children's books, published the pocket books of the eighteenth century. He was obliged to throw in sonnets from Shakespeare along with his Mother Goose to make it acceptable to the buying public of those days.

In selecting books today we are helped by the fact that we know more about children's development, including such facts as that rousing fear in them is damaging, that there is a readiness factor in learning, that children need help in understanding the world around them rather than in having it confused by things that are fanciful. These facts have changed our ideas about what constitute suitable books for children. We now feel that it is better to omit frightening elements from stories until the child has had time to develop secure feelings and confidence in his ability to meet the real world and to distinguish the possible from the impossible. This doesn't mean that stories for the child should lack action and suspense, but that terrifying elements should be left out. This, of course, precludes the use of stories like "Jack and the Bean Stalk" or "Little Red Riding Hood" with most nursery school children. Some children will, of course, be readier at an earlier age than others for folk tales, depending on their level of emotional development. The price of introducing such stories too early may be disturbed sleep and a child more timid than he need be in facing the new and unknown. Fanciful, unreal stories are better left until the child has had time to form a sound concept of what the real world is like. Imagination is fun when it is a play between the real and the unreal. Listen to the children's "jokes" to gain some concept of what is real and unreal to them. "How would you like to eat a horse?" draws a big laugh because they can perceive how impossible such a thing could be. They laugh at things like this because they know that they are not true, but what do they know about wolves and giants and what they might or might not do?

There are many unreal stories on bookshelves which make poor reading material for children. There are many stories of animals dressing and talking like people which are decidedly not among the best in books for children. As one child remarked, "I wonder why they make them talk like that." While "Little Black Sambo" is popular because of its repetitive element, it has many undesirable features, both frightening and confusing. Children can hardly be expected to understand tigers or the subject of butter any better after hearing it, and they have no experiences to correct the impression the book may give them. There are, of course, some delightful animal stories where animal personalities fit into their own animal world.

There are imaginative stories, too, on the young child's level. "Karl's Wooden Horse" is an example of a delightful, first fairy tale with a wish fulfillment element and a safe ending of being welcomed home after an adventure that will be appreciated by most four-year-olds. It constitutes a good beginning in the realm of the unreal where the child is still on "safe" ground. Perhaps we do not need to be too eager to offer fanciful stories to children. The real world is certainly sufficiently wonderful to stimulate the imagination of any preschool child. It is important that it be understood and that the child feel related to it. We need to look for books which will help him understand it better and which will do this with artistry and humor.

Science

Another important part of the nursery school curriculum has to do with science. The young child early comes into contact with physical forces and he is continually meeting the principles of physics. He lets his cars run down an inclined board, he pulls a loaded wagon up a slope, he balances on a teeter, he uses the pulley or the pump, he watches snow melting in the sun, or he sees the water frozen in a pan outdoors. If he has plenty of these kinds of

Fig. 21.   David is interested in wheels.

first-hand experiences, he will be able to understand the physical theories he meets later. He has many opportunities, too, to learn about biology—caring for plants and animals and watching them grow. When it is time for a garden in the spring, the teacher may increase the opportunities for learning by selecting seeds of different kinds and sizes so that the children's concept of "seed" is a broad one. The plants that they grow can include root vegetables as well as those that grow on stalks and vines. Watching and caring for pets teaches the children about the way different animals live, what and how they eat, and how they sleep and reproduce. Tadpoles change into frogs; fish only need to be fed occasionally while rabbits and chickens are hungry many times a day; the turtle moves slowly but the bird must be kept in a cage because he flies away so fast and far; the bird splashes in his bath while the baby ducks enjoy the water in a different way. Experiences like these go to make up a background which is the basis for understanding what will be learned about biology later. Every school should offer as wide a variety of experience in the natural and physical sciences as possible.

Fig. 22. *Panel board plus imagination.*

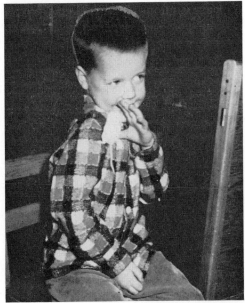

Fig. 23. *What does a mouse feel like?*

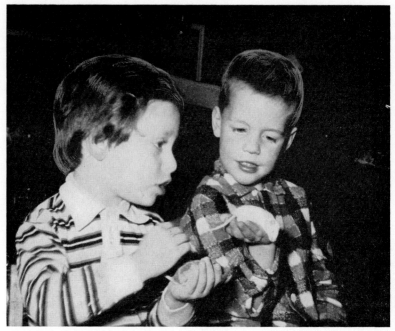

Fig. 24. What will a mouse do?

In one school it was usually possible each spring to have a lamb for a few weeks. The children loved to give the lamb his bottle of milk in the morning. He would play with them and often managed to slip in an unguarded door and make straight for the kitchen—the direction from which his bottle came—to the delight of the children. A young kid one spring proved himself as adept as the children on the walking boards and in jumping over boxes. The children enjoyed his companionship, too.

Baby animals are always a source of pleasure and of learning. Baby chicks with a mother hen, a litter of white rats, baby ducks, all illustrate growth. In fact the baby rats grow so fast that the children can see the changes from day to day. During the prenatal period, too, they learn to be careful in handling the mother rat "while her babies are growing inside her." Animal visitors have a place in the curriculum and a mother cat and her kittens or a litter of puppies are welcome additions for a morning. One of the most popular visitors that ever came to one nursery school was a baby pig. His curly tail, his short legs, round body and funny squealing delighted the group. A pet skunk who visited one day was the subject of a great deal of discussion, perhaps because the children had heard the word skunk used with a different connotation. They enjoyed getting acquainted with this friendly, attractive animal. Concepts are broadened in the course of experiences such as these.

Where Children Are Having Experiences with Animals, They Come in Contact with the Fact of Death

If barnyards are near, children will enjoy excursions there as much as to any other place. Horses, cows, sheep and pigs are all interesting to children because they are living and moving. If the children are having many experiences with animals, they are sure on some occasion to come into contact with the fact of death. The baby rats sometimes die, or a dog may get in and kill a chicken. The children may see a dead lamb when they visit the barn during lambing season, or they may discover a dead bird in the yard.

In their response to these experiences the children will reflect the attitudes of the adults with them. There is no need to hide the fact of death from children, or to try to escape from facing it with them. It is a mystery like life and sometimes far less of a tragedy. The children will want to understand why the animal died, and they may be helped in their acceptance of the reality of death by touching and feeling to see how the dead animal differs from the living ones they have known. They will not be greatly disturbed if the adult with them does not feel the need to dramatize or distort or escape from the fact of death herself. If the children can be helped to have sound, reassuring experiences in this area, they will be helped to face life as well as death with less fear.

Social Studies May Be Carried on by Taking Trips and Having Visitors

Trips to places other than farmyards are a desirable part of the curriculum and help broaden the children's concepts in the general area which we might call "social studies." The community offers services with which the children have some contact and which they can begin to understand. Fire protection is the outstandingly important example. If the firemen are cooperative, trips to the fire station belong in the curriculum of three- and four-year-olds. Because children are not yet concerned with letter writing, they are less interested in trips to a post office although they may enjoy getting acquainted with the local mail carrier and using the mailbox. Trips to the grocery store for needed supplies are always interesting. Other stores such as the feed store which supplies food for the chickens or rabbit may be a rich experience, especially if the store handles grain or hay in quantity. Back at the nursery school the children may turn the sandbox into such a store with chutes and elevators. Any local industries with which the children may have contact offer good material for learning and developing a clearer concept of what the community in which they live is really like. It is always necessary to guard against elements of possible danger, such as places where there may be machinery with moving parts or a great deal of noise which may be confusing and disturbing to children.

In planning trips the teacher will keep in mind that the children will learn most if there are familiar elements which they can relate to the unfamiliar. The child is likely to enjoy watching a cement mixer and men at work putting in a new driveway more than he will enjoy a trip to a factory with big machinery whose function is beyond his ability to grasp. A hatchery with incubators full of eggs and tiny chicks is of interest because the child already knows something about eggs and chickens. He gets the most satisfaction out of simple experiences which can be related to experiences he already has had, experiences where he can see clearly and perhaps touch things.

Any teacher must know her community and its resources if she is to offer the children, especially the four- and five-year-olds, the rich curriculum for which they are ready. She will make many excursions, taking small groups, so that she can be sure of the experiences that each child is having and can interpret what needs interpreting to him. On every trip there should be two adults, for emergencies arise, such as having to find a toilet. Many times parents are able and eager to help with transportation, and it may be of real value for a parent and teacher to share such an experience.

Many of the most valuable experiences outside the school lead directly to more variety and richness in the play experiences within the school. A trip to the fire station when the group has already developed an interest in "firemen" play will add detail and variety to the activities. A trip to a nearby grain elevator gave one group many ideas about how grain was handled and how cars were loaded.

The sandbox play took on new aspects after this trip which had as its purpose buying grain for the nursery school chickens.

Children's first-hand experiences may also be enriched through visitors to the nursery school. The man who delivers milk, the man who delivers groceries, the mailman, the taxi driver, are people whom we may take for granted. They are new people to the children. Meeting them, talking with them, watching them carry out their work, will serve to make community services better understood. The nursery school child may profit from watching an individual mailman as he delivers his mail and picks it up, seeing his bag or his cart, more than he might from a visit to the post office itself. When visits to a fire station cannot be arranged, a fireman can be invited to the school to show some of his equipment. A friendly policeman dropping in so that the children can get a close-up view of his uniform may change a child's idea of what policemen are like. Parents whose occupations interest children are also excellent resources for extending children's concepts about the life of a community and giving them more realistic ideas of what it is like.

REFERENCES

1. Arbuthnot, M. H.: Children and Books. Chicago, Scott, Foresman & Co., 1957.
2. Association for Childhood Education, Washington, D.C.: Bibliography of Books for Children, 1958. Music for Children's Living, 1955.
   Kintergarten Teachers Portfolio, 1951. Nursery School Teachers Portfolio, 1953.
   Creating with Materials for Work and Play, 1957.
   Recommended Equipment and Supplies for Nursery, Kindergarten, Primary and Intermediate Schools, No. 39, revised 1957.
3. Association for Childhood Education, Washington, D.C.: Children's Books for $1.25 or less. 1959.
4. Foote, Sarah: A Nursery School Evolves in a Brand New Building. Journal of Nursery Education, Spring 1958.
5. Friedman, David B., and Colodny, Dorothy: Water, Sand and Mud as Play Materials. National Association for Nursery Education Bulletin, 1959.
6. Green, Marjorie, and Woods, Elizabeth: A Nursery School Handbook for Teachers and Parents. The Sierra Madre Community Nursery School Association, Sierra Madre, California, 1954.
7. Green, Marjorie: Pets in the Nursery School. Journal of Nursery Education, Vol. XII No. 3, Spring 1957, pp. 14-18.
8. Greenlee, Julian: Teaching Science to Children (Rev. edition). Iowa, W. C. Brown Co., 1957.
9. Hartley, Ruth E.; Frank, Lawrence, and Goldenson, Robert: Understanding Children's Play, New York, Columbia University Press, 1952, Chs. 1, 4 and 5.

10. Haupt, Dorothy: Science Experiences for Nursery School Children. Chicago, National Association for Nursery Education, 1953.
11. Hochman, V., and Greenwald, M.: Science Experiences in Early Childhood Education. New York, Bank Street Publications, Bank Street College of Education, 1953.
12. Hymes, James L.: Before the Child Reads, New York, Row Peterson & Co., 1958.
13. Moore, Sallie Beth, and Richards, Phyllis: Teaching in the Nursery School. New York, Harper & Bros., 1959, Chs. 1, 2, and 3.
14. Packets for Nursery School Teachers, Bank Street Publications, Bank Street College of Education, New York.
15. Planning Space and Equipment: Home Economics in Colleges and Universities. Prepared jointly by American Home Economics Association and Home Economics Branch, Office of Education, U. S. Dept. of Health, Education and Welfare, 1956, pp. 25-30.
16. Rudolph, Marguerita: Living and Learning in Nursery School. New York, Harper & Bros., 1954, Chs. 6 and 7.
17. Sevens, Dorothy: A Sink with Running Water. Journal of Nursery Education, Spring 1959, Vol. 14, No. 2, p. 24.
18. Waechter, Heinrich, and Waechter, Elisabeth: Schools for the Very Young. New York, F. W. Dodge Corp., 1951.
19. Wolf, Anna: Helping Your Child Understand Death. Child Study, 1958.

II

Exploring Areas of
Common Experience

4

Initial Support Through

Guides to Speech and Action

We have described the nursery school itself and the needs it may serve through what it offers a child in the way of equipment and curriculum experiences. We have become familiar with our laboratory. Now we turn to the question of how we will fit into this laboratory as students. What guides are there to speech and action? How can we best meet the demands made on us by the school situation while we are increasing our understanding of human relationships?

We Are Likely to Feel Inadequate at First

Before we can follow any "guides," we must first be aware of what our responses to feeling inadequate are likely to be. Each of us will respond somewhat differently to the experience of beginning to work with children. Some of these responses may interfere with what we do while others may be helpful.

We discussed in an earlier chapter the necessity of accepting the fact that we may feel uncertain and uncomfortable in the nursery school at first. Too frequently we only increase these feelings by struggling against them, making it more difficult to develop constructive ways of acting. Sometimes we try to defend ourselves against feeling inadequate in a new situation by plunging into action as though to take our minds off the way we feel. In the nursery school we may do unnecessary things like talking to children when talking serves no useful purpose for the child. We may offer help which is not needed or try to start activities which have no real place at the moment in the child's pattern of play. Sometimes we may defend ourselves against feeling inadequate by withdrawing and taking no action at all. Sometimes we may fight against the necessity for direction at first by being very critical of the direction given; and at other times we may seek reassurance by trying to be completely dependent on instructions, insisting that these be specific and detailed so that there is no room for uncertainty.

These adjustments or defenses are part of a resistance to change which we all feel and which is sometimes a protection and often a limitation on growth. All of us have established certain patterns of reaction in new situations. These patterns are probably made up of more and less constructive adaptations. It is important for us to identify these adaptations and to select and add to the more useful ones. Growth is often an uncomfortable process. But growth is rewarding and satisfying when we have mobilized our resources and reduced the conflicts which interfere with our growth. Instead of spending energy trying to deny feelings, we can make constructive use of them.

Guides or Simple Rules Give Support

When one feels inadequate, one needs support of some kind. What are the supports available in the situation? In the nursery school, for example, what help can one get from the experienced teacher? What help can one find in one's own past experiences in related situations, in books or from discussion? In any new experience we begin to gain confidence when we assemble the useful, appropriate supports and build a framework in which to operate.

In this chapter we will list some techniques and principles which can be depended on at first as guides to action in the nursery school. These can be applied in an increasingly individual way with added experience. The success of some of these techniques depends in part on the relationship built up with individual children. Time is required to build as well as understand relationships, but during the process these "rules" will give clues to appropriate action. In time, with experience and increasing insight, each one of us will make her own generalizations and add new interpretations.

Set down alone, these statements may seem somewhat like letters in an alphabet. Only when they are combined by experience into larger units will they have much meaning. At this point they must be accepted as part of the alphabet which goes to make a "language" used in guiding behavior.

These fourteen points can observe as guides to speech and action in the beginning when the nursery school situation is an unfamiliar one. Here they are.

GUIDES

In Speech

1. State suggestions or directions in a positive rather than a negative form.
2. Give the child a choice only when you intend to leave the choice up to him.
3. Your voice is a teaching tool. Use words and a tone of voice which will help the child feel confident and reassured.
4. Never depend on changing behavior by words which may make the child feel less respect for himself such as by blaming or shaming him or making him feel guilty.
5. Avoid motivating a child by making comparisons between one child and another or encouraging competition.
6. Redirect the child in a way that is related to his own motives or interests whenever possible.

In Action

7. Avoid making models in any art medium for the children to copy.
8. Give the child the minimum of help in order that he may have the maximum chance to grow in independence, but give the help the child needs.
9. Make your suggestions effective by reinforcing them when necessary.
10. Forestalling is the most effective way of handling problems. Learn to foresee and prevent rather than mop-up after a difficulty.
11. When limits are necessary, they should be clearly defined and consistently maintained.

12. Be alert to the total situation. Use the most strategic positions for supervising.
13. The health and safety of the children are a primary concern at all times.
14. Observe and take notes!

Guides in Speech

1. *State Suggestions or Directions in a Positive Form*

A positive suggestion is one which tells a child what to do instead of pointing out what he is not to do. If a child has already done what he shouldn't do or we estimate that he is about to do this, he needs help in getting another, better, idea. We give him this kind of help when we direct his attention to what we want him to do.

It has been demonstrated experimentally that directions stated in a positive way are more effective than the same directions given negatively. This can be subjected to proof informally in many situations. For example, a teacher in nursery school demonstrated it in this situation. She was finding it difficult to weigh the children because almost every child reached for support when he felt the unsteadiness of the scale platform. When the teacher asked them not to touch anything, she had very little success. She changed her negative direction to a positive one. "Keep your hands down at your sides," and the children did just that. Telling them what to do, instead of what not to do, brought results.

A positive direction is less likely to rouse resistance than a negative one. It makes help seem constructive rather than limiting and interfering. Perhaps the child is doing the thing because he thinks it annoys us. By emphasizing the positive we reduce the attention and thus the importance of the negative aspect of his behavior. We usually help rather than hinder when we make a positive suggestion.

In addition, when we make suggestions in a positive way we are giving the child a sound pattern to imitate when he himself directs his friends. He is likely to be more successful, to meet with less resistance, if he puts his suggestions in a positive form. We give him a good social tool to use. One can tell something about the kind of direction that a child has received as one listens to the kind of direction that he gives in play.

More important still, having clearly in mind what we want the child to do, we can steer him toward this behavior with more confidence and assurance—with more chance of success. Our goal is clear to us and to him. We are more likely to feel adequate and to act effectively when we put a statement positively.

To put directions positively represents a step in developing a more positive attitude toward children's behavior inside ourselves. Our annoyance often increases as we dwell on what the child shouldn't be doing, but our feelings may be different when we turn our attention to what the child should be doing in the situation. We may have more sympathy for the child's problem as we try to figure out just what he could do under the circumstances. It helps us appreciate the difficulties he may be having in figuring out a better solution.

At first it is wise to allow oneself no exceptions to this rule, to discard negative suggestions entirely. It is too easy to slip into old habits and rely on the negative. Making only positive suggestions is a hard exercise because most of us have depended heavily on negative suggestions in the past and have had them used on us. We tend to resist the effort it takes to discover different words and different patterns of thinking. But it is worth correcting oneself whenever one makes a negative statement in order to hasten the learning of this basic technique. Every direction should be given in a positive form.

For example, the teacher will say:

1. "Ride your tricycle around the bench," instead of "Don't bump the bench."
2. "Throw your ball over here," instead of "Don't hit the window."
3. "Leave the heavy blocks on the ground," instead of "Don't put the heavy blocks on that high board."
4. "Give me the ball to hold while you're climbing," instead of "Don't climb with that ball in your hand."
5. "Take a bite of your dinner now," instead of "Don't play at the table."
6. "Take little bites and then it will all go in your mouth," instead of "Don't take such big bites and then you won't spill."
7. "Pull the plug now and dry your hands," instead of "Don't spend any more time washing," or "Don't you want to pull the plug now?"

HERE IS AN EXERCISE. Observe and record ten positive statements and contrast each with the corresponding negative statement. Estimate the effectiveness of the statements you recorded.

2. Give the Child a Choice Only When You Intend to Leave the Situation up to Him

Choices are legitimate. With increasing maturity one makes an increasing number of choices. We accept the fact that being able to make decisions helps develop maturity. But there are decisions which a child is not ready to make because of his limited capacities and experience. We must be careful to avoid offering him a choice when we are not really willing to let him decide the question. Sometimes one hears a mother say to her child, "Do you want to go home now?" and when he replies, "No," she acts as though he were being disobedient because he did not answer the question in the way she wanted him to answer it. What she really meant to say was, "It's time to go home now."

Questions such as the one above are more likely to be used when a person feels uncertain or wishes to avoid raising an issue which he is not sure that he can handle. Sometimes using a question is only a habit of speaking. But it is confusing to the child to be asked a question when what is wanted is not information but only confirmation. It is important to guard against the tendency to use a question unless the circumstances make a question legitimate.

Circumstances differ, but usually the nursery school child is not free to choose such things as the time to go home or the time to eat or rest. He is not free to hurt others or to damage property. On the other hand, he is free to decide such things as whether he wants to play outside or inside, or what play materials he wants, or whether he needs to go to the toilet (except in the case of a very young child).

Sometimes a child may be offered a choice to clarify a situation for him. For example, he may be interfering with someone's sand pies and the teacher may ask, "Do you want to stay in the sandbox?" A response of "Yes" is defined further as, "Then you will need to play at this end of the box out of Bobby's way."

A teacher sometimes puts a request in the form of a question when she herself is not clear as to how much responsibility to take in a situation. In using a question she avoids making a decision. Here is an example.

Marian is still at the easel painting. It is about time to put the equipment away to get ready for lunch. An adult approaches and asks hopefully, "Are you through?"

"No," replies Marian.

"Well, it's time to put the paints away," says the adult. "Let's call it done now."

A question is obviously not legitimate in this case and only serves to confuse Marian. The adult needed to state a fact. "It's time to put the paints away. Finish your painting now." She may have added a comment such as, "That's a nice picture. You've had fun painting today, haven't you!" to make the contact more friendly and pleasant, but the responsibility for pointing out what was to happen was clearly hers.

It is important to be clear in one's mind as to whether one is really offering the child a choice before one asks a question. Be sure that your questions are legitimate ones.

3. *Your Voice Is a Teaching Tool. Use Words and a Tone of Voice Which Will Help the Child Feel Confident and Reassured*

All of us have known parents and teachers who seem to feel that the louder they speak, the greater their chances of controlling behavior. We may also have observed that these same people often have more problems than the parents and teachers who speak more quietly but are listened to. A quiet, firm manner of speaking conveys confidence and reassures the child.

It may be necessary to speak firmly, but it is never necessary to raise one's voice. The most effective speech is simple and direct and slow. Decreasing speed is more effective than raising pitch.

It is a good rule never to call or shout across any play area, inside or outside. It is always better to move nearer the person to whom you are speaking. Children as well as adults grow irritated when shouted at. Your words will get a better reception if they are spoken quietly, face to face.

Speech conveys feelings as well as ideas. Children are probably very sensitive to the tone quality, the tightness in a voice, for example, which reveals annoyance or unfriendliness or fear—no matter what the words may be. One can try for a pleasant tone of voice and one may find one's feelings improving along with one's voice.

The teacher sets a pattern, too, in her speech as she does in other ways. Children are more likely to use their voices in loud harsh ways if the teacher uses her voice in these ways. Voice quality can be improved with training, and every one of us could probably profit from speech work to improve our voice. A well-modulated voice is an asset worth cultivating.

HERE IS AN EXERCISE. Listen to the quality of the voices around you. What feeling do the tones express when one pays no attention to the words spoken? Note the differences in pitch, in rate, and in volume in the voices of the teachers. Report a situation in which you feel that the tone of voice was more important than the words in influencing the child's behavior.

4. *Never Attempt to Change Behavior by Using Words Which May Make the Child Feel Less Respect for Himself, Such as by Blaming or Shaming Him or Making Him Feel Guilty*

One of the reasons why we study behavior is to gain understanding and skills so that we will not have to fall back on crude methods. We need to learn constructive ways of influencing behavior if we are to promote sound personality growth. Neither children nor adults are likely to develop desirable behavior patterns as the result of fear or shame or guilt. Improvement will be more apparent than real, and any change is likely to be accompanied by resentment and an underlying rejection of the behavior involved when these methods of control are used.

The wise parent or teacher will never use words which are calculated to make a child feel afraid or guilty or ashamed. This means that words like "bad boy" or "naughty girl" or "you ought to be ashamed" will never appear in the vocabulary of understanding parents and teachers.

It takes time to learn constructive ways of guiding behavior. The first step is to eliminate the destructive patterns in use. We must discard the gestures, the expressions, the tones of voice as well as the words that convey the impression that the other person should feel ashamed of himself. In passing judgment on another, we make the other person feel that we do not respect him. It is hard for a person to change his behavior unless he feels some respect for himself. The young child is especially dependent on feeling that others respect him.

If we believe that there are reasons why a person behaves as he does, reasons why patterns of reacting are established, we will not blame the individual for his behavior. We may see it as undesirable or unacceptable. We may try to change it but we accept and respect him. We will not add to his burden by passing judgment on him.

He will be helped if we accept him as he is and try to make it possible for him to find some success rather than if we reprove him because he does not meet our standards. Here is an example.

Mark, an active child with a short attention span who often acts destructively, runs up to the table and starts to work a puzzle, standing up and leaning over the table and saying, "I want to do this."

The teacher says, "Puzzles take time to do. If you want to sit down, I'll help you." (This is a steadying type of suggestion which will make it easier for him to stay with the task.)

Mark sits down and starts to put the puzzle together, whines when a piece does not fit in the first place he tries and throws the piece on the floor.

The teacher says, "Does it make you mad when it doesn't fit right away?" (She puts into words the feeling he appears to have, thus indicating her acceptance of it and of him. This probably helps him relax.)

She reaches down and gets the piece and passes it to him and he completes the puzzle successfully. She says, "That's fine. You did it." (She does not reprove him for throwing a piece on the floor or expect him to pick it up. He is not ready to meet such an expectation. It is more important for him to have some success. She helps him be successful and respects him for what he can do.)

5. *Avoid Motivating a Child by Making Comparisons Between One Child and Another or Encouraging Competition*

Comparing one child to another is a dangerous way to try to influence behavior. We may get results in changed behavior, but these changes may not all be improvements. Some of these results are sure to be damaging to the child's feeling of adequacy and his friendliness.

Competitive schemes for getting children to dress more quickly or to eat more of something may have some effects that are not what we want. Children who are encouraged to be competitive are very likely to quarrel more with one another. In any competition someone always loses and he's likely to feel hurt and resentful. Even the winner may be afraid of failing next time, or he may feel an unjustified superiority if the contest was an unequal one. Competition does not build friendly, social feelings.

Competition not only handicaps smooth social relationships but creates problems within the child himself. We live in a highly competitive society, it is true, but the young child is not ready to enter into much competition until his concept of himself as an adequate person has developed enough so that he can stand the strains and the inevitable failures that are part of competition. On the one hand, constant success is not a realistic experience, and does not prepare a child well for what he will meet later. Too many failures, on the other hand, may make him feel weak and helpless. Both are poor preparation for a competitive world. For sound growth it is important to protect children from competitive situations until they are more mature. It is important to avoid competitive kinds of motivation.

Some children place an undue value on success and failure. Children should not feel that their only chances for getting attention and approval depend on being "first" or "beating" someone or being the "best." They should feel sure of acceptance whether they succeed or fail.

This raises a question about what is sound motivation, anyway. Do we really get dressed in order to set a speed record or to surpass someone else? Motivation like this could logically lead to such useless activities as flagpole sitting. Isn't it true, rather, that the reason for getting dressed is to keep warm and comfortable? Isn't it also true that we dress ourselves because there is satisfaction in being independent and that we complete dressing quickly in order to go on to another activity? There may be a point in spending time enjoying the process of dressing if there happens to be nothing of any greater importance coming next. We may be better off when we get pleasure out of the doing of a thing, not just in getting the thing done. It is wise to be sure that we are motivating children in a sound way even though we may move more slowly. We ensure a sounder growth for them, and give them a better preparation for the years ahead.

One has only to listen to children on a playground to realize how disturbing highly competitive feelings are to them. Statements like "You can't beat me," or "I'm bigger than you," or "Mine is better than yours" increase friction and prevent children from getting along well together.

6. *Redirection Is Most Effective When Consistent with the Child's Motives or Interests*

What does this mean? It simply means that we'll be more successful in changing the child's behavior if we attempt to turn his attention to an act which has equal value as an interest or outlet for him. If he's throwing a ball dangerously near a window, for example, we can suggest a safer place to throw it. If he's throwing something dangerous because he's angry, we can suggest an acceptable way of draining off angry feelings—like throwing against a backstop or using a punching bag or pounding at the workbench. In the first case his interest is in throwing and in the second case it's in expressing his anger. Our suggestions for acting differently will take into account the different meaning in his behavior. We will always try to suggest something which meets the needs he is expressing in his behavior.

Bobby, for example, stands up in the sand and throws a pan at Susan who is startled and cries. Bobby has been playing in the sandbox for some time. The teacher assumes that he has lost interest and needs a suggestion for doing something more active. She says, "Bobby, Susan didn't like that. I can't let you throw pans but there's a ball over there. Let's fix a place to throw." She turns a barrel on its side and suggests to Bobby that he try throwing the ball through the barrel. He tries it and is successful. They throw it back and forth. Another child joins and takes the teacher's place in the game. It involves a great deal of running and chasing which both children enjoy.

If a group is running around wildly after a long period of quiet play, its members may need a suggestion about engaging in some vigorous and constructive play like raking leaves outside. Their needs will not be met by a suggestion about sitting quietly and listening to a story. The meaning of their behavior lies in a need for activity. The teacher's part is to help them find some acceptable expression for this need. If they are running around wildly, on the other hand, because they are fatigued by too much activity and stimulation, a suggestion about listening to a story meets their need for rest.

Effective redirection often requires imagination as in the following example where the teacher gave a suggestion which captured the interest of these particular children.

Donnie and Michael are at the top of the jungle gym and notice a teacher nearby who is busy writing. They shout at her, "We're going to tie you up and put you in jail." They have a rope with a heavy hook on it. Donnie climbs down with it saying, "I'm going to tie you up!" He flings it toward the teacher and stands looking at her. She says, "You don't quite know what I'm doing here, Donnie, do you? I'm writing down some things I want to remember," and she continues, "I can't let you throw a hook at me or tie me up, but I wonder if you could use the hook to catch a fish from the jungle gym. It would take a strong man to catch a big fish from the top of that jungle gym." He picks up the rope and climbs up the jungle gym and the teacher ties a "fish" on to the hook. The boys have fun pulling it up and lowering it for a fresh catch!

Effective redirection faces the situation and does not avoid or divert. The teacher who sees a child going outdoors on a cold day without his coat does not give him help when she stops him by saying, "Stay inside and listen to the story now." She is avoiding the question of the need for a coat. She helps him by saying, "You'll be ready to go out as soon as you put on your coat." On the other hand, suggesting a substitute activity may help the child face a situation as in the case of two children wanting the same piece of equipment. The teacher helps when she says to one, "No, it's Bill's turn now. You might rake these leaves while you're waiting for your turn." By her redirection she helps him face his problem. Redirection should help the child face his problem by showing him how it can be met, not by diverting him.

Guides in Action

7. *Avoid Making Models in Any Art Medium for the Children to Copy*

This may seem like an arbitrary rule. We hope that it will seem justified later. Of course it takes away the fun of drawing a man or making little dogs or Santa Clauses out of clay for an admiring crowd of preschoolers. All this may seem like innocent fun, but we must remember that art is valuable because it is a means of self-expression. It is a language to express feelings—to drain off tension or to express well-being. The young child needs avenues of expression. His speech is limited. His feelings are strong. In clay or sand or mud at the easel, through finger paints, he expresses feelings for which he has little other language. If he has models before him, he may be blocked in using art as a means of *self*-expression. He will be less likely to be creative and more likely to be limited to trying to copy

Art then becomes only another area where he strives to imitate the adult who can do things much better than he can.

Notice what happens to a group at the clay table when the adult makes something. The children watch and then ask, "Make one for me." It isn't much use to say, "You make one for yourself." They can't do it as well and they feel that the adult is uncooperative. Most of them drift away from the table, the meaning gone out of the experience. It is no longer art or self-expression.

You may see children cramped over a paper with a crayon trying to make a car like the one the adult made, or children who will not touch the paints because they are afraid that they can't "make something." They may well envy the joy of the freer child who splashes color at the easel, delighting in its lines and masses, and is well content with what he's done. He has had no patterns to follow.

The need for help with techniques comes much later after the child has explored the possibilities in different art media and feels that these can be used as avenues of self-expression. Then the child will want to learn how to use the material to express better what *he* wants to express, but not to imitate better.

The skillful teacher will avoid getting entangled in "pattern making" under any guise. She may sit at the clay table, for example, feeling the clay, patting it and enjoying it as the children do, but she will not "make" anything. It is possible, of course, for children to watch adults who have found in art a means of self-expression as they work in their favorite medium, and for this to be a valuable experience for the children. Being with an adult who is expressing himself through an art medium is valuable for any child, but it is a very different experience from having an adult draw a man or a dog to amuse one. Avoid patterns!

3. Give the Child the Minimum of Help in Order that He May Have the Maximum Chance to Grow in Independence

There are all kinds of ways to help a child help himself if we take time to think about them, such as letting him help to turn the door knob with us, so that he will get the feel of how to handle a door knob and may be able to do it alone someday, or such as putting on his rubbers while he sits beside us instead of picking him up and holding him on our laps, a position which will make it hard for him ever to do the job himself someday. Too many times the child has

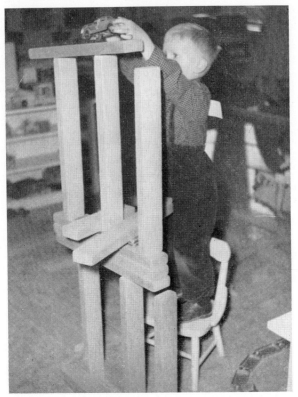

Fig. 25.   Look what I can do!

to climb down from the adult's lap when he might have started in a more advantageous position in the first place on his trip to independence.

Giving the minimum of help may mean showing a child how to get a block or box to climb on when he wants to reach something rather than reaching it for him. It may mean giving him time enough to work out a problem rather than stepping in and solving it for him. Children like to solve problems, and it is hard to estimate how much their self-confidence is increased by independent solving of problems. To go out and gather a child into one's arms to bring him in for lunch may be an effective way of seeing that he gets there, but it deprives him of the chance to take any responsibility in getting himself inside. It is important to give a child the minimum of help in order to allow him to grow himself as much as possible.

In leaving the child free to satisfy his strong growth impulse to be independent, we support his feeling of confidence in himself. "I can do this all by myself" or "Look what I can do," he says.

We must remember, however, that looking for opportunities to let the child do things for himself does not mean denying his requests for help. When a child says, "Help me" as he starts to take off his coat, he may be testing out the adult's willingness to help. The adult does not meet the test if she replies, "You can do it yourself." She reassures him if she gives help freely, with a full measure of willingness, or if she cannot, answers like this, "I'd like to help you but I'm busy just now," giving whatever real reason she has for not being in a position to help. A child may say, "Swing me," and he may be wanting assurance that the teacher really values him enough to do extra, unnecessary things for him. He seeks a relationship with the teacher. It is important to offer him a friendly, giving type of relationship. Confidence in self is based on a foundation of trust in others and a feeling of being valued by others. When a child *asks* for help, we listen to his request and answer it in a way that will make him less afraid of being helpless and dependent on us. This in no way interferes with our efforts to avoid giving unwanted help, with our efforts to leave the child free to act independently and with our efforts to help the child find ways to move away from his dependency on us. We will give only the help which the child feels he needs.

9. *Make Your Suggestions Effective by Reinforcing Them When Necessary*

Sometimes it is necessary to add several techniques together in order to be effective. A verbal suggestion, even though given positively, may not be enough in itself. "It's time to come in for lunch," may need to be reinforced by another suggestion such as, "I'll help you park your wagon," if the child is reluctant to leave his play, and then reinforced by actual help in parking. A glance at the right moment, moving nearer a child, a verbal suggestion, actual physical help are all techniques, and one must judge when they are to be used. Give only the minimum help necessary but give as much help as may be necessary.

One teacher says quietly, "It's time to go inside now" and moves toward the house. The child moves with her. Another teacher says, "It's time to go inside" and stands as though waiting to see what the child will do. He stays where he is for her behavior does not reinforce her words. Her behavior suggests something different.

When several children are playing together, some will accept suggestion more readily than others for different reasons. Success with one child will reinforce one's chances of success with others. It's wise to consider which child to approach first when one wishes to influence a group.

One of the most common faults of parents and teachers is that of using too many words, of giving two or three directions when one would have been sufficient. Anxiety and insecurity often take the form of over-verbalizing, showering the child with directions. Children will develop a protective "deafness" to too many words. It is important to have confidence in the child's ability to hear and respond to one suggestion, given only once. It is better to add different techniques together until one is successful rather than to depend solely on words.

10. *Forestalling Is the Most Effective Way of Handling Problems. Learn to Foresee and Prevent Rather Than Mop-up After a Difficulty*

We all are aware that "an ounce of prevention is worth a pound of cure." This is true in working with children. The best strategy depends on foreseeing and forestalling rather than mopping-up operations. Success in forestalling problems comes with experience. It takes time to learn what to expect in certain types of situations or with particular children or combinations of children.

Learning to prevent problems is important because, in many cases, children do not profit from making mistakes. The child who approaches others by doing something annoying may only learn that people don't like him and this may become a reality. He may learn acceptable ways of approaching others if the teacher, observing that he is about to go up to a group and knowing what he did previously in a similar situation, says to him, "If you'd like to play with them, you might knock first or ask Michael if he needs another block," or some other suitable suggestion. She may move into the situation with him to give him more support or interpret to the group what his intentions are or even help him accept his failure and find another place where he might have a better chance of success. If she waits until he fails, he may be unable to learn anything constructive. He may only run away.

Learning from experience may not be possible for the child, too, because we cannot permit him to experience the consequences of his action in some types of situations. The consequences would be too serious. In some cases, also, even if the child does suffer consequences, he may interpret them incorrectly. He may not really understand what is involved. This is often true where responses of others or their values and standards are concerned.

Sometimes children tell us what they are going to do. In these cases we need to listen and prevent what may be undesirable, not wait until the damage is done and there is little chance to learn from the experience.

Douglas says to Robert, "There's Pam. Let's hit her." They run over and hit Pamela and run away. The teacher comforts Pam and goes after the two boys. They have already gotten interested in digging with a group and appear resentful of her interfering with their activity. If she could have stopped them firmly and quickly as they started toward Pam, she might have made it clear to them that she expected them to control such an impulse and that she was there to help them. She could perhaps have helped them by asking a question about what other possibilities there were for action. They were readier to learn the lesson of not hitting before they hit rather than afterward!

The timing of a suggestion may be as important as the suggestion itself. Through experience and insight one can increase one's skill in giving a suggestion at the moment when it will do the most good. When a suggestion fails to get the desired results, it may be due to the "timing."

Advice given too soon deprives the child of a chance to try to work a thing out for himself. It deprives him of the satisfaction of solving his own problem. It may very well be resented. A suggestion made too late may have lost any chance of being successful. The child may be too discouraged or irritated to be able to act on it.

Help at the right moment may mean a supporting hand *before* the child loses his balance and falls, or arbitration *before* two boys come to blows over a wagon, or the suggestion of a new activity *before* the group grows tired and disorganized. Under a skillful teacher a group functions more smoothly because of all the things that never happen. Effective guidance depends on knowing how to forestall and prevent trouble by the proper timing of help as much as on knowing what to do when trouble occurs.

11. *When Limits Are Necessary, They Should Be Clearly Defined and Consistently Maintained*

There are some things which must not be done. There are limits beyond which a child cannot be allowed to go. The important thing is to be sure that the limits set are necessary limits and that they are clearly defined. Much of the difficulty between adults and children which is labeled "discipline" exists because of confusion about what the limits are. In a well-planned environment there will not be many "no's" but these "no's" will be clearly defined and the child will understand them.

We are very likely to overestimate the child's capacity to grasp the point of what we say. Our experience is much more extensive than his. Without realizing it we take many things for granted. The child lacks experience. If he is to understand what the limits are, these limits must be clearly and simply defined for him.

When we are sure that a limit is necessary and that the child understands it, we can maintain it with confidence. It is easy to feel unsure or even guilty about maintaining limits. Our own feelings bother us here. We may be afraid to maintain limits because we were over-controlled, and we turn away from the resentment and hostility that limits arouse in us. Because of our past experiences we may not want to take any responsibility for controlling behavior. Gradually we should learn to untangle our feelings and handle situations on their own merits with confidence and without hesitation.

The adult must be the one who is responsible for limiting children so that they do not come to harm or do not harm others or destroy property. Children will feel more secure with adults who can take this responsibility. They will feel freer because they can depend on the adult to stop them before they do things that they would be sorry about later.

12. *Use the Most Strategic Positions for Supervising*

Sometimes one will observe an inexperienced teacher with her back to most of the children as she watches one child. On the other hand, the experienced teacher, even when she is working with one child, will be in a position to observe at a glance what the other children are doing. She is always alert to the total situation.

Turning one's back on the group may represent, consciously or unconsciously, an attempt to limit one's experience to a simple situation. It is quite natural that one should feel like withdrawing from the more complex situations at first, or that one should take an interest in one particular child because other children seem more difficult to understand. It is a natural tendency but one should guard against it. It is important to develop skill in extending one's horizons. Observation of the total situation is essential to effective guidance. It is essential if the children are to be safe.

It is important to develop skill in being aware of all that is happening in a situation instead of only one part of it if one is to make the most of the opportunities for helping children. Safety requires teachers who are alert to see that all areas are supervised and not just one area. Enrichment of experience also will come when a teacher is observing all the children and their interests, not just one child. The teacher who is reading to children, for example, may encourage a shy child to join the reading group by a smile or she may forestall trouble by noticing a child who is ready for a change in activity and by encouraging him to join the group before his lack of interest disrupts the play of others.

Sitting rather than standing is another technique for improving the effectiveness of one's supervision. One is often in a better position to help a child when one is at the child's level, and children may feel freer to approach the adult who is sitting. It also makes possible more unobtrusive observation.

In the laboratory nursery school where there may be many adults, it is important that the adults avoid gathering in groups, such as near the entrance or in the locker room or around the sandbox. Grouping calls attention to the number of adults present. It may limit the children's feeling of freedom and may increase any tendency they have to feel self-conscious or to play for attention. Too many adults in one place may also mean that other areas are being left unsupervised.

Where one stands or sits is important in forestalling or preventing difficulties. A teacher standing between two groups engaged in different activities can make sure that one group does not interfere with the other and so can forestall trouble.

"Remote control" is ineffective control in the nursery school. Stepping between two children who are growing irritated at each other may prevent an attack, but it cannot be done if one is on the other side of the playroom. Trouble in the doll corner, for example, may be avoided by a teacher moving quietly near as tension mounts in the "family" and suggesting some solution. Her suggestion is more likely to be acceptable if her presence reinforces it. Trouble is seldom avoided by a suggestion given at a distance.

Depending on the physical plan of the school, certain spots will be more strategic for supervision than others. If the teacher is standing near the entrance to the coat room, it will be easy for her to see that the child hangs up his coat before he goes on to play. If she is standing on the far side of the room, she is not in a position to act effectively if he chooses to disregard her reminder. Some places are favorable because it is possible to observe many corners and others are "blind spots" as far as much observation goes.

Choose the position for standing or sitting which will best serve your purposes. Study a diagram of the school where you are teaching and check the spots which are strategically good for supervision. List places where close supervision is needed for safety, such as at the workbench.

13. *The Health and Safety of the Children Are a Primary Concern*

The good teacher must be constantly alert to the things which affect health such as seeing that drinking cups are not used in common, that towels are kept separate, that toys which have been in a child's mouth are washed, that the window is closed if there is a draft, that wraps are adjusted to changes in temperature or activity.

The good teacher must also be alert to things which concern the safety of children. Being alert to safety means observing and removing sources of danger such as protruding nails, unsteady ladders or boards not properly supported. It means giving close supervision to children who are playing together on high places, or to children who are using such potentially dangerous things as hammers, saws and shovels. The point is familiar but clearcut and important. The skillful teacher never relaxes her watchfulness.

HERE IS AN EXERCISE. List ways in which you have observed a teacher protecting the health and safety of the children in the nursery school.

14. *Observe and Take Notes*

Underlying all these guides is the assumption that teaching is based on ability to observe behavior objectively and to evaluate its meaning. As in any science, conclusions are based on accurate observations. Jot down notes frequently, statements of what happens, the exact words that a child uses, the exact sequence of events. Make the note at the time or as soon after the event as possible, always dating each note. Reread these notes later and make interpretations. Skill in observing and recording is essential in building understanding. Improve your ability to select significant incidents and make meaningful records.

REFERENCES

1. Child Welfare League of America: A Guide for Teacher Recording in Day Care Agencies. Bulletin, 1954.
2. Cohen, Dorothy, and Stern, Virginia: Observing and Recording the Behavior of Young Children. Bureau of Publications, Teachers College, Columbia University, 1958.
3. Dawley, Edith: Cues for Observing Children's Behavior. Childhood Education, Nov. 1953.
4. Shuey, Betty: Written Records on Children. Journal of Nursery Education, Spring 1958.

5

Helping Children
Adjust to New Experiences

We All Know What It's Like to Be in a New Situation

We suggested earlier that the first step for us to take in the nursery school was to accept the feelings which we had because we were new and strange there. These feelings probably included feelings of inadequacy which led us to defend ourselves in some way against the inadequacy we felt. Some of our defenses may have been handicapping to further learning. One of our first problems was to recognize and accept the feelings that are part of being new in any situation and handle these feelings in a constructive way, so that the new situation could contribute to our growth. We had to learn to feel comfortable about being new and strange.

Each Child Has Characteristic Patterns of Response to
New Experience

The child faces the same problem when he meets new situations such as entering nursery school or accepting the approaches of strange people. He may defend himself against the uncertainty and inadequacy he feels by inappropriate behavior or by rejecting the experience. Because we know what it is like to feel strange, without skills and inadequate, we will find it easier to understand the child's behavior. We may be able to recognize the meaning which lies behind what the child does. We may be better able to help him as he goes through a new experience because we ourselves know what it is like to feel new and strange.

By observing the child we can see more clearly the kinds of defenses people use, including ourselves; and as we help him, we can understand better the way people respond to support. The behavior of the children will teach us a great deal about adjustments to new experiences.

For the child as for the adult new experiences call forth defenses, tendencies to retreat or, on the other hand, to explore and find satisfactions. What the child or the adult will do depends on his individual makeup and his past experiences.

What kind of adjustment is a "good adjustment" in a new situation? Obviously fear is very limiting. An uncritical acceptance sometimes reveals a lack of awareness which may lead to undesirable consequences. What we might consider most desirable is a readiness to accept differences, an ability to pick out familiar elements and relate the unknown to the known.

There Are Reasons for Differences in Adjustment

What lies behind differences in children in adjustment to the same situation?

For one thing, we can be sure that it is not the same situation to all children. Every organism differs in its response to a situation or experience. Demonstrable differences in responsiveness to stimulation are present at birth or soon after birth. One child, for example, will be more disturbed than another by a sudden, loud noise or a difference in the intensity of light. Experiences will have different meanings for each depending on the sensitivity which is part of his native equipment.

Each child also brings to a new experience his own past experiences. These have prepared him differently. It would be easier to understand the child's adjustment in the present if we knew all that had happened to him previously. As this is impossible, we can watch his behavior for clues that we must use with understanding. In one nursery school, for example, where the wagons and tricycles were kept in a shed, one of the four-year-olds refused to go in and get a wagon or to put one away. On talking to his mother the teacher learned that he had had an unfortunate experience in being shut up in a shed by someone who was temporarily crazed. Because of this association with a shed he could not use the shed in the same way as the other children.

We cannot safely ignore the child's past experiences. We must accept him as he is. It does not matter if we do not know specifically what these past experiences have been as long as we accept the child's present behavior *as having some meaning*. Being taken to a new place may mean pleasant possibilities to one child and disturbing possibilities to another. We can expect and accept different behavior in different children. Each child is a different organism. Each has had different past experiences.

Single events like moving or having a fright happen against a background of experiences already past. The child who had been locked in the shed had spent his four years in an unusually comfortable, loving family. He had had plenty of experiences of being safe and protected and the unfortunate experience in the shed was an isolated experience which disturbed him remarkably little. It did not affect many areas of behavior. A less secure child might have shown many disturbances of behavior instead of a disturbance only in a directly related area.

The many daily experiences which a child has are probably of more importance in influencing his adjustments than single traumatic events. In other words, the sum total of the child's experience is usually more important than any single experience. It is desirable, therefore, to have each experience contribute to making the child feel more secure and more adequate. We are not likely to gain strength by being hurt; we are sure to acquire scars. Children who are forced into making adjustments for which they are not ready are less prepared for further adjustment. They may try to conceal their feeling as is sometimes the case with the child whose mother declares, "He doesn't mind being left anywhere." The damage they suffer may be evident only in indirect ways as in a loss in creativity, greater dependence, or increased irritability. But many experiences of feeling strange or frightened, however small and seemingly insignificant, add up to a total which may be disastrous for sound adjustment.

ENTERING NURSERY SCHOOL IS AN IMPORTANT EXPERIENCE

The first and one of the most important of these new experiences is the experience of entering nursery school itself. Entering the nursery school is a big step for the child. It means leaving his familiar home and depending on adults other than his parents. It means finding a place for himself in a group of other children of about his own age. There are new toys, different toilet arrangements, a strange play area. He meets a variety of responses from the other children, some of them apparently unreasonable responses. He must trust the teachers to understand him and keep him safe through these new experiences.

The child's feeling of confidence in himself may be strengthened if he can meet these new experiences successfully. He may be able to recover to some extent from the fear and uncertainty left by past experiences. For many children there are valuable opportunities at this point to "work through" problems and take steps in rebuilding a shaken sense of trust.

Readiness for Nursery School

What makes a child ready for nursery school? Why do some children enter eagerly and others hold back from the new experience? What can we do to reduce the difficulties to manageable proportions for all children?

Here we will refer to the concept of developmental tasks as outlined by Erickson. According to this concept the development of a sense of trust is the first and basic task for a healthy personality. The sense of trust grows out of experiences of being cared for by loving parents. In the first year of life the infant finds the world a safe place if his needs are met, if he does not suffer because he is little and helpless. He learns to trust because his parents care for him. Feeling safe with his parents, he can proceed to feel safe with other people. If he has good experiences with other adults and children, he adds to his sense of trust. There are many reasons why one child may not feel as safe or secure as another. Many moves, leaving little in the way of familiar physical surroundings to tie to, may make it harder for a child's sense of trust to develop. Frequent separations from parents, or separations coming at critical times in development may be another reason.

Because feeling secure contributes significantly to healthy personality development, it is important to reduce the difficulty of the new experience of entering a school, so that it may add to the child's feeling of being safe rather than threaten it. Safeguards include avoiding starting a child in nursery school shortly after a new baby has arrived, or after the family has just moved, or after there has been some upsetting change in the family. If it is necessary for the child to start school under circumstances like these, he should be given much more time to make the adjustment.

The Significance of the Experience for the Child

Because the experience of entering nursery school may contribute to growth in important ways, let us try to understand its significance for the child and his parents, and then outline steps to follow which will promote healthy growth through the experience.

The tasks facing the child in entering nursery school are twofold. First, he must go out to meet a new experience, rich with possibilities for growth and for sensory and social contacts, but full of the unknown for him. The second and perhaps the more significant task which the child faces is that inherent in growth itself. He must resolve the conflict inevitably felt in leaving something behind in order to go on to something else.

The conflict to be resolved in this case is lessening the close dependency on his mother in order to live in the world the nursery school offers and find the new satisfactions it makes possible for him. In going forward, he must leave behind a measure of dependency in order to take a step in the direction of independence. He must resist his desire to cling to the relationship with his mother which has been the main source of his satisfaction and security up until now. He must act on the wish to separate himself from her and be ready to explore new relationships which may also prove to be sources of satisfying experience.

Each Child Comes Differently Equipped

In meeting these tasks each child brings different equipment with him. His own constitutional endowment will differ, the senses with which he perceives, his tempo of living and the intensity of his response. One child may delight in sounds, another in color, another in movement. One child may respond quickly, reacting to a variety of stimuli; another may be content to experience slowly. What each child has known in the past will differ even more although affected to some extent by the differing endowments of each. Some children will come to nursery school having had limited opportunities for sensory experience, while others may have had many opportunities to touch, taste, smell and hear. Some children will come having known much uncertainty and fear. Others will have known more often the familiar and the safe.

The quality and number of relationships with people which each child has known will also differ. The way a child faces the second task presented by entrance to nursery school will usually depend to a large extent on the relationships he has had with people in the past.

Relationships with His Mother and His Teacher Are Important

Of these relationships, the one with his mother will probably have the most effect on the way he proceeds toward independence. If his mother has been able to give him a basic experience in trust, she will have satisfied in large measure his pressing infantile dependency needs. He is now free to move on to include new relationships which will meet new needs. The conflict he feels in separating himself from her is more easily resolved when he does not carry a heavy burden of "unfinished business" in the way of infantile dependency.

The teacher plays a significant role because of the help she gives the mother as well as the child. They both face a new experience in the need to move from dependency toward greater independence. The teacher can make the new seem more manageable and the unknown seem more attractive. She can give support to the child's desire to move toward independence as well as support to the mother's desire to leave the child free. The teacher will do this best when she sees clearly the significance of what the experience of entering nursery school may contribute to growth for both child and parent.

It is not simple for the teacher to move with certainty for each child differs in what he brings and needs. In addition the teacher herself may be handicapped by set patterns of the way school entrance is handled, or handicapped by her own fears, by her own need to control or by the way her own dependency needs have been met. But as she develops sensitivity and skill she will find satisfaction in working out this problem for it is here that the nursery school makes one of its most significant contributions. If it can help the child with these tasks, it has given him help which will be of value in many future experiences.

THE PROCESS OF HELPING THE CHILD AND HIS PARENTS

How does the teacher proceed in helping the child and his parents? What is the best use of the growth opportunities which the experience offers? How may the philosophy of nursery education be translated into action in this particular experience? What are steps in the process of entering nursery school?

We will suggest a series of steps which may be taken in helping a child enter nursery school. Our goal in these steps will be to use the experience of entering nursery school so that it may contribute to the child's satisfaction in the world around him and his growth in confidence and adequacy.

One Step in the Process Is a Conference

The first specific step is a conference between the teacher and one or both parents. In this conference the teacher explains to the parents the policies of the school, makes clear the matter of fees, health regulations, hours and steps in admission. She tells them something of the program, of their part in it and tries to answer the questions they have. She learns something of the child's past experiences and the parents' expectations. She may ask them to fill out a home information record to be kept by the school.

One of the important parts of the conference will be the discussion of the steps to be taken in entering the child in the nursery

school. These steps will need to be clarified in subsequent conferences, but the parents should have clearly in mind a general idea of
what the steps are before the child starts school. The teacher will
confer often with the parent in the first days, informally at school
or over the telephone. Timing and details of the procedure of entering will be adapted to each child as she comes to know him. But it is
essential for the parent to understand, especially for the mother who
may be employed or have other obligations, that someone from the
family must participate with the child in the first days of school.

Another Step Is Visiting the School

The next step is to give the child some concept of what nursery
school is like through a visit to the school. The child needs a picture
in his mind when he hears the word "nursery school." He needs to
be anticipating what lies ahead in as realistic a way as possible.

Visting the school at a time when school is not in session will
enable him to meet the teacher and become familar with aspects of
the physical setup. He can give his attention to particular toys or
activities. He can discover areas in which he feels secure. He can
choose his impressions. He is free to proceed at his own rate in per-
ceiving and experiencing. He will begin to build a concept of what
nursery school is like.

Visiting the school when other children are not present keeps the
situation simple and manageable for him. There are not as many
new and unknown factors. He is protected against the unpredictable-
ness of other children's behavior. He has an opportunity to enter
into a relationship with the teacher without the competition of other
children dividing her attention. She has a chance to become acquainted with him and take a step in understanding what his needs
are likely to be and what role she may play as his teacher.

Attending for Part of the Session Is Another Step

The third step, following this visit, is for the child to visit with his
mother at the nursery school when school is in session. School as a
place where children are present is added to the concept he is forming about a nursery school. As a visitor he can watch, make the
contacts he wishes and participate only as he is ready.

Children will differ in the way they use experiences in this visit.

Some will make many contacts with children. Others will follow, watching from a distance. Still others will return to the play materials which they enjoyed on the earlier visits, seeming to pay little attention to the other children around them.

The teacher will add to her understanding of a particular child by observing him in this new situation. She also has many opportunities to help him. Seeing his interest in something, she may place this material near him, bringing it easily within his reach. If he looks at a child painting at the easel, she may walk nearer with him, and say a few words about the paint, the colors, etc. She does not push him into activity. She only moves with him if she feels this makes him feel more secure. He may find the piano and together they may share some music, with other children joining them, perhaps. If he is most interested in watching what other children are doing, she may comment on what is going on, mentioning the children's names. Some children do not need as much help, and still others may be made anxious by much attention from the teacher until they feel more at home. The teacher can limit her help to a reassuring smile when such a child looks in her direction and be ready with more active help later.

Fig. 26.   Discovering each other. (H. Armstrong Roberts.)

When a new child enters a group, he holds a special place as a visitor. Other children have a chance to become aware of him as a "new" child. They may become aware of the "newness" and the fact that there are steps in proceeding from being "new" to feeling familiar and at home in a group.

A wise teacher may use the opportunity to support growth in individual children already in the group. "Remember when you were new and visited?" perhaps recalling some special incident and adding, "Now you know where things go and what we do. You have friends." In this way she points out and strengthens the movement the child has made toward independence and greater security.

There Must Be Opportunities to Develop a Relationship with the Teacher

Through experiences with the child during his visits the teacher makes an effort to establish a relationship with the new child which he can accept. Her task is to help him discover a teacher as a person who is there to be depended on, who cares for and about him. He must feel sure of this before he can let his mother go with confidence. He must feel able to depend on the teacher. For this reason it is important for the teacher to have time to spend with the child or to be available to him. It is not enough just to have someone able to look out for him at this point. He needs the same person to whom he can turn if he is to make the separation in a constructive way.

In order to make the best use developmentally of the experience for the child, the teacher will bring only one new child at a time into the group. It is difficult to be able to give the needed reassurance to more than one new child at a time in a group. We are speaking here of bringing children into a group. If a group is just forming, it represents a different situation. The teacher may then plan to bring perhaps four children together for an hour with their mothers. Four new children are not likely to enter into sustained relationships with each other or to demand a great deal from the adult immediately. She can be available to them all as she introduces the possibilities of the school environment to them. Another group can come at another hour to go through the same process and, in a few days, the two groups may come together to become a school to which a new child may later be added.

A Clear Understanding About the Length of Time the Child Is to Stay Helps in the Adjustment

The wise teacher will have a clear understanding with the parent as to the length of time the child will be staying on his first visit to the school. An hour is a reasonable and safe time to plan on. The hour should be scheduled at a time when the teacher is not likely to be busy with other activities as she is at the opening of school. Since the first visit offers the teacher an opportunity to observe the child in the school situation and to start building a relationship with him, she must have time for this.

More than an hour spent in an environment which calls for as much responsiveness as the nursery school is too fatiguing for most children. The child needs to be protected from fatigue. Some children could, of course, stay longer and many children will wish to do so, but there are advantages in setting a definite length of time for the first visit and maintaining it.

One of the most important reasons for a clear understanding is that it helps the mother to feel sure about what is expected of her. If she knows that she is to bring the child and stay with him for an hour and then they are to leave, it reduces her uncertainty. She may be better able to relax and use the time to add to *her* picture of what nursery school is like. It is not up to her to decide the length of time they should stay. Here, too, the teacher has a chance to gain some understanding through the way the mother reacts to this time limit. Does she find it difficult to accept? Does she try to change it, saying as the time for departure approaches, "He's getting along so well. I think he might as well stay on, don't you?" Is she afraid she may not be able to get the child to leave? Does she comment anxiously, "I'm afraid he won't want to go. What do you do about that?" Does she needlessly disturb the child with warnings, "You haven't much time left. It's almost time to go." Is she comfortable with the time limit set?

What is the mother's part during the visit? We have suggested that she may be helped by having a definite idea of the length of time that she and her child are expected to stay. She may also be helped if she is clear about what the teacher feels it is wise for mothers to do during a visit. In the conference with the mother in preparation for the child's entrance the teacher will discuss the kind of help a child needs from a parent. She may indicate that he needs to feel that his mother is glad to have him going to nursery school, that she thinks it is a good place for a child to be and that she believes that he will find it good. He needs to feel, too, that she is not leaving him but that she is letting him leave her and will always be glad to have him return.

The Mother's Feelings Influence the Child in His Adjustment

The way the mother really feels about sending the child to nursery school will have a profound effect on the way the child adjusts there. If she feels reluctant or unsure or overanxious about his attending, she hinders his accomplishment of the task of meeting the new experience and growing more independent. It is sometimes hard for both parent and teacher to realize how completely a child senses what the adults who are close to him may be feeling.

There are many reasons why a mother can feel uncertain. She inevitably feels some conflict between wanting to hold on to the child, to prolong his dependence, and wanting the child to be strong and independent. The teacher needs to stand ready with reassurance. She needs to strengthen the mother's acceptance of the reality of what nursery school really is and the mother's confidence in her child's readiness for it. A parent may want very much to have a child in nursery school and yet still not want him there. She may be afraid of the disapproval of people. She may be afraid of her own feeling of not wanting him home all the time. It is for the teacher to encourage those feelings in the mother which will support the growth of the child toward independence and reduce the conflict for them both.

What does the mother do to show the child how she feels? In this first visit she may say, "I will be right here. I am staying with you. I won't leave." She may find a chair where she can see and be seen easily by the child and stay there. She does not push him away from her with words like, "Why won't you go play with the blocks or with that little boy over there."

It is the teacher's responsibility to encourage the child to move away from his mother, not the mother's responsibility. The mother may show him by a smile that she is glad to see him when he returns to her side, but she indicates her pleasure in what he has done on his own. If he is hurt or is rebuffed by another child, she gives him the comfort he seeks, but she accepts the incident as part of the reality of existence with others, trying to look at it in the way she hopes that he will. She shows confidence in his ability not to be upset just as she will not be unnecessarily upset.

The Teacher Finds Ways to Help Both the Child and the Mother

The teacher is the one to take the responsibility for helping the child try to participate again when he is ready. Always she is alert to the need to give him support in the efforts he makes to move toward greater independence. When he does leave his mother, she stays near him to give him the protection he needs at first. Things are more upsetting to someone who is already feeling uncertain. Later he will be ready to hold his own. By staying near him she is also demonstrating both to him and his mother that she is there, looking after him. Later he will be able to come and find her when he needs her, but in the beginning she must be there so that he can be clear about her role. In this way she makes it easier for him to leave his mother with confidence. She makes it easier for the mother not to interfere but to leave the child free.

Some children are helped to make the adjustment if they bring something from home to keep with them at first. While it may not be the usual practice of the school to encourage children to bring their own toys to school, it may be desirable to permit it during the initial adjustment period. It is unlikely that the child will be able to "share" this possession if he is depending on it for support, and he should be protected against having to share it. A simple explanation by the teacher such as, "Mary is new at school and needs to keep her doll. Later when she knows us better, she'll let us play with it, too," will serve to deepen understanding all around.

Some mothers find time spent at nursery school full of interest. Others are restless, seeing little to interest them. If a mother is interested, she will find it easy to respond to the child's requests to come and look at things, but she also needs to make him feel that it is *his* school. She looks at what he shows her, but she will avoid trying to point out many things to him. The teacher, for her part, will look for ways to help the mother appreciate the significance of what is occurring. As she has time, she can sit with the mother, pointing out and explaining things that are going on. Many people have had little background for understanding the development of children. They lack interest in it because they know little about it. Parents

are almost sure to be interested if they are helped to see the significance of the play experiences children are having. The teacher and
the school may open up possibilites to parents for growing in understanding which will be valuable through the years.

Regular Attendance for Part of the Session without His Mother Comes Next

The fourth step for the child in entering nursery school is to attend
regularly for part of the session and to begin the process of having
his mother leave him at school.

It is at this point that individual differences become most evident
and the teacher is called on to exercise judgment and skill. The time
which needs to be spent in this step may be one or two days or it may
be one or more weeks. The point to keep in mind is that a relationship of trust in the teacher and interest in the school program itself
are the sources of support which will enable the child to be successful in staying at school by himself with confidence and a sense of
achievement. The first visits have been steps in preparation for the
separation. Most children will need their mothers with them for a
few days until they feel at home in the school and with the teacher.

It is interesting to note that most mothers overestimate their children's capacity to adjust. One cannot depend on a parent's assurance
that "He'll be all right without me; I've left him lots of times." He
may be a child who stands quiet and withdrawn, the very child who
needs his mother most because he cannot express his insecurities. He
may have had too many experiences of being left! Entering nursery
school with his mother may mean the chance to overcome some of
the past, to reassure himself by this present situation that his mother
really will stay with him when he needs her. This may be the feeling
that he needs if he is to be free to explore and enjoy the new. The
tendency on the part of most parents to expect too much of their
children in the way of adjustment probably indicates how universally
we fail to perceive what is involved in an experience for a child.
We are not accustomed to observing behavior for clues to feelings.
We look for what we want to see and not for what is really there.

To feel secure is basic to sound personality growth. There is no
greater source of insecurity to the very young child than to be separated from his mother when he feels he needs her. He should be
protected from this experience. Most three-year-old children, however, have built up sufficient trust in the world and their mothers

so that they are not made unduly anxious by a short separation under favorable conditions. In fact, by this age they may be ready to test themselves by just such a separation. They are working on the task of achieving a sense of being independent people. Being able to stay apart from the mother brings them real satisfaction. They may feel more secure for knowing that they can be safe and content in a larger world. There is a real sense of achievement in gaining this measure of independence. One of the reasons that authorities agree that three is usually a desirable age for beginning nursery school is that the evidence which we have points to this age as the period of readiness for some separation from the parent.

The Teacher Plays an Active Part in Helping the Child Separate Himself from His Parent

It is usually necessary for the teacher to take an active part in the process of separation. The major responsibilty is hers, not the mother's. The mother's role is a passive one. She must be able to let the child go but neither push him away nor try to hold him. The teacher is the one who must actively give support to the child as he shows signs of readiness to leave his mother. She must make it seem desirable for him to take the step.

The child cannot be expected to take responsibility for this step unaided. If the teacher plays a passive role and leaves the major responsibility up to him, she is greatly increasing the conflict he faces. "Do you want your mother to go now?" or "Is it all right for her to leave?" demands an answer which he is not ready to give in most cases. It is unfair to ask it of him. This is the very question to which the nursery school experience and others like it will give him the answer someday. As a result of these experiences, he should be readier to answer it later with, "It is all right. I know I am safe. I am an independent person." We know that forcing a separation when the child is not ready is very damaging, but forcing the child to be responsible for a decision which involves unresolved conflicts also puts heavy burdens on a child. He is likely to cling to dependency.

Some sensitive teachers today, concerned about the danger of forcing a separation, lose sight of the growth potentials in the child. They fail to pick up the clues he offers as to his readiness to move toward independence provided he can get help. Prolonging his dependency in the new situation may interfere with his growth toward independence which is the task at hand developmentally. We must not push a child, but neither should we hold development back. We must trust the child's capacity and desire to grow, and we must develop skills as teachers which will aid him in this growth.

During this fourth step in the process of entering nursery school, the child will come for only part of the session. Until he has successfully completed the stage of separating from his mother, it is better for him not to stay for the full program. For one reason, it will probably make too long a day for him. For another reason, postponing the full session will be an incentive for him to make the effort of staying without his mother in order to achieve the goal of full time attendance. If he can have his mother and the nursery school, too, he has less incentive to become independent.

The teacher will plan with the mother as to the length of time he should stay. Having observed the child during his visit, she must decide with the help of the mother how long he can stay without undue fatigue. For several days most children should stay less than two hours. The teacher will also decide with the mother on the best time in the morning for his attendance. It is important to give consideration to family schedule in planning here. The child is not helped if the running of the home is greatly disrupted by the demands made by nursery school. The needs of other members in the family must be considered.

During these first days it is important for the child that his mother come without bringing other children in the family if it is at all possible to plan it this way. Entering nursery school is a significant event in the life of the child and his mother. If she is free to give him all her attention, she may reaffirm for him his sense of being valued by her. It may be especially important to him if there is a baby at home who has necessarily been taking much of her attention. It becomes important in helping him realize that she cares for him at this moment of approaching separation.

After the child has begun to relate to the teacher in nursery school as a person whom he can depend on, he may be helped by having her visit at home. She may make a visit to his home arranged beforehand with him and his mother, so that he can show her his toys and his bed and the things important to him. This contact may help the teacher, too, in her understanding of the needs of the child and what she may be able to offer him in the school.

The Mother Helps with Her Understanding

As soon as the mother and teacher agree that the child is feeling comfortable at nursery school and is able to accept help from the teacher, they will plan for the mother to leave the child by himself for a short time. In the case of a secure parent and child, well prepared for the experience, the mother may be able to leave for a short time on the second day. One mother reported to the teacher on the first day that as they were on the way to school, her three-year-old son said to her, "Now I want you to go home, mummy." Wisely they decided to follow his request. He was telling them clearly that he felt ready to be left for a while, and they showed him that they, too, had confidence in him. Other children may not be ready for several days to have their mothers leave, but the skillful, experienced teacher will help the child reach this goal in the shortest time possible. She will not encourage the child's dependency on his mother as we pointed out above.

The timid child may be helped by having his mother out of sight but in a place where he can reach her whenever his anxiety grows great enough for him to need her. It may be wise for her to sit in the teacher's office, reading, but quietly glad to see him when he leaves the playroom and comes to her for reassurance. If she is a mother who is concerned over whether he can stay without her, she herself may need a good deal of help from the teacher in accepting the fact that it is good to give the child this support and that his behavior is not a cause for anxiety. She needs to see it as an opportunity to help him deal with fears which exist for him and which cannot safely be ignored.

The child is likely to feel secure at school more quickly, not only if his mother has confidence in the school but also if she gives him confidence in her willingness to stay. When three-year-old Phil started going to nursery school, his mother stayed with him for several days, hoping each day would be the last day that he would need her. She kept suggesting that it was about hime for her to go, but he looked distressed every time. The teacher finally suggested that perhaps Phil had never felt really sure that his mother wanted to stay. The next day when they came to school Phil's mother sat down, saying, "I will stay just as long as you want, Phil," and she sounded as though she meant it. Phil seemed more relaxed as he played. In the middle of the morning he turned to her and said, "You can go home now, mummy." He seemed pleased at being able to stay by himself. Too often we are kept from giving freely to the child what he needs because we are afraid of spoiling him. Yet it is the quality of our "giving" which may mean the difference between security or uneasiness. If we give of our time and our attention, we can afford to give freely. Children are not spoiled by this kind of giving.

The mother will find an opportunity to prepare the child for her leaving, saying perhaps, "Today, I may do some errands while you are playing at nursery school. I will be gone a little while, and when I get back, I'll see what you are doing." If his response is, "I don't want you to go," she may answer, "I won't go for a while after we get to nursery school, not until you are having fun and I know you are ready. I will tell you and I'll only be gone a very little while."

It is almost never wise for a mother who is helping a child to accept her leaving to go immediately after she has brought him to school. She needs to sit down in her usual place and wait until he has found something he enjoys, his favorite corner or a story or music session with the teacher, or perhaps a tricycle outdoors. It is usually the teacher who should be responsible for indicating that it is a good time for the mother to say good-by. The teacher can then prepare the child for what he already expects by saying quietly, "Your mother is going now, John. She will be back very soon." With the teacher there, the mother can say good-by to the child and leave for a short time. If they have estimated the child's readiness correctly, the teacher will be able to help the child handle the anxiety he feels until his mother returns. She will be careful to stay near him.

The first separation should be a very short one. Even fifteen minutes may seem a long time when one feels unsure of oneself and under some strain. When the mother returns, she will speak to him and then stay for a while, giving the child time to enjoy his play before they go home together. This may need to be repeated for several days with the length of her absence increased if he has seemed able to accept it. In this way his mother is showing him the pattern which she will follow. She goes but she comes back. He is discovering the satisfaction of feeling more and more comfortable about being able to stay at school without his mother.

During this period it is important that the teacher talk over with the mother the reactions of the child at home. Is he showing signs of undue fatigue? What about his sleeping and eating? Is he wetting his bed? The child's reactions will be the determining factor in deciding how long he should stay at nursery school and how long his mother should be away from him.

The Child Is Ready for Full Time Attendance without His Mother

When the mother is able to leave the child almost as soon as they arrive at school and stay away for as long as two hours without his becoming uneasy, the child is ready for the fifth and last step—that of full time attendance by himself.

Few children reach this in less than a week. Others take much longer. Sleep disturbances, toilet accidents and increased irritability may be the result of trying to move faster than the child is ready. Good adjustment requires time, and there are less likely to be relapses if the adjustment has not been either hurried or prolonged unduly.

It often happens that a child who is disturbed by some event at home or at school will revert to an earlier level of dependency, wanting his mother again. Again, it is important that his real needs be accepted and met. If his adjustment is sound, he is usually quickly reassured by his parent's willingness to stay with him for a time, and it does not take long for him to become independent. Again, the teacher helps him by accepting him but by giving all the support she can to his desire to be more self-sufficient.

To Summarize

We may summarize the steps in entering nursery school in this way:

1. The teacher has a conference with the parents in which, among other things, the procedures to be followed as the child enters school are defined.

2. The child and his parent or parents visit the school when it is not in session to become acquainted with the physical setup and establish a relationship with the teacher in the school.

3. The child and his parent visit during the regular session of the school for a limited, specified time.

4. The child begins attending school regularly for part of the session and begins the process of separating himself from his parent as soon as he feels comfortable there. The teacher takes the re-

sponsibility for planning with the parent the time and method of separation. She may visit in the child's home so that he and she can become better acquainted.

5. The child attends school without his parent for increasingly longer periods until he is coming for the full session.

If the step of moving toward independence and away from the dependency on his mother is taken so that it does not produce more anxiety than the child can manage easily, he is free to enjoy and profit from the new experience. He gains in self-confidence. We may wonder whether children who have had this kind of help in a significant experience in separation will be as likely later to suffer from panic in strange situations or to be disorganized by feelings of homesickness.

Here are some examples of the ways in which different children have made the adjustment to entering nursery school.

Ralph, Whose Mother Could Give
Him Time to Grow in Feeling Secure

Ralph was an only child, a little over three years of age, with a father and mother who were very fond of him. Although they were gentle and kind, they were very anxious to have Ralph come up to all expectations, perhaps because they were not too secure themselves.

On his visit to the school before he entered, Ralph enjoyed playing with the cars and blocks, but he called his mother's attention to everything and referred to her constantly. It was apparent that he depended on her and would not be ready to have her leave for some time even though he was eager for school and friendly with the teacher.

When he came on the first day of school, he held his mother's hand tightly. She went into the playroom with him and sat down near the block corner. Ralph immediately began playing. When other children approached, he seemed pleased and made attempts to join their play. One of the boys took a block from him in spite of his mild protest. Tears came into his eyes as he relinquished his hold on the block. He turned toward his mother but did not go to her. She smiled sympathetically and encouragingly, not quite sure what to do, and the teacher quietly reassured him, "That was your block, wasn't it? I'll ask Bill to give it back. There are other blocks for him.

There are plenty for both of you to build with." It was easy to get Bill to return the block, and under the teacher's watchful eye the two had a satisfactory play, side by side. Ralph returned to his mother's side finally, flushed and happy.

Ralph was inclined to stutter when he got excited. This was further evidence that it was especially important to proceed slowly in introducing him to experiences. The stuttering showed that he was sensitive to strain. It was also apparent that there would be some strain for him in adjusting to the realities of three-year-old behavior because of the somewhat "adult" standards to which he had been accustomed. But he had shown a capacity to enjoy not only the play materials, but the other children on that first day, and to accept help from someone other than his mother.

Ralph and his mother went home at the end of an hour and a half to return the next day, both eager for more. Ralph's mother watched with interest the things that went on in school. At Ralph's request she sat by the window while he went outdoors to play. He looked toward the window frequently but he appeared to enjoy his play, again welcoming approaches by the other children and accepting help from the teacher when the children's approaches were not just what he expected. Again it was apparent that he was depending on his mother's presence to feel comfortable even though he did not stay near her. His mother stayed at school for four mornings, taking him home before the lunch period. On the fifth day she told him that she was going to see one of her friends while he was playing at school, but that she would be back soon and see what he was doing. He agreed and turned to the blocks. With the teacher sitting in the chair where his mother usually sat, he played busily building a garage for his cars. He smiled at his mother when she returned, but went on playing.

His mother and teacher then agreed that Ralph no longer needed his mother, but that he still needed a short day at school. He came happily the next morning, knowing that his mother was not staying. When she started to leave, however, he asked her to go to the store and not to go home without him. Apparently he could not quite bear to think of a mother at home without him. She went shopping and he had a good morning at school. It was nearly a week later that he decided he would like to stay for lunch like the other children, and did. His adjustment had proceeded smoothly. His mother smilingly remarked one day that she missed being at nursery school, adding,

Fig. 27. Discovering what one can do.

"It was such fun and I learned so much. They're all different, aren't they?" The days had been worth almost as much to Ralph's mother as to Ralph. She had gained confidence in the school, too.

Not long after this as Ralph was leaving one day he ran back and threw his arms around the teacher's neck and gave her a kiss. It probably showed that he felt he belonged to the school and to the adults who helped him feel comfortable there as his mother did at home. As the result of this experience in adjustment he had probably grown less tense and felt himself to be a more adequate person, more secure because he knew he could handle an experience at his own rate.

Walter, Who Found It Easy to Have Fun

Walter illustrates the case of a child for whom starting to nursery school was as pleasant as opening the door on Christmas morning to discover the delightful surprises. Walter was the youngest of four children in a busy, accepting kind of home. When he visited the nursery school, he had plunged into activity immediately and had enjoyed himself thoroughly. His mother reported that he was a happy child and had always been easy to live with. On his first day at school he ran from one activity to another, seeming to feel completely free to explore. When the time came to leave, he was squatting down watching some boys dig and he definitely didn't want to go. His mother repeated her statement that they both had to go and then she picked him up without any show of concern. He accepted this just as casually and smiled broadly at the teacher over his mother's shoulder as they went out the door. The next day his mother left him at the door with a "good-by" and he ran to the playground. From then on he lived at nursery school as freely and comfortably as he did at home. The teachers and children alike were glad to see him arrive.

Peter, Who Wanted the Teacher to Help Him

Peter is nearly four years old. He has a ten-month-old brother and the family has recently moved so that Peter has had to make many adjustments in the last year. He is a thin child and his face has an unchildlike expression. When he visited the nursery school he seemed interested in a variety of materials, explored hastily both indoors and outside. He wanted his mother to accompany him and avoided the teacher and seemed defensive and self-conscious. He didn't talk much but when he did, he used big words although many of his speech sounds were infantile.

When he began coming for part of the morning with his mother, he showed interest in all that went on. He watched intently but did not participate directly with the other children. Although he checked frequently on his mother as though to be sure she was there, he did not stay beside her. At any suggestion that she might leave he seemed to get panicky and clung to her.

His mother assured the teacher that she was willing to stay as long as Peter wanted her. She reported that they had had a very difficult time leaving him in the past and she was eager to try to overcome this problem.

The teacher was careful to spend as much time as she could near Peter and to suggest and participate with him in interesting experiences as he seemed ready. In time he seemed to build a close relationship with her and a real smile appeared on his face when he saw

her in the morning even though he often hid his face in his mother's
coat. He would not allow anyone but this teacher to do anything
for him and began staying near her. She was careful to let him know
where she would be so that he would never feel that he had "lost"
her.

Since Peter seemed to find it easier to start playing when there
were not many children or adults around, she suggested to his
mother that they arrange to come early rather than arrive after the
others had arrived. This arrangement helped. Peter had told his
mother there were "too many big people" at school.

But each time his mother attempted to leave, Peter clung to her,
crying desperately and insisting on going with her. Even though
Peter seemed to have a warm, close relationship with the teacher
and was participating with obvious pleasure in many activities, he
continued to become almost hysterical at any suggestion that his
mother might leave him. He had been coming with her for about
three weeks.

The teacher was not sure that she understood just what Peter's
behavior meant. She felt that his mother lacked confidence in herself and seemed very anxious not to upset Peter by anything she did.
It was at this time that the teacher had an experience with Peter
which helped her see more clearly how he felt.

One day as she was helping him get ready to leave, they had the
following conversation:

Peter: (half-teasingly) Miss Williams, will my locker be here when I come
          back?
Miss W: Yes, Peter, it will be right here waiting for you.
Peter: If my locker starts to run away, will you hold it?
Miss W: Yes, I'll hold it tight and tell it to stay right here because Peter is
          coming tomorrow.
Peter: You just hold it; I want it right here.

As she thought about this incident, she felt that in an indirect way
Peter was telling her that although he wanted to run away, he really
wanted to stay. He needed her help in resolving the conflict. He
wanted her to "hold" him, like the locker, if he started to leave. He
wanted to take the step of separating himself from his mother and
staying at nursery school, but he needed help from the teacher.

Acting on this impression, the teacher telephoned to Peter's mother
suggesting that she felt it was time to plan for a separation even
though Peter might protest verbally. She suggested that the mother

and father talk it over and if they, too, felt Peter was ready that the mother might plan to leave him by himself for a while.

On the way to school the next day, Peter's mother told him she would be leaving for a while that day. To her surprise he ignored her remark and talked about something else, but when his mother did attempt to leave, he cried loudly and clung to her. The teacher took Peter in her arms and held him as his mother said "good-by" and left. Peter kicked at the teacher, crying, "Let me down, let me down. I want to go to my Mommy."

The teacher kept repeating quietly, "I'm right here. I'm going to stay with you until your mother comes back." Suddenly he stopped crying, "You walk me home."

She replied, "I will walk home with you some time, Peter, but now I'm staying with you here and your mother is coming back. You remember we said that someday your mother would be going and that I would stay with you until she came back. I will be right here with you."

Just then another child, Christine, who was watching anxiously while building with blocks, said, "Here, Peter, would you like a block?"

Peter ignored her and instead turned to the teacher saying almost gruffly, "Do you have a red truck here?"

"Yes, we do," said Miss Williams.

Together they found the truck and Peter and Christine began playing with it. He laughed more loudly than he usually did but otherwise showed no sign of being disturbed. He was busy playing at a table with puzzles when his mother returned. When she came into the room, he looked up and then quickly looked back with a frown, "I don't care. I have to finish this." "We said Mother would be back and she came and she's ready to go home now," said the teacher. His mother went to the table and knelt down beside him and he turned to her and they hugged each other. When she suggested that they finish the puzzle, he refused, so they left, Peter saying "good-by" cheerfully to the teacher. Miss Williams refrained from replying, "See you tomorrow" but just returned his "good-by."

The next day Peter came with his father. He stood by his father for a few minutes and then joined the teacher who was reading to Christine. In a little while the teacher spoke to him:

Miss W: Peter, your daddy will be going home now and then he'll be back later.

Peter: Is he going now? (but without starting toward his father)
Miss W: Yes. We'll tell him "good-by."
Peter: (turning to his father) You going home now? I want to go with you.
Miss W: (to the father) Peter is saying "good-by." Will you be back after juice?

The two hugged each other and the father said, "I'll be back for you." Peter said "No!"

"I'll give you another kiss," said the father and he did. Miss Williams picked Peter up and he cried for two or three seconds but without any violence. She walked with him back to where Christine was waiting and held him on her lap as she read to them. In a few minutes they went outdoors where Peter played vigorously and more freely than he had formerly.

The next day there was no crying on Peter's part when his father left and the following day he stayed for lunch, at his own request. He had become a full member of the group! He had wanted to have the teacher help him actively in order to succeed in his wish to be independent.

ADJUSTING TO OTHER NEW EXPERIENCES

All New Experiences Need to Be Handled Carefully to Build Greater Confidence in the Child

Parents as well as teachers help a child when they are able to accept the needs a child expresses through his behavior and give him support by meeting his needs.

Entering nursery school is a big adjustment but it is not the only new experience which the child may face. Any moment during the day may bring something new. When the children go on walks, for example, they may see unfamiliar or even frightening things. New experiences, wherever they are found, need to be handled carefully. They serve to build confidence or to destroy it. A visit to the fire station may mean strange noises, unfamiliar people, as well as the sight of the huge fire engine itself. Some children will need to proceed slowly. One child may be able to watch the fire engine comfortably if he holds the hand of the adult. Another may need the safety of being held in the adult's arms. Others may need the reassurance of knowing that they can leave the situation whenever they want.

The necessity of keeping each experience within the level of the child's ability to take part in it without anxiety means that at least two adults must go with any group from nursery school to all but the most familiar places. On a walk to the barns, for example, a child may shows signs of fear about going inside. An adult will need to stay outside with him, accepting the fact that for some reason he is not ready for the experience of going inside. They both can have a pleasant experience outside a barn. Later the child may want to go inside or he may want to return. With his fear accepted and with time to proceed at his own rate, a child will gain confidence in himself as he succeeds in handling the fear. If he is pushed into entering the barn when he is still afraid, he may only learn to conceal his fear or to depend on adult support. In such a case if anything happens which startles him while he is in the barn, such as a cow mooing, he may be thrown into a panic because of the feelings of fear inside him which are released by the sudden noise. He becomes more afraid and loses confidence.

Fig. 28. *The first spring tulip.*

Fig. 29.   A dog at a safe distance.

The Adult's Feelings Influence the Child's

The attitude of the adult influences the child, and in any emergency it is imperative that the adult meet the situation calmly for the sake of the child. A group of four-year-olds were visiting the fire station one day when the fire alarm sounded. One of the firemen directed them calmly, "You all stand right against the wall and watch this fire engine go out." His composure steadied the teachers and in a matter of seconds everyone was against the wall and the fire engine pulled out before the eyes of the thrilled line of four-year-olds. It was the best trip to the fire station they had ever had. The reports of experiences during the bombings of the last war showed that children reacted in the way the adults they were with reacted. If they were with calm people, they were not likely to be upset even when the situations were terrifying. They grew hysterical for much less cause when they were with hysterical people.

In planning any experience for the children the teacher must always be familiar with it herself. She must have made the trip so hat she can prepare the children for what they may expect. What will it be like? What will they do? What will they see? Will they hear a noise? If there is much that is unfamiliar, it helps to go over t in words so that the children have some framework into which to fit the situation. Often a lively review on the way home of what each one saw will help place the experiences among the "known" things.

It's usually important to talk to the non-nursery school adults about what will help the children enjoy the experience more. Not all adults understand the needs of young children. Some firemen think it's fun to startle children by blowing a whistle unexpectedly or ringing a bell. If the adults are not helpful, it may be better not to visit the fire station, or at least to be very careful to take only the children for whom such possibilities will not be frightening. People who work with animals can usually be counted on to be gentle and quiet and to help rather than hinder the children's sound adjustment to the experiences they are having.

Watching Children Meet New Experiences Gives One Insight into the Way They Feel

Observing the way children explore the world outside nursery school is one way to become aware of the different patterns of adjustment which children already have. Some children go out to meet new experiences with confidence. There are others whose areas of confidence are limited, and there are others who are disturbed by the smallest departure from the familiar. Experiences offered to children must be adapted to what they are ready to accept.

When a child stops to watch something, the wise adult will wait. It is a sign that the child is absorbed in the new, attempting to relate it to what he can understand. He may ask questions or he may not. Moving on before he is ready will only mean leaving behind some unresolved ideas. The habit of exploring an experience fully is a sound one and builds feelings of adequacy.

Most children in the first few months at nursery school need to have their experiences limited to the school itself, to have plenty of time at school before going on any trips. There are many new experiences inside the school. By watching, questioning, participating, the child digests the new, whether it be a wasp's nest brought in by the teacher, or a visitor in a foreign costume, or just a new toy. When he repeats an activity over and over, he is assimilating it, making it his

Fig. 30.   Learning about animals.

own. He is adding to his feeling of being an adequate person by making it an "easy" experience.

Childen's attempts to fit a new experience into what they can recognize may lead to amusing interpretations on their part. Bill revealed an unexpected aspect of the routine of nursery school. He was a quiet child, accepting everything that happened and appearing to find it pleasant. He said very little at school but at home he reported, "When I come, the teacher looks in my mouth to see if there are any words there." He wasn't familiar with inflamed throats and medical inspection, but he knew that words came out of mouths, and he was keeping his safely inside.

Children Have Defenses When They Feel Unsure

Children, like adults, have defenses that they are likely to use when they feel uncertain because the situation they are in is new and strange. When children feel unsure of themselves, they may withdraw or retreat from any action and play safe by doing nothing and thus run no risk of doing the wrong thing. This is a type of denial of the situation—like turning one's back on something.

For example, Helen came to nursery school and made no protest at her mother's leaving her. She simply stood immobile on the spot where she had been left. If an adult took her hand and led her somewhere, as to the piano, she went passively. She had had many new situations to meet in her short life and much unfriendliness. A frail child, she had protected herself in the only way she could—by being passive. She was not far from being a "dummy" in one sense of that word. The teachers made no attempt to push her into any activity but gave her friendly smiles, often sat near her, and sometimes took her to the piano or the finger-painting table. Very slowly she began to show some responsiveness. It was interesting to observe that only after she had been in the nursery school some months did she begin to make a fuss over her mother's leaving and beg her to stay. It seemed likely that only then was she feeling free enough to dare to make some demands on her mother—to indicate how she really felt. Unfortunately her mother could not accept her demands and refused to "baby" her so Helen stopped this behavior, but in spite of her mother's denial she continued to progress at school, making some demands on the teachers and joining an occasional child in play. When the situation changed in any way, as when there were visitors, she became quite passive again. One wonders whether Helen would have been less passive if her mother could have accepted the child's demand that she stay. Would she have felt less helpless? Would she have been less likely to retreat into passive behavior?

Sometimes a child who feels strange and uncomfortable will suddenly begin to play for a lot of attention or act "silly" as though seeking reassurance by surrounding himself with attentive adults. Another child will be aggressive and try to bully others as though to prove to himself that he is really big and strong and not weak and helpless as he fears. This child is doing something actively about his problem. He gives us a chance to help him.

Children Need Help When They Act Defensively

It is not unusual to see a child who has been frightened by something startling or unusual turn and hit a companion on almost no provocation. In this way he drains off the feeling of fear which is uncomfortable. The adult's role is to help him face the feeling and find some acceptable outlet for it. Fear is a less uncomfortable feeling when one is not ashamed of it. It may help if the teacher can say, "That noise made you feel afraid, didn't it? Lots of people feel afraid when they hear a big noise like that. It's all right. Take hold of my hand and let's walk farther away and then it won't sound so loud. There's no need to hit Billy. He may be afraid, too." And Billy will need some help with, "I think he hit you because he felt afraid. I'm sorry." This kind of handling will help them both in understanding why people behave as they do.

Often children will actively reject a situation or some part of it because they feel strange and insecure. In the laboratory nursery school the large number of adults may increase any difficulty a child has in accepting adults. Because he feels uncomfortable with so many unfamiliar adults around, he will try to protect himself by rejecting them. Frequently he will meet a friendly advance with the words, "Go 'way. I don't like you." It's like getting in the first blow when you're expecting the worst. For the child's sake, it's important to recognize the real feeling back of these words, to understand its meaning as "Go 'way. I'm afraid of you." It usually *is* better to go away until the child has had more time to make an adjustment. It is sometimes possible for a teacher whom the child does know to interpret his feelings to him in such a case, saying, for example, "I think that you don't like her and want her to go away because you don't know her yet. When you know her, you will like her. Her name is ——. She might help you find a shovel for digging."

In a situation in which the child feels inadequate, he may regress or return to some early stage of adjustment in which he felt more secure and comfortable. One child who entered nursery school would often lie on the floor, sucking his thumb and rocking himself back and forth much as if he were a baby again. His mother had encouraged him to be a baby and kept him very dependent on her. He liked the teachers and enjoyed his school experiences, but many times during the first weeks at school he would retreat to this infantile position. After a few months when he felt more adequate, he was never observed retiring into babyhood in this way.

It is important to be able to identify children's defenses and to help them make adjustments which are really appropriate to the situation or to help them discover how to drain off their disturbed feelings in acceptable ways. It is equally important to see that children have experiences in which they feel adequate so that they will have less need for defenses. When adults can do these things, they offer real help to the child.

REFERENCES

1. Allen, Frederic: Mother-Child Separation: Process or Event. Emotional Problems of Early Childhood, edited by Gerald Caplan, Basic Books, 1955, Ch. 15.
2. Beller, E. K.: Dependence and Independence in Young Children. Journal of Genetic Psychology, 1955, pp. 23-35.
3. Gerard, Margaret, and Dukette, Rita: Techniques for Preventing Separation Trauma in Child Placement in the Emotionally Disturbed Child. Child Welfare League of America, New York.
4. Heathers, G.: Emotional Dependence and Independence in Nursery School Play. Journal of Genetic Psychology, 1955, pp. 37-59.
5. Heincke, Christoph: Some Effects of Separating Two Year Old Children from Their Parents: A Comparative Study. Human Relations, Vol. 9, No. 2, 1956, pp. 167-171.
6. Hymes, James L.: Three to Six—Your Child Starts to School. Public Affairs Pamphlet, No. 163, 1950.
7. Klein, Donald C., and Ross, Ann: Kindergarten Entry: A Study of Role Transition. Orthopsychiatry and the School, edited by Morris Krugman, New York, American Orthopsychiatric Association, Inc., 1958, pp. 60-69.
8. Littner, Ner: Some Traumatic Effects of Separation and Placement. Child Welfare League of America, 1956.
9. Murphy, Lois Barclay: Learning How Children Cope with Problems. Children, Vol. IV, July 1957, pp. 132-136.
10. Peller, Lili: The Child's Need to Anticipate. Childhood Education, March 1947.
11. Peller, Lili: Nursery School Readiness. Childhood Education, Sept. 1946.
12. Rudolph, Marguerita: Living and Learning in Nursery School. (Ch. 1—When Babies Leave Home.) New York, Harper & Bros., 1954.
13. Steinert, Atkins, and Jackson: The Child Entering Nursery School: A Study of Intake Principles and Procedures, Bulletin. New York, Council of Child Development Center, 1952.

6

Helping Children
in Routine Situations

Understanding Is Important in Everyday Experiences

We have seen how new experiences can contribute to building confidence and security in a child. Having new experiences such as
going to nursery school, visiting a fire station, taking a walk, even
hearing a strange noise, will help a child develop more confidence
if we accept and respect the child's level of readiness for each experience. If we fail to do this, we may find, however, that these experiences only increase his feelings of being little and helpless.

The need to understand and accept the child's readiness for an
experience is as important with everyday experience as with new
experiences. Experiences which occur daily may pile up feelings and
set patterns in a way that influences growth even more significantly
than do unusual or new experiences. Teaching which includes an

awareness of the child's level of readiness is needed here, too. If we are to achieve the goal of developing secure, adequate people, free to make use of all their capacities, we will do this kind of teaching wherever children are having experiences, either new or everyday ones.

Experiences in the Toilet Room Offer Opportunities for Teaching

The child's daily experience with toileting are important in the development of his feelings and his behavior. Some of the best opportunities for teaching in the nursery school occur in the toileting situation, for toileting is a significant experience in the young child's life. It is one about which his feelings are sure to be strong. It offers the chance for a great deal of growth.

For the child, toileting is associated with many intimate experiences with his mother, with her care of him, with his efforts to please her, perhaps with conflicts over her attempts to train him. Toileting may even be tied up in his mind with ideas about "good" and "bad" behavior. One parent used to leave her child at nursery school with the admonition, "Be a good girl today." What she really meant by these words was "Stay dry today." Morality such as this is confusing.

When the child is ready for nursery school, about the age of three years, he has probably only recently been through a period of toilet training. He is not likely to have emerged from this training period completely unscathed. His behavior will tell us something of what the experiences have meant to him.

Early Experiences with Toileting

Let us review what is likely to take place in regard to toileting before the child starts to nursery school.

In infancy, urination and defecation are involuntary processes. With time the child begins to be conscious of a feeling of pressure in his bladder and of the pleasurable sensation which follows the emptying of the bladder. The passing of stools brings him a relief which is pleasurable, too. This is often followed by a pleasant contact with his mother in addition. These feelings are very important in the child's development. Psychiatrists tell us that there is probably something creative for the young child in producing stools. They are his very own. The way they are received by those around him has significance for him. If his stools are acceptable, he feels accepted himself. If they are received with disgust and if his interest in them meets with disapproval, he is apt to feel himself rejected. He may get a confused notion of his "badness." The child wants to please for he needs the safety that comes from being loved and accepted, so he must reject what he has produced if the adults reject it. Doing this makes him feel less adequate and confident. He may begin to distrust his own impulses.

Usually during the second year of the child's life the situation changes. The child is expected to learn to control his elimination following the pattern of those around him. If this control represents too great an interference with the child's natural rhythm of elimination, or if it is imposed before he is physiologically ready, or if it is imposed along with many other restricting demands, the child tends to resist or to feel overwhelmed by the process of learning. Training becomes a long-drawn-out struggle in which the child develops a good deal of negativism and the parent-child relationship becomes a relationship of issues. Or it may become a process of submission in which the child fears failure and feels resentful and helpless. In either case the child pays a heavy price in his personality development. We may see some of the results reflected in the behavior he exhibits when he reaches the nursery school.

Training for Toilet Control Has an Effect on Many Areas of Behavior

Excessive negativism is perhaps the most common result of toilet training which is not based on a child's readiness. The child who says "no" to everything, who looks on any contacts with adults as a possible source of interference and restriction, may have acquired this attitude during his training period. One of the most resistant, hostile children in one nursery school had been subjected to an early, rigid period of toilet training. She defied adult suggestions and could not share with children. The quality of the relationship she had with her earnest parents can be pictured in the note which she brought to school one day, "Ruth has *refused* to have a bowel movement for four days."

Inhibitions of many types may stem from the same source. If the child has been forced to achieve bowel and bladder control before he is able to comprehend and differentiate patterns, his "control" may include the inhibition of spontaneity and creativity in many areas. We see children who were trained early to stay "dry and clean" who are unable to use play materials in ways that are creative. They cannot get dirty in other situations, play in mud, or savor the ordinary joys of childhood and the social contacts that occur in the society of the sandbox crowd.

Loss of self-confidence may also characterize the child who has been subjected to early and rigid toilet training. In his experience the products of his body have been rejected and his natural impulses denied expression. He loses confidence in his impulses in other directions. His inevitable failures in the training process do not help him feel like an adequate person, either. Because he has had to give up too early the pleasure of eliminating as he wants, he is likely to "give up" easily in other ways—unless he goes to the other extreme of asserting himself to compensate for his loss.

The child whose parents have treated the acquiring of toilet control in the same manner as any other developmental step such as learning to walk or talk is likely to be a more comfortable child. Learning to control elimination is not nearly as complicated a process as learning to talk, for example. The child who is left free to proceed at his own rate is likely to learn rather easily sometime after he has started walking. He will show an interest in the toilet and in imitating the behavior of the people he observes. Parents can make it easy for him to do this and can show the same satisfactions in his successes here as they do in his other developmental accomplishments. They should accept any sign of resistance as a sign that he has lost interest and is not ready, and drop any efforts they may be making to train him. They should not make an issue out of learning toilet control any more than they would out of learning to walk or talk. When there is no pressure, the child himself usually begins to take on the patterns of the adult in regard to toileting sometime between the ages of fifteen and thirty months.

Pressure of Public Opinion Is Often an Obstacle for Parents

For many parents the biggest obstacle to letting the child take his own time lies in the pressure of public opinion. The "trained" child too frequently stands as the symbol of success in the eyes of the average parent today. A mother may be more influenced by the attitudes of friends and relatives toward the subject than by a desire to reduce the amount of laundry for herself. One mother whose struggle over toilet training had resulted in a great deal of resistance and antagonism in her son reported that she started training him because she "felt humiliated to have him wet." Her mother-in-law was very critical of her lack of success with the child and could not see an excuse for her inability to keep him dry. In other words, the toilet situation here was the center of much hostile family feeling.

Another mother who understood what the toilet situation meant to her child and was determined not to impose standards on him before he was ready found it hard to resist the pressures of the neighborhood. At twenty-four months her son was still wetting frequently while her neighbor's two-year-old had been "trained" since he was a year old. She had enough confidence in her child to allow him to take his own time. She resisted the influence of her less understanding neighbor, but it was not easy! Around the age of twenty-seven months her son suddenly "trained himself" with very little help from her. As a three-year-old in nursery school his control was stable. He used the toilet there as easily as he did at home and accepted the adults and what they had to offer him. The neighbor's son at the same age was more subject to accidents and more resistant to adult directions.

Adult Attitudes and Standards May Complicate the Toilet Problem

Toileting is sometimes complicated for the child by parental anxieties. A parent may give a great deal of anxious attention to the child's elimination. It then becomes unduly important to the child, and even disturbs him. He feels anxiety and this interferes with his behavior.

A mother may express her anxiety in this way if she is not sure of her ability to be a "good" mother. She tries to find reassurance by seeing that her child eliminates properly. She may use this means of expressing anxiety if she is having some difficulty in accepting the changes she has had to make in her life because of the child. She may wish that she could do the things she used to do, but she tries to hide her feelings, even from herself, by concern over the child's elimination. Mothers who have these feelings are likely, too, to undertake training early, in a determined way, as part of their efforts to prove themselves "good" mothers. Thus they complicate further the problem for the child. The child in turn may use the withholding of his stools as an unconscious means of "punishing" his parents for withholding acceptance from him. It becomes hard for healthy attitudes to develop under these circumstances.

More confusion for the child is added by the standards about toilet behavior which adults sometimes impose before the child can understand them. Separation of the sexes, demands for privacy, disapproval of many kinds of behavior in relation to the toilet situation can have little meaning for the child except to confuse him. These standards add feelings of uncertainty or fear or guilt to the situation.

Children Gain from Sound Handling of Toilet Experience at Nursery School

The important thing for us to remember as students in the nursery school laboratory is that children will be coming to school with many different backgrounds. Some will have healthy, matter-of-fact attitudes, with no doubts about their ability to handle the toileting situation and expecting to meet friendly, accepting adults there. They will not be disturbed about toilet accidents. Other children will be confused and insecure. They will resent attempts by the adult to help them and will be upset by their failures to control their elimination. Some will use the toilet situation to express their anxiety or their resentments or their defiance. Some will not be able to use the toilet at nursery school until they feel comfortable there. According to their different needs they must be helped. All of them, no matter what their background, will gain from a sound handling of the toilet experience at the nursery school.

If the handling is to be sound, the children must meet adults in the school who are themselves comfortable in the situation. This is not always easy, for many of us have had experiences in our past which have included being ashamed or confused about the subject of toileting. Many of us have unfortunate emotional attitudes to overcome. Being with children who have matter-of-fact attitudes will often help us. Learning how to work with a child who needs guidance in overcoming his problem may also help us in reorienting ourselves. If we can appreciate the meaning the toilet situation holds for the child, we will be helped to free ourselves from the conflicts generated by our own past experiences.

The interest that children show in the subject of toileting can be seen in the frequency with which it appears in their dramatic play. Again and again they will act out with their dolls what is for them the drama of the toilet. This is a desirable way of expressing any conflicts they may feel and making these conflicts seem more manageable. The good nursery school will supply equipment in the doll corner which can be used to represent the toilet room.

Be Alert to the Meaning of What the Child Does at Toilet Time

Because insecurities are so often evident in behavior in relation to toileting, it is important to be alert to the meaning of what the child does at toilet time. Toilet accidents, for example, are likely to be common in the first weeks at nursery school and are indications of the strain that the child is feeling in the new situation. They should be treated as a symptom and the strains reduced for the child in every way possible. The child will be reassured when he realizes that he does not need to be afraid of having a toilet accident. This removes one possible strain. He will gain confidence if he finds friendly, accepting adults to help him when he is wet.

Some children will react to the new situation of being in nursery school by holding back from the experience. They will be unable to use the toilet. This will be one symptom of the way they feel. It is hardly necessary to say that no pressure should be put on a child to use the toilet until he is ready. He may need to go home after a short stay, or he may be comfortable after he has wet himself. One child who was unusually resistant and suspicious of adults had a long and difficult period of adjusting to the nursery school. She refused to go near the toilet room and could stay only part of the morning. Gradually she gained confidence and became more relaxed and less defensive. One morning she stood in the middle of the room and urinated in a big puddle. The teacher realized that this was a real step forward for this very inhibited, hostile little girl. She accepted the behavior in a casual way but with some satisfaction.

"You'll be much more comfortable now. I'm glad," she said as she wiped up the puddle. The child seemed to respond to her friendliness and acceptance. She walked with her to the coatroom where she took the dry pants the teacher offered and put them on herself. After that she went to the toilet room frequently to watch the other children. She wet her pants on several other occasions and then began using the toilet, insisting at first that the adult leave the room.

Before the year was over she had no problem about going to the toilet and she was a happier, freer little girl in all situations.

Sometimes a child who has been attending nursery school will suddenly have a series of toilet accidents. These accidents are a sign of emotional strain and should be regarded as a significant symptom. It is our job to make every effort to discover and remove the sources of the strain. We should not increase the strain by disapproval. The child's behavior gives us a clue as to how the situation is affecting him.

Occasionally a child will wet himself as an expression of resistance against the efforts that have been made to train him. Parents can threaten, punish and shame a child, but they can't make him stay dry! It's one of the few areas where a child is in control. If a child is wetting to resist domination, we need to stop trying to control him and to accept the fact that it is his responsibility. This may mean letting the child get wet as often as he wants to—without showing any disapproval or making any efforts to prevent his wetting—until he is convinced that we really mean to leave the matter up to him. We may have a child in the nursery school who needs this kind of handling. These children are likely to be children who will assume control quickly when they feel responsible, for they already have control. They are almost sure to be children who have experienced the training process as a series of issues with their parents. When the responsibility for toileting is left up to them, they will probably become less resistant in other ways.

A Child Is Reassured by the Casual Attitude of the Adult

It cannot be emphasized too strongly that a matter-of-fact attitude about toilet accidents on the part of adults is exceedingly important. If a child knows that toilet accidents are not condemned, he feels much freer and safer. He can proceed to acquire control at his own rate and accidents do not damage his confidence in himself. We do not need to be afraid that he will fail to learn or that wetting will become a habit. Children establish the habits that they observe in the people around them unless there is some very good reason such as emotional strain which makes this impossible.

The child who is unsure of himself is reassured by casual handling. It restores his confidence and removes a source of possible conflict with the adult. Under no condition should a child ever be made to feel disapproval or be shamed for his failure to stay dry and clean.

Shame is not a healthy feeling. It does not contribute to the development of the confidence and adequacy we all need.

It Is Better to Have a Wet Child Than a Resentful One

Forcing or insisting on toileting builds resistance and conflict
around an area where it is important that poor attitudes be avoided.
Forcing is usually done by adults who are trying to satisfy a need in
themselves to control others. It is better to have a wet child than a
hostile, resentful one. It is better to be an accepting adult than a
dominating one.

When the child does have a toilet accident, we can try to make
the experience a comfortable one for him. We can give him any help
he may need in changing his clothes although sometimes children
feel more adequate if they can put on dry clothes themselves. Whenever the child has to depend on the adult for help, he is likely to
feel less adequate and take less responsibility. The type of clothing
the child wears becomes an important factor here. Small buttons,
complicated belt buckles, fastenings in the back or tight clothes
make it hard for a child to take responsibility.

We must free ourselves, too, from anxiety about the child's ability
to achieve control. We must accept the fact that he will achieve control when he is ready. While we can show pleasure in his successes,
we must not value success too highly. An undue emphasis on success
may rouse anxiety in the child. If success is valued too highly, the
child may find it hard to meet the inevitable failures. He will get
the needed support when we have confidence in his capacity to
learn, and can accept him as he is. The adult who succeeds in making the child feel that she is his friend in the toileting situation is
the adult who can give him support at other times. It will be easier
for her to help him grow in feeling confident and adequate in other
situations.

Acceptance of Children's Interest in Each Other at Toilet Time Promotes Healthy Adjustment

Sound handling of toileting also includes a matter-of-fact attitude
in meeting situations in which the children show an interest in each
other in the toilet room. Children need a chance to satisfy their
curiosity without becoming confused. Girls will be interested in the
fact that boys have a penis and stand when they urinate. The way

this interest is received by the adult will influence the development of their later attitudes toward sex. At this stage their interest is not very different from their interest in anything new in the school experience. A girl may not notice sex differences the first time that she uses a toilet beside a boy, but when she does notice a difference, she will usually want to watch boys frequently as they urinate until her interest is satisfied. She may comment and ask questions. If she does, she will be helped by the teacher's casual acceptance of her comments. It may help her to have the teacher verbalize in some way as, "Bill has a penis. He stands up at the toilet. Boys stand up and girls sit down there."

Psychiatrists tell us that an important factor in later sex adjustment is the acceptance of one's sex. In this situation it is usually easier for the boys to feel acceptance because they possess a penis. Many times a girl will try to imitate the boy by attempting to stand—with not very satisfactory results! She learns from the experience and no particular comment is needed. But some girls may need help in feeling that being a girl is desirable. The teacher may remark, "Mothers sit down, too."

The girl who persists in trying to imitate the boy over a long period of time is probably suffering from a deep-seated conflict and needs help in many areas. It is unwise to express disapproval of her behavior but every effort should be made to reassure her about the role of a girl and help her feel more adequate. One child who was observed in a group of four-year-olds persisted in trying to imitate boys at the toilet and showed other evidences of disturbance about sex. Her father did the disciplining in her home. He was harsh and inconsistent and he often put her in the bathroom as punishment because there was no other isolation space in their small home. She felt her inferiority keenly and was making an attempt to overcome it by trying to identify herself with the punishing parent and to become more like a boy. The unwise handling she was receiving was already interfering with her chances for a good sex adjustment later.

Procedures That Are Constructive

How do we use the toilet period to build up constructive feelings? What are specific procedures?

The physical setup plays a part in building positive feelings. If the toilet room is a pleasant place, light and attractive, the child is more likely to feel that it is a safe room in which to be. The teacher may help him feel comfortable by talking about the room and what goes on there as, "There's room for three people to use the toilet at the same time here at nursery school, isn't there?" or "I think that mirror over the bowl needs washing. Would you like to wash it?" Just ordinary, pleasant conversation on any topic will help make a child more relaxed and comfortable. Some children, of course, who already possess a comfortable feeling, will not need such distraction, but conversation and participating in activity may help some children whose feelings may be mixed.

Interest in the plumbing usually rises to a peak around the age of four and observation of the inside of the toilet while it is being flushed and discussions about water pipes and sewer systems are of absorbing interest. These have values. Any attempt to hurry the child out of the situation or to discourage his curiosity will make it harder for him to develop and maintain a healthy attitude. The wise adult will be prepared to spend time and feel comfortable in the toilet room with the child.

The easier it is for the child to manage independently, the more he will gain. Small-size toilets are desirable. If they cannot be obtained, a step can be made to fit in front of the toilet seat. A hinged seat to make the opening smaller may be desirable, too. A door to the room is a handicap and it is usually easy to have one removed if one is there. Doors present hazards for fingers and interfere with the casual matter-of-factness of the situation as well as with the ease of supervision.

Children at the nursery school level can be expected to be independent about their clothing at toilet time if they are properly dressed. Girls can pull down their panties and boy can use a fly. There are well-designed coverall suits with drop seats for both boys and girls. Boys can be reminded to raise the toilet seat before urinating. Both boys and girls can be reminded to flush the toilet after they have used it. When an occasional child refuses to flush the toilet, we can safely assume, as we can with any refusal, that there is some meaning behind it. Children are sometimes frightened by the noise and movement of water in a flushing toilet. They will be reassured in time as they watch others and as they gain more confidence in other places. Their refusal should be respected.

A question may be raised about the necessity of handwashing

after toileting. For most children it is an unnecessary interference to insist that they stop and wash their hands after they have been to the toilet. It increases time away from play. Handwashing can be encouraged after toileting but it is hardly an essential part of the routine for young children. It is a habit they will acquire in time if they live with people who practice handwashing. They are not likely to appreciate its significance during their preschool years unless they happen to enjoy the washing process itself. To impose it arbitrarily may interfere with its being adopted later. Handwashing is definitely necessary before eating. This is where its value should be stressed. A child can see the point here.

In the nursery school, boys and girls use the toilets freely together while adults are present. Occasionally a child may find this difficult and the teacher can explain, "Here in nursery school we all use the toilet room together." Standards do differ in different places. Because it is customary to do a thing one way in one place does not make another practice in a different place wrong. Adults sometimes ask, "But won't this make it harder for a child when he has to learn a different custom, as in a public school?" We must remember that the important thing is to be able to accept the customs that are in use. Toileting on a picnic differs from that done at home. Little boys accompany their mothers into public restrooms but learn to make a distinction later when they are older. Patterns of behavior differ with age, place and society. The child learns to accept differences as he is ready to understand them.

Establishing a Schedule for Toileting

When a child starts nursery schools, the teacher can soon discover how frequently he needs to go to the toilet by talking with his mother and by observing what happens in the school.

For the younger child she can establish a schedule to fit his rhythm. She will take most of the responsibility herself, saying to him, "Time to go to the toilet now," and attempting to time her interruptions to a shift in his activity. In this way she will avoid building resistances in him. If she is pleasant and friendly, he will welcome this opportunity for adult contact and attention. Going to the toilet will bring him satisfactions.

A new child usually adjusts more easily if he has the same adult helping him each time. He feels secure more quickly and may begin to come to her when he needs to go to the toilet.

As a next step the teacher may ask the child, "Do you need to go to the toilet now?" rather than simply telling him that it is time to go. This begins to shift the responsibility onto him where it will belong entirely in the end. If the number of toilet accidents show that the child is not ready to take this much responsibility, the teacher can drop back to the earlier stage. Many factors change a child's rhythm, such as cold weather, or excitement, or drinking more liquids than usual. Even older children will not always remain dry under unusual conditions.

A set schedule for going to the toilet has the disadvantage of not meeting individual needs, or not meeting changing needs in the same individual. Nevertheless, as children's needs are likely to follow a similar pattern, it is possible to have a framework within which to expect toileting and this simplifies management. If we remember that the goal of any schedule is to help the child go to the toilet when he needs to go—and not any oftener—we can work out a schedule which will be flexible. For example, some children may need to use the toilet when they first come to school, depending on their last toilet period at home. The next logical time for an interruption is around juice time which is usually in the middle of the morning. Children whose interval is short or who are dependent on the teacher can be taken then. A toilet period before lunch ensures a lunch period less likely to be interrupted by a trip to the toilet. The more mature children, those who have taken over responsibility for their toileting, will follow their own schedule, but the teacher will find it wise to suggest toileting before lunch for them all.

Examples of Problems in the Toilet Situation

Let us consider some specific problems which may arise.

John was a child who seemed to grow increasingly reluctant to use the toilet at nursery school although he got along well in other situations and there was no report of previous difficulty with toileting. When he went to the toilet, he preferred to go when there were no other children in the room. The teacher noticed that John sat on the seat when he urinated instead of standing as most of the boys did. It seemed reasonable to conclude that he had become aware of this difference in nursery school and was uncomfortable about it. A conversation with John's mother revealed that John sat on the seat at home, and his mother had not considered handling his toileting differently from that of his older sister. She accepted the teacher's suggestion that it was time for John to follow his father's pattern. The teacher felt that in this case the shift should be made at home before it came at school. John's father helped him and it wasn't long before John was standing up, and he appeared pleased to use the toilet at nursery school with the others.

Mary was a delightfully imaginative child with a fine sense of rhythm. She loved music and often played and sang at the piano or danced when music was played. She was friendly with other children and enjoyed "homemaking" play in the doll corner. She was curious about many things, played actively outdoors and enjoyed expeditions outside the school. Toward adults she responded in a very negative way. She resisted suggestions and was likely to become self-conscious and "show-off." She found rest difficult and at the table seemed to concentrate on behavior that she felt might not be acceptable, putting her fingers in the food, throwing it, or running away from the table. She was wet several times a day, and consistently refused to go to the toilet. She always changed her panties immediately, leaving the wet ones on the floor in the toilet room. Her mother reported that she had been toilet trained early and then had suddenly begun wetting again within the last year. They had "tried everything" to make her stop, even to shaming her and making her wear diapers. At first she would stay wet but they had succeeded in impressing on her how "dirty" that was and now she wouldn't stay wet a minute.

It was easy to see where Mary's negativism came from. It seemed likely that here was an able little girl trying to assert herself. The methods of training and disciplining that her parents had used with her more docile older brother had only increased her resistance. She was defiantly insisting on being independent.

Since she was out to defeat "bossing," it was evident that pressure for conforming to standards, no matter how desirable the standards, needed to be reduced before she could be expected to change her behavior. The whole matter of toileting was dropped in nursery school, and no comment was made on her wetting. There was no insistence put on her to use the toilet. It was hard for her parents to see that before she could accept adult standards she must be convinced that she was a "free agent" and that they could convince her of this only by accepting her right to wet as she pleased. They themselves valued conformity. However, they were friendly, intelligent people and very fond of their small daughter. Somewhat reluctantly they followed the suggestion of saying nothing, perhaps because there was nothing left for them to do. It was several months before Mary began using the toilet at nursery school. It might have happened sooner if her parents could have been more wholehearted in turning the responsibility completely over to her. Whenever she was subjected to domination, Mary would revert to a series of wet pants. It was the area in which she felt she could win in the battle to assert her independence. When left to accept things at her own rate, she was an unusually social and capable child with a wholehearted enjoyment of experience.

A child does not always express his resistance to pressure as directly as Mary. In a less friendly and understanding home a child may have to conceal his feelings of resistance and resentment.

Sam was a child whose mother reported that she had felt that "the sooner I started him on regular toilet habits the better." She began when he was six months old and he responded "perfectly." He now says to his younger brother, "I never got my panties wet when I was little." But he chews on his blanket, sucks his finger, and is very inactive. He often sits passively instead of playing. His mother reports, "He doesn't enjoy anything that I can see." This child, with perhaps more against him, has not felt strong enough to protest in a direct way as Mary has been able to do. With many other strains added to the pressure to be clean, his position is far less favorable. He is dry but not free! Spontaneity and creativeness have been sacrificed to conformity.

Alice was a child whose toilet training had begun at six months and had proceeded smoothly and quickly. Her mother felt that the early training was successful and it certainly had made matters easier for her. Alice had no toilet accidents at the nursery school and she was not a resistant child. In fact she was anxious to please. She was lacking in confidence in herself and somewhat tense and easily disturbed by new experiences. She needed reassurance and support from the teachers.

Alice enjoyed nursery school and was friendly with both adults and children—friendly with children who did not get wet, that is. If a child had a toilet accident, Alice avoided him or even actively rejected him in play. One day, for example, Alice was in the toilet room when Gary happened to come in. Gary was thoroughly wet, having had one of his not infrequent toilet accidents. Gary was one of the youngest children in the group but he managed well in spite of the short time he had been in school. He was friendly and eager to play with the other children. Alice watched the teacher help Gary get into dry clothes but she kept as far away as possible and made her disapproval evident. "He's a bad boy," she remarked to the other children. Throughout the rest of the morning she refused to play with Gary. When he approached her, she would say, "We don't like you," although usually she found it easy to include other children in her play.

Alice had succeeded in staying dry herself because of the way her mother felt about wetting, but she was not able to accept people who failed to keep dry. How will she feel about her own children someday? Will she impose dryness on them, together with tenseness and fear and a rejection of those who do not meet her standards?

MEALTIME

Strong Feelings also Exist in the Eating Situation

Eating is another area which is important in the development of feelings and behavior. When children enter nursery school, they enter with a long past as far as eating goes. They have had many previous experiences with food. These experiences have been satisfying or unsatisfying in varying degrees. The child's attitude may consequently be favorable or unfavorable toward the meal situation.

Like the toileting situation, the meal situation is highly charged with feeling. "The way to a man's heart is through his stomach" is true in more ways than one. The child's earliest feelings of comfort or discomfort, satisfaction or deprivation, helplessness, or adequacy, have come from what happened to him when he felt hungry.

Adult Behavior and Attitudes Influence the Child

From the very beginning the child is affected by the way the adults act and feel about his eating. While his toileting functions are not interfered with during the first months of his life, he is at the mercy of adults from birth on as far as eating goes.

If his first days are spent in a hospital nursery, the infant is probably fed at a three- or four-hour interval because this schedule is part of the hospital routine, not because he necessarily feels hungry then. He is expected to adapt himself to the hospital schedule even though he is adapting himself at the same time to the extreme changes which birth itself has brought. The generations of babies who were fed when they were hungry and cried, and who were kept close to their mothers, probably had an easier time developing positive feelings of trust than babies under modern conditions. Hunger pangs are an individual matter and usually occur without much regularity in the newborn baby. They are acute and distressing to him. If they are not relieved by food, he is acutely miserable, and he is helpless to meet his own needs.

Some hospitals have a "rooming-in" plan where mother and baby are together and shortly after his birth the mother can begin taking some care of her baby and can feed him according to his needs. She can thus not only meet the baby's needs for food and for comfort and reassurance, but satisfy her own need to be close to her child and care for it. The enthusiastic reports of parents who have been able to follow this plan, especially parents of first babies, make us hope that someday more children will be protected by this kind of start in life.

The more experienced a parent is, the more likely she is to trust her child and feed him when he indicates he is hungry. This may account in part for the easier adjustment which is frequently seen in later children in families. Even being awakened to be fed constitutes an interference which may be annoying to a baby.

Parents today are more likely to feed their babies on a "self-regulating" schedule than they were a generation ago. They try to follow the child's rhythm rather than feed him by the clock! Sometimes, of course, an overanxious mother may interpret every cry as a demand for food until she learns to know her baby. Parents who follow the child's rhythm instead of imposing a rhythm on him usually find that he wants frequent feedings at first, at somewhat irregular intervals, but that he gradually establishes a regular pattern of his own which slowly shifts with his growth changes. After a few months it is not difficult to adjust the child's feedings to a schedule suitable both for him and for the family.

Some Basic Attitudes Develop in the Feeding Situation

Since the child's earliest and strongest feelings are related to the feeding situation, some of his basic attitudes develop around it. Because of what has happened to him here, he may be satisfied and sure of being loved or unsatisfied and full of resentment.

From the child's behavior in the meal situation at nursery school we can get clues to his feelings, to the kind of adjustment he is making. Appetite is a sensitive index to emotional adjustment. Mary who resisted efforts at training over toileting also defied every convention at the table. This behavior was part of her effort to assert her right to be an independent person. When Jane made progress toward becoming a freer, less inhibited individual, she used her fingers more as she ate. She began to dabble them in her melting ice cream in a deliciously relaxed way at about the same time that she began playing more freely with the other children. It is important, not only nutritionally but from the standpoint of personality development, that the child's behavior at mealtime be understood.

What Are Our Goals for the Meal Situation?

In handling the meal period in a constructive way, we must keep in mind our goals and their relative importance in the child's development.

The most important goal is that of ensuring a positive, accepting attitude toward eating. If the child enjoys his food, he has the prerequisite for building other learnings about eating. No other learning must be allowed to interfere with the development of this positive feeling.

Another goal is to help the child enjoy a variety of nutritionally desirable foods. No one diet is the only "right" type. But wherever the child lives, he will be better nourished if he enjoys a wide variety of foods.

Still another goal is to help the child learn the accepted customs in regard to eating, whatever these may be.

While the child is learning these things, he should also be growing more independent and secure. In the eating situation as in other situations all our goals for the development of sound personalities apply, too.

How do we further these goals?

Without Interference a Healthy Child Enjoys Eating

In helping children enjoy mealtime we have nature on our side.

Unless he has had unpleasant experiences in connection with eating, a healthy child is likely to enjoy his food. We don't need to do much more than refrain from interfering. A child enjoys eating because eating satisfies a basic need. To be hungry and then to eat is one of the most satisfying things that anyone can do. We can help by seeing that the child has plenty of chance to be outdoors and to play actively, for this will increase his appetite. But growth needs are great in childhood and normally the healthy child is a hungry child. Problems arise when we emphasize other learnings which interfere with the urge to satisfy hunger as, for example, when we emphasize "manners" or try to introduce new foods too rapidly.

The teacher is responsible, however, for making it easy for him to eat all he needs and may want. To do this she will help him stay at the table. She will prevent distractions and will call his attention back to the business of eating if it strays for any length of time. She may give him help with finishing. She will expect something of him although even here she may be flexible at times. But children gain from a known framework in any situation. They have something to work toward or even to resist if there are some expectations, such as finishing one's milk or tasting everything and finishing at least one thing.

Having Sensory Experiences with
Food Are Part of Learning to Like Food

Touching food with the fingers is usually a real help to the child in learning to like it. This raises the question of how fast we should go in expecting children to meet adult standards at the table. Again, we must consider the factor of "readiness" in learning. If we move too fast in teaching manners, we may interfere with the child's enjoyment of food. When a child is young his need for sensory experience is very great. He wants to explore the world by touching. If he has a chance to satisfy this need, he will be more, rather than less, ready to move on to more mature forms of behavior.

Children who enjoy their food when they reach nursery school are likely to be, if other things are equal, children who have used their fingers, who have had a "messy" stage in eating. A mother who was having many problems with her young son admitted that she was still feeding him at the age of three because she didn't want him "to get the habit of being messy." Being messy in eating is a stage which normally precedes the stage of being neat, just as creeping normally precedes walking. I remember a three-year-old who ate like an adult but who ate practically nothing at the table. She did eat between meals when she did not have to conform with painful effort to the standards expected of her at the table.

A child will usually continue to use his fingers at times long after he has begun to use a spoon. It will be easier and he will drop back to the easier level when he is tired. If we believe that it is important for him to enjoy his food, we will not interfere. Gradually he will depend more and more on a spoon and fork. The kind of manners he will acquire in the end will depend on the example set by the adults around him and not on how much pressure they have exerted on him to meet their standards. On the other hand, his interest in food will be adversely affected by their pressure. We need confidence that the child will acquire the eating patterns of those around him *as he is ready* just as he acquires their speech.

Emotional Disturbances Affect Appetite

Because feeling and appetite are so closely related, we must recognize that any emotional disturbance will affect the appetite. Probably we all know what this means. We have at some time had the experience of losing interest in food for a time because of strong feeling. We turn away from food until we have recovered our emotional balance. The child who is suffering from anxiety or some other emotion may have little appetite even though he may be physically well. When the emotional problem is solved, his appetite will respond to the normal demands of a growing organism.

Attacking the loss of appetite directly may do a great deal of harm. Try making yourself eat a big dinner when you have no appetite! The immediate effect on the child may be vomiting or at least regurgitation or storing of food in the mouth. The more serious and lasting result may be a strong conditioning against food. Being made to eat when one is not hungry is a very unpleasant thing. If eating is to be a pleasant experience for the child, we will avoid forcing him in any way.

Small Servings May Mean More Food Eaten

Perhaps one of the best antidotes to increasing resistance and diminishing appetite is the small serving. A child will usually eat better if he is served small amounts of all foods except those that he is known to like very much. When he is free to have more if he wishes, he will get what he needs. He is likely to eat more than when he is served large helpings.

Small servings are better than large ones and the child can be encouraged to have additional servings. Children often enjoy serving themselves and can learn to regulate servings to amounts that they really want with a little help from the teacher.

We need to remember that there are big individual differences in the amount of food that one child will eat in comparison with another. He will eat different amounts on different days. He may eat a great deal of one food and very little of another and reverse his preference at the next meal. It is well if we do not have any preconceived ideas about how much any child should eat at any one meal. If we have no fixed expectations, we will find it easier to accept the fluctuations in appetite which are common in children. We will not be as likely to put pressure on him to eat as we expect him to eat.

We Should not Try to Extend the Child's Food Horizons too Rapidly

Another step in making sure that the child enjoys his meal is to avoid putting pressure on him to eat a new food or a food that he dislikes. We want children to like a variety of foods, but we must keep in mind that there is a "readiness" factor in all learning. We must not expect the child to learn to like many new foods in a short time. As we think of a three-year-old, for example, we might remind ourselves of how many foods he has "learned to like" in the space of three short years. If we move too fast in introducing variety into a child's diet, we may meet resistance. We should not try to extend his food horizons too rapidly if we want good results in the end.

Children have a tendency, in common with the rest of us, to resist the new and unfamiliar. A child often tends to reject a food because it is new. He may spit it out or make a face. But this may be the first step in learning to eat it. This kind of behavior does not constitute a real rejection. The child will gradually overcome his initial resistance to the food if his behavior does not receive a lot of attention or if he is not forced at the time. He will try the food again and, as he acquires familiarity with it, he will probably learn to like it. In the nursery school, foods that are new or disliked should be tasted to promote familiarity but no pressure should be put on the child to eat even a small serving. He can fill up on other foods. He may be helped by meeting the food under other circumstances. Helping prepare it or tasting it in the kitchen may help in introducing a new flavor to the child. One child who spit out cottage cheese when it was on her plate enjoyed licking the cheese from the carton cover and later came to accept it as part of the meal.

Feelings Influence Food Habits

There are important emotional factors and emotional consequences to what we do in the eating situation. A secure child, for example, may be able to accept a variety of new foods more easily than a less secure child who may need to cling longer to the familiar in food, as in other things, to gain reassurance. The emotional balance of the insecure child may be threatened if he is pushed into eating too many new foods. One extremely insecure child who had met with tremendous obstacles in his life wanted custard every night for his supper. It might have been disastrous for him if someone had insisted on introducing variety into his diet while he was still depending on custard for a stability which he had not found in other areas of his world. A sound way to obtain acceptance of a variety of foods is to build greater security and confidence in the child in every way possible. Feelings of security and confidence will influence the child's ability to accept new foods.

What the child eats will often depend on who is offering him the food. Infants seem to be sensitive to the likes and dislikes of the person feeding them. They are also sensitive to other feelings in the person feeding them. A baby may take his bottle well or accept his cereal when the person who gives it to him is relaxed and enjoys feeding him. He may refuse the same food if it is offered by someone who dislikes the "messiness" of his eating and is tense and uncertain in her relationship with him. Some children eat very little when there is a new teacher at the table, for example, but will taste new foods or eat everything on the plate when the familiar teacher is there with whom they feel safe.

There Are Ways in Which We Can Help

There are many indirect ways to help a child enjoy eating. An attractive-looking table appeals to children. Bright-colored dishes, flowers, a neatly laid table, all add to the child's pleasure and interest in food. Food that "looks good" with a contrast in color is important. Colored junket, for example, usually disappears faster than plain white junket.

Children's tastes differ from adults' in that children usually do not care for very hot or very cold foods. They do not like mixed flavors, either. A casserole or loaf may be unpopular even though each individual flavor in it may be relished separately. They care less for creamed foods or sauces over foods than adults do. All this makes cooking simpler and should be a welcome advantage to a busy homemaker. Strong flavors or unusual textures in a food are usually less acceptable to a child.

A child will enjoy eating more if he is comfortable at the table. He needs a chair in which his feet can rest on the floor and a table that is the right height for him. He needs implements that are easy to grasp. A salad fork rather than a large fork, a spoon with a round bowl and a small glass add to his comfort and his pleasure. He is more comfortable if he is not crowded too close to others at the table.

When a child feels independent and adequate, he enjoys the situation. If there is a marker at his place at nursery school so that he feels no uncertainty about where he is going to sit, he may feel surer of himself. If he can put on his own bib, he will be happier. Even the youngest child can pull on a bright-colored wash cloth with an elastic across the end and such a bib is absorbent and easily laundered. The child will also enjoy getting up and down without help, clearing away his own dishes and getting his dessert. If he can wait on himself, he may be less restless, too.

Behavior at Mealtime Has Meaning

It is necessary that children are handled in the eating situation according to their individual needs and stages of development. Eating is an activity in which a great deal of meaningful behavior is evident. Because of its importance emotionally as well as nutritionally, it is worth understanding why children behave as they do in the eating situation.

Frequent demands to be fed should be regarded as a symptom, and may be part of a pattern of dependence. Perhaps the standards for eating behavior have been set too high. The problem to be attacked is not the asking-to-be-fed but, in this case, the changing of what is expected of the child, so that he has confidence that he can live up to expectations. Often a young child will ask to be fed when he grows tired because of the demand on his coordination that eating makes. As his motor skill improves, he will need less help. Sometimes a child asks to be fed because he wants to find out if the adult is willing to help, to be reassured about his ability to get help when he wants it.

Companions can be distracting at times. Eating with other children is fun and one good eater will influence others, but sociability may need to be kept within bounds by proper spacing and placement of the children. The main business at the table is eating!

The teacher may need to help children by influencing the amount of conversation taking place. Conversation sometimes interferes with eating for children have not mastered the art of talking and eating. In his enthusiasm for communicating with others, a child may forget about eating. If he is a child for whom the teacher estimates that talking to others has more value at the moment than eating, she may give him time to finish later or feed him herself, as in the case of a shy, withdrawn child who is just "blossoming out" and needs to be encouraged to continue. A different child who is already socially adequate may need to be reminded to "eat now and talk later."

There may be practical limitations inherent in the situation which determine how much time a child can be permitted to spend at the table. There may also be limitations which are desirable for particular children depending on their individual needs. But eating should not proceed by a clock. Just as a "set" toilet schedule does not meet the needs of children, so a "set" length of time to eat cannot mean the same thing to all children. Some are deliberate and some are quick. These differences are reflected in the time they take for their meals. Meals are served because we need food and we enjoy eating. There is no special virtue in eating to get through a meal.

REST

Rest is something children need but often resist. Active children who are easily stimulated may find it hard to relax with other children near. They may want to continue their activities. Rest time comes as an interruption. It is imposed by the adult. Nursery school experience encourages independent choices in most areas. Children may resist having no choice here and try asserting themselves by opposing the adults' demands that they rest.

The teacher herself must feel very sure that a rest period is good for children if she expects to communicate such a conviction to them. One wonders if some teachers are really sure that they want children to rest. They may be carrying some seeds of rebellion against rest in their own feeling about it which make it hard for them to be effective in their efforts to help children here.

What the Teacher Does Is Important

Children often recall the resting period at nursery school without much pleasure. This fact should raise some questions about the procedures used. What are our own feelings toward a rest period? Are we clear about what we mean by rest and do we make this clear to the child? Are we too ready to make the child feel he is failing here?

The way a teacher approaches a child at rest time may give him reassurance or indicate her disapproval of him. A teacher can look in a friendly, reassuring way in the direction of a child who is beginning to be disturbing, reminding him of her presence or she can look at him with a frown, suggesting her disapproval. She can move quietly to him, patting him in a comforting way, whispering a reminder to him and even adding a few whispered words about something he did earlier that was fun and that she and he both can remember with pleasure. On the other hand, by going to him with a different manner, she can make him feel uncomfortable about his behavior. The result may be resistance on his part.

The teacher will start by creating an atmosphere which suggests rest. She will move quietly and perhaps speak in a whisper. She will make her expectations clear, that is, she will expect the children to be quiet, not to be disturbing to others, but her expectations will be reasonable. She will give each child time to settle down. She will not expect him to be perfectly quiet but just to be relaxed and to refrain from interfering with others. Some schools use music during the rest period as a way of creating an atmosphere conducive to relaxation.

Dependency Needs Are Greater at Rest Time

It is especially easy for the child to feel uneasy at rest time because resting is closely associated with experiences with his mother and her care. His need for her may come closer to the conscious level. He reverts to earlier dependencies. He may need the teacher's attention. He may want to have a blanket straightened just to have some contact with her. Failing in this, he may be noisy which is another way of getting attention. He may be less able to bear her disapproval at rest time than when he is feeling more independent. It does not help him to feel he has failed. He needs her reassurance. He needs to have his dependency need met in some way and he needs to be helped to move back to being independent and responsible for himself.

It does not help him to have her give him an unnecessary amount of attention. At rest time children are likely to be jealous when the teacher's attention goes to other children. The teacher must make each of them feel that she is willing to give enough attention so that they all will have what they need. If an individual child needs an extra amount of attention, she will remove him from the room so as not to make the others unduly anxious. The resting room is a place where the children can take a step toward resolving rivalries if the situations are handled with understanding. It is a place where their need for care must be accepted while they are being helped to find satisfaction in independence. The confident, maternal person will be most successful in helping the children grow through the nap room experience. Since the limits in the nap room are set by the adult because she knows something about the whole group's need for rest, they are limits which she is responsible for maintaining. They are not limits which she can expect the children to maintain easily without her confident support. The inexperienced person is likely to have difficulty here until she gains confidence in herself. We will discuss this point further in the chapter on limits.

THE RELATION OF ROUTINES AND
THE DEVELOPMENT OF INDEPENDENCE

We have discussed some of the meanings which toileting, eating and rest may have for children. We have indicated some of the problems which arise in connection with these routine activities.

Problems Occur at "Transition Points"

From the standpoint of the teacher many of the difficulties she faces in managing these routines exist at "transition points," or the point at which she interrupts the child's own activity to direct him into the routine. He delays. He resists. He defies. He asserts himself, in other words, and such behavior is appropriate to his developmental level. He needs and wants to direct his own activities, to do things for himself, to assert himself against others in order to test himself. Is he really an independent person? How much independence does he have?

Since he is striving to be more independent, the child often makes an issue at these times of transition from free play to a more directed situation. If the teacher keeps the child's needs in mind, she may find it easier to meet his resistance without adding to it. She can value the fact that he is working at growing into a more autonomous, independent person. She can respect his right to assert himself and his desire to do it. But she should also recognize her responsibility to maintain certain reasonable demands. The child cannot do just as he likes all the time even though he grows best if he can do what he wishes a good deal of the time when he is young.

He also needs experience in finding that he does not lose his independence just because he accepts some restrictions and meets some demands. It is important for him that his teacher feel clear about what she expects him to do and sure about her right to expect this of him. If she acts with confidence, she makes it easier for him. Acting confidently, she is likely to give him more definite and specific directions, to show less impatience and be more imaginative in the kind of help she gives him in making the transition. He may be able, in the end, to turn his desire to be independent into working with her and make it a matter of self-direction. We all must do necessary things which, at the moment, we may not really want to do. Transition points can be growth points but this may take time!

Changes Can Be Made

Some of the problems which arise in connection with routines may be related to the physical setup of the school. A crowded locker room creates problems when children are pulling on their wraps. Cots set up in the playroom may make resting difficult. A change in the situation may be possible. Sometimes making a change in the schedule itself, the time or the sequence as well as the physical arrangements, may reduce the difficulties which have been arising.

The Child Wants to Be Independent

We see children's great interest in being more autonomous and independent appearing in many places. Children find great satisfaction in doing a thing unaided. Shoes laced in irregular ways, a shirt on backwards, hands only partly clean may be sources of pride to a child because these things were achieved independently. The process of achieving is more important than the product. If we can be aware of the overwhelming importance to children of being independent, we can relax at this point in our own concern for the end result. We can give them time to grow and find satisfaction in freedom from dependency. In doing this we are accepting them and their developmental level.

Our Own Need to Help May Interfere

But the drive to be independent which every healthy child feels comes up against one of our own needs, the need to help. This need is especially strong when we feel least sure that we can help. We may feel this way when we first start working in a nursery school. By helping, by doing things for a child, we try to prove to ourselves that we are in fact competent and able. The child's dependency on us reassures us that we have a place in the school. Incidentally, children are aware of this when they approach a new teacher with a request for help. By asking for help and making the stranger feel friendly toward him, the child reduces his anxieties about a strange person. This type of contact may be a satisfactory one in the beginning, but if it continues the child is deprived of opportunities for growth.

Watch what happens in the coatroom. The inexperienced teacher is the one who steps in and expertly buttons the button that the child has been fumbling intently with. She takes the child's coat from its low hook and holds it for him and then may be surprised that he runs away instead of putting it on. She puts in the plug when he is ready to wash his hands, pushes up his sleeves and hands him the soap. She deprives him of many chances to do things that he can do for himself. She herself needs to help and she acts out of her own need. If she is to handle her strong feeling about wanting to help, she must be aware of this feeling as well as of the values for the child in being independent. Keeping his need in mind, she will plan the situation so that he has a maximum chance to do things for himself. She will keep from helping him needlessly.

The Child Reverts to Dependency at Times

When we have recognized the importance of the child's need to be independent as well as the likelihood that we will feel a need to offer help unnecessarily at times, we must still be ready to accept the fact that there are times when the child needs to be dependent on us. Erikson makes it clear that no development is completed at any one stage. This means that we carry on to the next stage the uncompleted tasks of earlier stages. A child may ask for unnecessary help because he wants reassurance that he can still be dependent if he wishes. It may be important to help him with his coat if he asks us, as we mentioned earlier. When we help him at his request, we are responding to his need and not to our own. He is better off for this kind of help. In routines we must only be sure that we do not deprive the child of the chance to be independent when he is ready.

REFERENCES

1. Buxbaum, Edith: Your Child Makes Sense. New York, International Universities Press, 1949, Part 2.
2. Farnham, Maryna: Helping Boys to Be Boys and Girls to Be Girls. Parents' Magazine, Jan. 1953.
3. Hymes, James L.: How to Tell Your Child About Sex. New York, Public Affairs Pamphlet No. 149, 1949.
4. Ridenour, Nina: Some Special Problems of Children, Aged 2 to 5 Years. New York, National Mental Health Foundation, 1947.
5. Spock, Benjamin: Pocket Book of Baby and Child Care (Revised) (Sections on eating, thumb-sucking, toilet training and sleep.) New York, Pocket Books, Inc., 1957.

III

Understanding

Feelings in Areas

Where Feelings Are Strong

7

Building Feelings of
Confidence and Adequacy

Feelings of Confidence and Adequacy Are Important for All of Us

"Look here, teacher, I'm bigger than you think. I'm going to have a birthday soon. Let me do this by myself," said Katherine to a well-meaning adult who was trying to help her.

Her words remind us how often adults handicap children by acting as though children were unable to meet situations. A child has a difficult time developing confidence when he is surrounded by people who "help" him all the time. Children are often bigger than we think! Katherine was able to express her confidence in herself as a person able to do things. Few children can do this because they lack not only the verbal ability but the feeling itself.

As adults most of us probably wish that we had more self-confidence. We realize that we are likely to do a thing better when we

157

feel confident than when we are afraid of failing. We realize, too, that we get more pleasure out of doing something when we feel adequate and are free from anxiety. For all of us, feelings of insecurity and inadequacy are handicapping. They do not arise entirely from lack of skill, for the person who has confidence in himself may enjoy undertaking something new in which he lacks skill. But most people are not free enough of doubts about themselves to feel that the unfamiliar is a challenge to them.

One of the important ways in which we will use the nursery school as a laboratory will be in trying to understand better how people grow secure and confident as well as how security and confidence are sometimes destroyed. As we observe people in nursery school, we will look for the meaning of their behavior in terms of the degree of security revealed by it. As we work with the children, we will seek for ways of strengthening their feelings of confidence and security. We will ask ourselves at least three questions. First, where do feelings of security and adequacy come from and what helps or hinders their development? Second, how can we identify these feelings in people? Third, what can we do in the nursery school to increase these feelings?

DEFINITIONS. Before we consider these questions we must in some way define the terms, "security" and "adequacy." Let us say that security refers to the feelings that come with having had many experiences of being accepted as we are rather than rejected, of feeling safe rather than threatened. It refers to a person's relationships with people and develops from the way these relationships have been experienced by the individual. Adequacy refers to the feelings which an individual has about himself, his concept of the kind of person he is. This concept, too, grows out of the responses other people make to him. Security and adequacy are closely related. It will be easier to consider them together in our discussion for, as we help the child with one feeling, we are likely to help him with the other.

FOUNDATIONS FOR FEELING ADEQUATE AND CONFIDENT

First, where do feelings of security and adequacy come from?

We have already suggested some of the important areas. They arise out of the way the child's basic needs are met, his experiences with feeding and later with toileting, the kinds of responses he gets from other people, the satisfaction he finds in exploring the world. Out of these early experiences the child builds a feeling of trust in the world, his first task developmentally. Having learned that he can trust others he is ready to trust and have confidence in himself. The attitudes and feelings of his parents are the most important factors in building confidence because he depends largely on his parents for the satisfaction of his basic needs.

If the child's first experiences have made him feel adequate and confident because he has been able to have his wants satisfied, to obtain response from people, to have satisfying sensory experiences, he has laid a firm foundation for confidence and security. If he was fed when he was hungry and had attention when he felt the need for it, the world seems a safe place to him and he can face it with the assurance that he will be able to meet the problems it presents. If, on the other hand, his wants have been unsatisfied, if he has failed to get response when he needed it, he has already experienced insecurity and felt inadequate. If he constantly heard the words, "no"

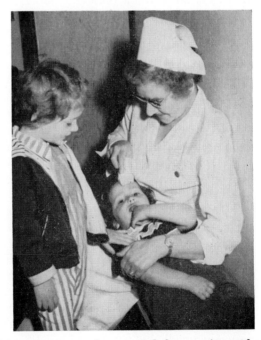

Fig. 31.   Recovering from a bump and finding comfort with friends.

and "don't," when he reached for experience, he has already grown to distrust his own impulses. The world does not seem to him a place where he can feel safe, and he builds a picture of himself as a person who is not very adequate to meet the problems it presents. He thinks of himself as a person who is likely to do the wrong thing.

As Will said dejectedly when he looked down at his muddy boots one day in nursery school, "It's sure hard to please anybody when you get right in the mud." He had been having fun in the mud but he knew from past experience that what he did in mud somehow made him unpopular.

Children Are Influenced in Their Feelings by the Attitudes of Adults

Children tend to behave as they feel they are expected to behave, or according to the concept of self they have built up out of the responses of other people to them. Charles, for example, thinks of himself as a boy who gets into trouble. As he and his father came into nursery school one morning, his father remarked, "See how nice and quiet this place is until you get here!" What is a boy like who hears words like these? He is a boy who is noisy and defiant and "difficult." He lives up to the picture his father paints.

When Jim's mother brought him to nursery school, she explained to the teacher as Jim stood beside her, "Perhaps he'll learn to ride a tricycle here. He doesn't know how yet. He doesn't like to learn things. He just tries for a minute and then gives right up." It was not surprising that Jim lacked confidence, and did not persist and was unfriendly with both children and teachers.

Ella was timid, too. She didn't join other children in play, but she did like to paint. She was at the easel painting carefully around the edges of the paper when her mother came for her one day. Her mother saw the picture and she said half scornfully, "Nobody paints like that!" How can one have much confidence if one is considered a "nobody"? Ella didn't expect to be liked!

After Ella had been in nursery school some time and had gained confidence through feeling more acceptance and approval, after she felt more of a "somebody," her behavior changed in an interesting way. She quietly but persistently tried to put herself in as important a place in every situation as she could. For example, she and another child were pretending that their block structure was a truck. "I'll be the driver," said Ella. "No," insisted her companion, "I'm the driver." After a moment's hesitation Ella said, "Then I'll be the man who owns the truck and hires the driver."

Ella's solution was very different from that of Mary who had always felt sure that she was loved. "Can I play with you?" she asked Dick. "No," shouted Dick, and Mary answered calmly, "I could be the maid and sweep and then two people could play together." In the same kind of situation, she was only interested in finding a playmate and did not need to depend on having an important place.

Leighton and Kluckhohn in *Children of the People* make an interesting comment on the attitudes which appear in another culture than our own. They describe the way the Navaho people treat young children in these words, ". . . the Navaho toddler is given self-confidence by being made to feel that he is constantly loved and valued."* Would Ella and Jim have behaved differently if they had lived under conditions where they were "constantly loved and valued"? There are many children in our culture who are "constantly loved and valued," but there are many others who are treated as "nobodies" like Ella and Jim even though there is no conscious intent on the part of parents to treat them this way.

The frequency with which the word "big" appears in children's conversation, as "We're big truck drivers," and "Mine's the biggest car," or "I have the most," is perhaps a reflection of the many occasions when we have made the child feel that he is "too little" and not sufficiently loved and valued. They are words which are in part a defense against the inadequate feelings which result from being "too little" on many occasions in a world that favors those who are big and have the most.

We live in such a highly competitive society that it is often hard for us to recognize the values that may exist outside of achievement. Parents feel the pressure for accomplishment. They want children who will learn to ride tricycles or who paint good pictures. They push their children, even their toddlers. They do not value them as they are.

* Leighton, Dorothea, and Kluckhohn, Clyde: Children of the People: The Navaho Individual and His Development. Harvard Univ. Press, 1947, p. 33.

We Tend to "Nudge" Children

Dr. James Plant described this tendency of parents to push their children as quickly as possible from one stage to the next as "nudging" the child in his growth. We are likely to "nudge" children on rather than allow them to take time to satisfy their needs in each stage. We do this even though it has been demonstrated that growth proceeds in certain sequences, one stage following another, and that the soundest growth occurs when the child is given time in each stage, "living it out completely" before going on to the next. Dependency, for example, precedes independence and the child who is most independent in the end will be the one whose dependency needs have been most completely met, not the one who was pushed the soonest into being independent. "Nudging" a child from one stage to the next serves to make him feel less secure and more defensive. Children who have been pushed through a stage frequently have to go back and experience it again before they are free enough to go on, before they are secure enough to develop further.

We Make Children Feel Guilty

Children sometimes find it hard to develop confidence in themselves because they feel they are to blame for things that happen. A child may enjoy an experience such as playing in the mud or exploring a bureau drawer only to find that what he has done is considered very naughty by the adult. With little basis for real understanding of adult values, with a great need to please adults because of his dependency on them, he comes to feel uncertain about himself and his behavior. Many times he thinks that his mistakes are much more serious than we really consider them. He suffers from a load of guilt that may be very great. When we blame him for what he does not understand or understands only in part, we damage his feeling of confidence and trust in himself.

By making events conditional on a child's good or bad behavior, we may increase his sense of uncertainty and lack of confidence since good or bad behavior is what we chose to call it. He may feel responsible for events which have no connection. Betty said, "Next week if I'm a real good girl, know where we're going? To the beach!" Let's hope that her parents were not too busy or tired that week or that nothing interfered with their plan!

When unrelated events are made conditional on each other, the child gets the idea that he causes things to happen by his behavior, by being good or bad. He may feel that some unfortunate circumstance such as an illness occurred because he was bad. If he can bring about a trip to the beach by being good, he can cause a calamity by being bad. Without enough experience to correct his concepts, he is the victim of his misapprehensions. Pam, for example, arrived at nursery school one morning and didn't see the ducks. She was very interested in them and inquired anxiously, "I can't see the ducks." Then she added, "I made a noise. Do ducks get headaches?" We may not suspect a child's real feelings or the heavy load of guilt he may feel for events. We may have helped make such misconceptions possible with words like, "If you're a real nice girl, this will happen," or "If you aren't a good boy, this will happen."

We Are Afraid of "Spoiling" Children

Sometimes people are afraid to accept children as they are and to meet their needs because they are afraid of "spoiling" them if they do. They deny and interfere with them needlessly out of ignorance of the growth process. They make it hard for the child to think of himself as an adequate person. "Spoiled" children are in fact those who get attention *when the adult wants to give it* rather than when the child himself needs it. They are those children who are subject to inconsistent interferences rather than given the support of consistent limits by parents who are willing to take responsibility for limits. A "permissive" type of handling which allows the child to live on his own level tends to build secure feeling in the young child rather than to "spoil" him. It reduces to the minimum the denials and interferences which are likely to shake a child's confidence in himself. It accepts him as he is. It helps him feel adequate.

What Does "Permissiveness" Mean?

The word "permissiveness" is misunderstood or at least interpreted very differently by different people. It may be worth explaining what we mean by it. By permissive type of handling we do *not* mean handling which allows the child to do whatever he likes and which leaves the entire burden of responsibility for his behavior up to the child. Few of us as adults are mature enough to take this much responsibility. We find that laws are necessary and police are needed to enforce them. The adult who lets the child do just what he want is an adult who is avoiding his own responsibilities. Children nee limits set for them to protect them from acting in ways which wil have damaging consequences or frighten them. But the limits can b set at quite different points. One person will not interfere with child or stop him in what he does unless he or she feels sure th action will result in undesirable consequences. This person wil permit anything short of behavior with such consequences. The chil is free to explore and experiment with materials, to act in all kind of childish ways and learn for himself.

Another person will interfere or stop a child in what he is doing unless he or she feels sure that what the child is doing is desirable There is much less room for discovery and for trying out ways o acting under this method. The first person's attitude is a "permis sive" one in contrast to the restrictive attitude of the second person For example, a three-year-old was digging in the yard with a shovel He carefully dug around some bricks laid to serve as a path. He removed them and made a wall with them to dam up water as he poured it on a slope. He was delighted with what he had accom plished. It had taken effort and purposefulness on his part. His mother had observed him at work but had not interfered. Although she might have preferred to have the bricks left where they had been placed, she knew it would do no harm to move them. They could be replaced later and meanwhile her small son was enjoying a satis fying experience. He was using bricks as a child, not as an adult. He carried out his own purpose. She would not have allowed him to do just anything with the bricks. She would have stopped him if he had used one to hit the car parked in the drive or to hit another child. She was handling him in a "permissive" way, giving him as much freedom as was possible in the situation. She was not restrict ing him just to what she thought might be done.

Parents Need to Be Secure People

Accepting the child as he is and meeting his needs freely are easier for people who are themselves secure. A secure person is relaxed, comfortable, permissive and giving. He or she does not feel as much need to make demands on others. Secure people are likely to create the kind of environment in which it is easy for the child to think of himself as an adequate person.

Insecure people are defensive and often demanding. They are likely to set standards which the child can meet with difficulty, if at all. They are likely to be very concerned with what other people say about them as parents. If they are to accept children, parents need to be secure people; yet there are many reasons why parents have a hard time feeling secure today. They are handicapped not only by economic insecurities, tensions and conflicts in the world, by inadequate housing and limited community resources in health and recreation, but by an education which offers little guidance in understanding the parent-child relationships. Charles' father, who spoke in such a belittling way to his son, is typical of many parents. He wants to be a successful parent but he is without experience or preparation for his role. Like most people he values success highly and is striving for it in a professional field. His concept of a successful parent is one whose child behaves like an adult. He feels his failure to achieve this goal with Charles. His love for the child is hidden under his constant criticism. He is not a secure parent. He makes Charles an insecure child.

A Child May Be Offered Many Different Kinds of Experiences by Adults

By the time the child reaches the nursery school he will have had many experiences which will determine how secure and adequate he feels. He may have come from a home where he has been accepted by parents secure enough to be permissive and giving. He may have come from a home where there has been little permissiveness, and his parents are too insecure themselves to be able to accept his immaturities. The experiences that he will have in nursery school will add to the foundation he has laid. The acceptance he finds in the teachers, the care with which experiences are adapted to his readiness to meet them, beginning with the experience of entering the school itself, will bring growth in the direction of being more secure and adequate or will handicap this growth. We will consider further the significance of his nursery school experiences as we discuss ways of strengthening his positive feelings.

RECOGNIZING THE CHILD'S FEELINGS

We will raise the question here of how we may recognize a child's feelings. How do we identify feelings so that we may be of help to a child?

Children reveal their feelings through behavior. Sometimes they do it openly and directly. They act as they feel. Sometimes their feelings come out in ways that are harder to identify. We must learn to understand; then we can recognize how plainly they speak to us through behavior.

Observe Behavior First

Perhaps the first step in understanding the meaning of behavior is to be able to look at the way a child behaves without feeling a necessity to change his behavior. We must learn to look at behavior as it is rather than in terms of what we want it to be. We are likely to confuse the meaning of a child's behavior with our own feelings if we try to judge it, if we decide that the child should or should not be behaving as he is.

We learn by observing. We are interested, at first, in learning to understand what feelings are being expressed through each bit of behavior. It may be dangerous to strive for change before we fully understand the forces with which we are dealing. Damage has been done many times when people have acted without sufficient knowledge. Men cut down trees and cleared land only to discover that the soil washed away and that water supplies were endangered because of what they had done. Too much of our energy is spent trying to repair the consequences of hasty action. In the field of behavior as in all fields, we need to observe and learn before we can evaluate a course of action.

There Are Clues to a Child's Feeling in Behavior

We have already pointed out how children differ in the kinds of adjustments that they make in new situations. These differences have meaning. The person who wishes to understand a child will observe carefully how he responds in a new situation. He will not decide how the child should respond and try to force this pattern of response on him. If he does, he may be burying a clue to understanding. He may damage the child and his development.

Children reveal characteristic attitudes in everyday, familiar situations, too. These may be seen in such things as in the way the child walks, runs, holds his hands, in his posture, etc. Posture is, of course, influenced by constitutional and environmental factors, but over and above these, reflections of the child's emotional patterns can be seen

n his muscle tensions. One child's hands are relaxed and another's
re tense and constantly moving. One child clutches our finger tightly
s we walk along with him, a sign of his need for support and the
ntensity of his feeling. Another lets his hand lie limply in ours, suggesting perhaps the nongiving quality of his relationship with others,
n contrast to the warm, responsive grip of still another child who
welcomes closeness without clinging to it. These are all clues to help
is understand the child's feeling.

Sometimes a conflict the child is feeling is expressed in the movements of his hands, as in the case of the child who is attracted to
finger paints yet cannot use them because of the inhibitions he has
built up against getting dirty. He may stand at a distance, wiping
his clean hands on his suit or wringing them together, showing us
he conflict he feels between the desire for sensory experience and
the force of the restriction he has known against satisfying this
desire.

There Are Clues in a Child's Speech

Voice quality and speech offer clues to feelings. The quality of a
child's voice may be strained and tight, or relaxed and easy. It may
be loud and harsh, or soft and faint, or it may be confident and
well-modulated. Even the amount of speech may give some indication of the extent of the child's assurance or of his hesitation. One
child talks very little; another chatters almost constantly. These
extremes may be a reaction to strains and pressures which are making him feel less confident and less secure than he should feel. Many
insistent, needless questions are sometimes a symptom of insecurity,
a seeking for reassurance more than for any specific answer. Too
often these questions meet an impatient rebuff, not calculated to
satisfy the need they express.

Spontaneous singing usually indicates confidence and content-
ment. The child who sings at play is probably comfortable, and it is
worth noting the times and places when singing occurs spontaneously. We can learn from this in what areas or on what occasions a
child feels secure. We can provide more of these kinds of experience. We have an important clue here.

For further clues as to how secure and adequate a child feels, we
need to listen closely for the meaning which lies behind the words
he speaks. An anxious little boy, new at school, talked to the teacher

as he lay on his bed, resting. He kept telling her, "I live in Corvallis," and then asked her if she had a car. When she answered, "Yes," he said, "You could take me home." His words clearly indicated the insecurity he was feeling and the way he was trying to reassure himself by clinging to the idea of where he lived and by working out a plan for getting himself safely there. The teacher understood, and reassured him about how his daddy would come for him as he had the day before and how she would stay with him until his daddy came. She did stay near him and helped him to find satisfactions in his present environment.

Martha cried one day and wanted her mother to stay at school with her. Her mother consented, somewhat reluctantly. Later she said to the teacher, "You know, I was pretty cross with Martha this morning. Do you suppose that has anything to do with her wanting me to stay with her?" They both agreed that this was probably the explanation of Martha's behavior that day. She was seeking reassurance from her mother. An increase in dependency often means the child is seeking more reassurance that he is loved.

The child who asks the teacher, "Do you want to go outdoors with me?" may really be saying, "I'm afraid to go out by myself. It would help if you wanted to go with me." The teacher needs to understand the meaning back of what he actually says.

The child who says happily, "Isn't this going to be a good gate? I'm building it all myself," is telling us something about what comfortable feelings he has about being an adequate person. This same boy's father once remarked about him, "I think he's one of those fortunate people who like themselves." The child liked himself—and everybody else, and was one of the most likeable children one could meet. He had been "loved and valued" in his family like the Navaho toddler in his.

There is a real consciousness of an emerging self in these words of Katherine—the same Katherine who is "bigger than you think"—when she says, "I'm different from all the other people. When other people laugh, I don't, even if it's silly." Katherine feels secure enough to be different.

Patterns of Behavior Give Clues to Feelings of Security and Adequacy

Defensive behavior is usually a sign of insecurity. Only too often children express their insecure feelings in a defensively aggressive

way. They try to conceal the uncertainty they feel by being aggressive. They hit without much provocation. They reject the approaches
of other children. One can get valuable clues by observing the way
a child reacts to the approaches of another child as well as the way
he himself approaches others. The secure child is not on the defensive. He does not feel threatened when another child approaches,
but finds it easy to be friendly. The insecure child is likely to be
hostile and unfriendly at any approach even before he finds out what
kind of an approach it is. While the secure child can share easily
when he is ready for group experience, the insecure child cannot
afford to share because he fears any loss. His problem is not one
of unfriendliness or selfishness but one of degree of security. This
is the real problem which needs to be handled, not the symptom.

When someone knocks over Ralph's blocks, for example, he bursts
into tears or he may hit at the offender frantically. He exhibits behavior characteristic of the insecure child. It is worth noting that
Ralph does not behave this way every time something happens.
There are a few children in the group with whom he feels sufficiently
comfortable, sufficiently sure of himself, to be able to accept interference without being overwhelmed with feelings of helplessness.

It is important for us to note the people and the areas in which a
child shows us by his behavior that he feels secure, if we are to help
him. Steven and Sheila behave in a way that characterizes children
who feel secure. Steven was pushing a block train along the floor
when Sheila, who was riding a tricycle, happened to run into it and
knock it over. "Excuse me, Steven," she said. "That's all right," he
replied and he hooked the cars together and continued playing.

The child who is very insecure will often be unable to accept even
a suggestion by the adult that he (the child) has made a mistake.
Jane, for example, had known very little safety and security in any
of her relationships with people. She was passive and inhibited,
risking very little action. She had been in nursery school several
weeks when this incident occurred: During rest, one of the children
sat up and began playing. The teacher glanced in his direction,
indicating that he needed to be quiet. Just then Jane sat up and the
teacher indicated that she, too, needed to be quiet. Jane instantly
burst into a storm of weeping, unable to face what seemed to her
to be failure. She needed more time to grow secure before she could
accept limitation without feeling threatened by it.

Margaret was another extremely insecure, defensive child who acted as though she did not expect friendliness from anyone. After a long period of holding herself back from any contacts in nursery school, she began to play with individual children. She had her first spontaneous, friendly play one morning with Betty. The two of them sat together in the sun playing with clay. It was growing hot so the teacher suggested that they stop playing long enough to take off their sweaters. Betty protested; then she acquiesced, for she was a secure, friendly child. Margaret's reaction was entirely different. She put her head down on the table and began sobbing. All the feelings from which she had momentarily escaped seemed to return. She may have interpreted the request as a threat to deprive her of this rare moment of companionship. Contacts with adults still represented a hostile limitation which she felt helpless to combat. She was the defensive, resentful little girl again. It was a long, slow process, lasting many months, to help this child grow in confidence to the point where she came to trust adults and accept their requests, or protest them without fear. During these months the adults made almost no demands on Margaret and accepted the resistance and defiance she increasingly began to show. Gradually, as she came to trust adults, she was able to accept and conform to requests or limitations from them without being overwhelmed by feelings of helplessness. She showed herself a responsive, warmly affectionate little girl with a real strength of purpose and a capacity to defend the self that she now knew that others would respect.

Thumbsucking May Be a Symptom of Insecurity

When we are in nursery school, we are likely to see a child sucking his or her thumb at rest time or when the group is listening to a story or even during a play period. Like all behavior, thumbsucking is a symptom and may indicate a need in the child for more reassurance and greater security than he has found in his experience. He may seek the comfort associated with the earliest satisfactions in nursing because his world seems too difficult to face. It may be a difficult world for him because he is expected to be more grown-up than he is ready to be. He may be expected to be quiet, to inhibit his impulses for touching things, to take over adult ways of behaving at the table or in social situations, to comprehend and maintain the rules for property rights, etc. The strain of living up to all these demands, or of failing to live up to them, may be so great that the child

eeks an infantile source of comfort. He turns to his thumb as a
efuge.

In some cases the world may be a difficult one for the child be-
:ause he has to respond to many different adults and the attention
hat they give him and expect from him in return. "Show her how
'ou do this," or "Come give me a kiss," and then "Don't bother me
10w," all put a strain on a child and confuse him. By sucking his
humb he is retreating into a situation which is not so demanding.
Γhe world may be difficult for a child because it is always changing.
Γhere may be moves from one house to another, from one town to
ιnother. The adults in the home may shift. The coming of another
:hild may change the pattern of relationships.

Whatever the reason in individual cases we can be sure that the
:hild who persists in sucking his thumb after he has become a tod-
ɪler is finding his world difficult, with more strain and tension in it
than he can handle comfortably. He is telling us something through
his thumbsucking, and we need to understand. We should not increase his strain by taking away the avenue of comfort that he has
found, but we should try to make his life simpler and more comfortable. We should try to reduce the tensions he is under and offer
him a greater chance for feeling secure and adequate, so that he
may seek other kinds of satisfactions.

Mary Lou Took Her Own Thumb Out of Her Mouth

Mary Lou was a round little girl of three who sucked her thumb
most of the time at nursery school. She was timid and often held
onto the teacher's skirt with her free hand. She didn't venture into
activity with other children or even play alone actively.

Mary Lou was the oldest of three children and had always been
a "good" girl according to her mother. She had been easy to care for
and could even be depended on to watch out for her little sister
while her mother was busy with the baby. She seemed content with
little to do and never disturbed the babies. It was not hard to imag-
ine that Mary Lou had had very little chance to have the satisfactions that usually come with being a baby. She had had to grow up
very quickly, and had had to seek approval by behaving in unchildlike ways. It would have been an empty world for her without her
thumb. She remained dependent on the teacher at nursery school
for many months, but her interest in the children was plain as she

watched a group having fun together. Sitting close to the teacher she sometimes became part of a group at the piano or at the clay table. She had a real capacity for enjoying experiences and a sense of humor which was evident as she felt freer to act. She thoroughly enjoyed the sensory experiences at the clay table, in the sandbox and later in the mud hole in the nursery school yard. She often played alone in the doll corner after she felt more at home.

Some months later she ventured into more active play. She still stood around with her thumb in her mouth part of the time but she was busy in the sandbox or riding the tricycles more of the time. The most marked change came in her behavior after she gained enough courage to use the slide. Sliding was a popular activity and Mary Lou would often stand watching, but resisted any suggestion that she join the group at the slide. At last on a day when no one else was at the slide, she tried it, with her favorite teacher near to hold her hand. It was an effort but she succeeded and went down again and again. She waved gaily to her mother when her mother came that day and showed off her newly acquired skill. From then on she participated more freely in every group. Mastering the slide seemed to give her a great deal of confidence. She even did a little pushing to hold her place in line there and began to stand up for herself in other ways. She was busy and happy. She hardly ever had time for her thumb. By the end of a year some of the adults had even forgotten that she used to suck her thumb. The fact that she no longer needed her thumb told a great deal about the change in Mary Lou and what nursery school had meant to her.

All Nervous Habits Are Symptoms

Other children may express the tensions they are feeling by biting their nails, twisting on their clothes, or sucking other objects. Masturbation is another means of finding satisfaction and a defense against strain. We may do a great deal of harm by attacking the symptom directly and denying the child an avenue of expression while he is still feeling tension and seeking relief and satisfaction. We need to look on all of these so-called "nervous habits" as symptoms whose cause must be sought and treated before the symptom itself can be expected to disappear. Treating the symptom only will tend to make some other form of expression necessary for the child and increase the strain he feels. The thumbsucking child may become a nailbiting child or a masturbating child, for example, if the symptom and not the cause is attacked. We must keep in mind the fact that all kinds of behavior have meanings which we cannot afford to ignore.

Speech Reveals Adjustments

Through his manner of speech a child tells us something about himself, too. In the nursery school we are likely to hear children whose words tumble out in broken rhythm or with many repetitions. Preschool children are just learning to talk and they often cannot form or recall the words as fast as they wish to get their ideas across. In some children this blocking is marked and begins to resemble stuttering.

Because children's speech is in its formative stage, it is especially important for us to handle its development with understanding. The repetition and broken rhythm which sounds like what we call stuttering or stammering is in itself a sign of strain and tension in the child. These strains may be temporary ones such as the piling up of unusual experiences which have fatigued the child or too much excitement just at the point in his growth when he is making rapid progress in learning to talk. Speech may be the most vulnerable spot at the moment and breaks down under the strains. Or the strains may be of long standing such as conflicts over relationships in the family or the piling up of hostilities which are allowed no avenue for expression.

If the emphasis is put on the symptom—the imperfect speech—the result may be a serious and lasting speech disorder. Some speech specialists feel that stuttering does not become true stuttering until the child recognizes and grows afraid that he will stutter. If this is true, it is essential that we exercise care to avoid calling the child's attention in any way to his speech. It is important to avoid asking him to "stop and say it more slowly" as many people will do. It is important for us to accept his speech and attack the conditions which are causing it. We can make it a point to stop and give the child our full attention when he is speaking, so that he will not feel the need to hurry. We can speak slowly ourselves when we speak, so that we will set a pattern in speech that will be easier for him to adopt successfully. But most of all we need to accept the fact that speech like this is a sign that pressures and demands made on this child must be reduced if his speech patterns are to change. Demands for staying dry, demands for standards in manners at the table, demands for staying clean, must be reduced or better yet eliminated if we are interested in helping him with his speech problem. All of the things which we will say later about emotional development can be applied here, but at this point we will only remind ourselves that we must be careful to avoid creating a problem for the child in the way we react to defects in his speech.

Infantile mispronunciations are common and reflect patterns of feeling as well as of speech. The independent experience of going to a nursery school will itself be of help to the child. We can treat the symptom which is established by making sure that the child hears correct speech. Rather than asking him to repeat the word or sound which is not spoken correctly, we can ourselves repeat it so that he has a chance to hear it correctly. If he is interested in books, we can read a great deal to the child whose speech has defective sounds in it, and we can read slowly and enunciate carefully as an aid to him.

It is of interest that types of speech defects vary in different culture patterns. This observation suggests that different ways of bringing up children may have different effects. Among certain Eskimo and Indian tribes, for example, no case of stuttering has ever been recorded. In our culture stuttering is much more common among boys than girls, while there are cultures where the reverse is true. Speech seems to be a sensitive index or response to the pressures which an individual feels. We need to try to understand more than just the words which are spoken.

ACCEPTING THE CHILD'S FEELINGS

We Must Face and Accept Feelings if We Are to Offer Help

In all these ways a child shows us how he feels. After we have learned to recognize the child's feelings, we must find ways of adding to his feelings of security and adequacy and reducing his feelings of insecurity and inadequacy.

What are some of the ways in which we can do this in the nursery school?

The most important step is to make sure that we really accept the child's feelings—that we do not condemn or blame him for feeling as he does. Perhaps he feels afraid or angry or unfriendly. These may be feelings of which we do not approve, but approval and acceptance are different things. Acceptance means recognizing without blaming. We may not approve but we must accept the feelings that the child has if we are going to help him with them. Our very acceptance will reduce the feeling and make the child less defensive about his fear or his anger or his hostility. Instead of hiding his feelings he can bring them out where he—and we—can do more about them.

Accepting Our Own Feelings May Be Difficult

We usually find it most difficult to be accepting about feelings which we have had to deny in ourselves. When we were children, we often felt jealous or resentful or hostile, but we may not have been permitted to express these feelings. They were not accepted by the adults around us. We had to act as though we loved a little sister, for example, and were willing to share our dolls with her, or we had to let the neighbor boy ride in our wagon because the adults insisted that children must be generous. Resentment piled up inside us as well as guilt for the feelings that we knew existed in us. We had to carry this burden alone. Now, as adults, we find it hard to be accepting of the child who refuses to share her doll or who pushes another out of the wagon. We project onto her some of the resentment which is associated with this kind of situation for us because of the experiences in our past. We identify ourselves with the adult role now, and feel like punishing the little girl who doesn't want to share her doll or her wagon today. This helps us deny that we were ever like this little girl. But in handling our feelings by denying them, we cannot offer help to children who face problems with their feelings.

The story of what goes on unconsciously is over-simplified by the description we have given, of course, but we can be sure that whenever we feel strongly rejecting of a bit of behavior, there are strong emotional reasons lying in our experience for such a rejection. For some of us there will be more of these emotionally toned areas than for others and our feelings will be stronger. Few of us will have escaped without some areas of behavior about which we find it hard to be accepting.

If, on the other hand, we were helped to accept our real feeling when we were children, we will now find it easier to be accepting of children as they show their feelings. If the adults with us when we were children said, "It's easy to get mad with someone who takes your things, I know" instead of saying "She's your sister and you must love her and share with her"; then we would have felt understood and could have faced our feelings with this kind of support. Because the adult could accept our feelings, we would not have been as likely to feel afraid or guilty about them. It would have seemed easier to feel and act more generously. This is the kind of help that we want to offer the children we are now caring for.

It is important if we are to help children in this way that we free ourselves of our old defenses. As adults we can now take the step of accepting the reality of any feeling that exists. We have less need to fear the knowledge that we are not always loving and generous. We know that we all found sharing and loving hard at times when we were children and that we felt like hitting. Some jealousy is in fact almost inevitable as children adjust to changing patterns in the family or at school. It is not necessary to deny the existence of feeling. Hostile, aggressive feelings exist in all of us. They must be accepted if we are to relieve ourselves, as well as the child, of guilty feelings about them.

Acceptance Helps the Child

The child who refuses to share a toy isn't helped by disapproval and shaming. Neither is the child who is afraid. All these children need to be accepted as they are if they are to feel secure. There is always a reason for their behavior. As we work with the little girl who refuses to share her doll or who pushes her companion out of the wagon, we will accept her feelings and use her behavior as a clue to understanding. We will not ask her to cover up her feelings. We will not be satisfied merely with changing her behavior. We will try to make it possible for her to develop different feelings which will be expressed through different kinds of behavior. We will ask ourselves some questions. What kind of little girl is it who is trying to keep the doll? What unmet needs are driving the child to behave this way? Is she craving affection and substituting the doll for the love she seeks? Does she depend on possessing things to give herself a feeling of security? How can we help her?

We Can Voice Our Acceptance of Feeling

In the first place, we can express our acceptance in words: "I know how you feel. It makes you cross because it's Timmy's turn on the swing and you want it to be yours," or, "It makes you feel cross to have your blocks tumble over, I know," or, "You're pretty mad with me right now because I can't let you play outdoors." Words like these help if they express a real acceptance of the feelings which exist. They are very different from words like "You didn't mean to hit Bobby, did you?" which are untrue, as the child's reply, "I did, too," tells us. We must be honest and state what is true.

We Can See That Feelings Are Expressed

Next comes the question of what one can do about a feeling that exists after it has been accepted. It's important that feelings be put into action, that they be drained off in ways that are not destructive. If all of us would *do* something, when we *felt* something, we'd be much healthier emotionally. We wouldn't be carrying around hidden feelings that are apt to come out when we are off guard in ways that make us unhappy. We should encourage expression of feelings at the time that they arise. We can be much clearer then as to what the feelings are. We will feel more secure because we will be more likely to handle them in ways that are appropriate.

In Words

There are all kinds of ways to express feeling. Words are one good way. As adults, we tell a friend how we feel and then feel much better. Children are likely to talk things out directly on the spot. They call names, shout lively descriptive insults, and put themselves in a better frame of mind. When they use speech like this, they may be using as good a means of handling feeling as they have at their disposal. It may not be a mature way, but they are not mature people. They cannot write poetry or denounce with eloquence some measure or some person or some oppressor. The language in which they express their rage is limited but it is adequate for them. It expresses their feeling directly instead of hiding it. If they can use language now to drain off feelings, their later responses may be more reasonable. In many cases we are wise to accept their words as expressions of the way they feel. Words like this do no damage to us if we are mature people ourselves, and if we understand what they really mean in a child's development. Listening to an insult or a swear word may not be too high a price to pay in helping a child drain off negative feeling. We can well afford it.

In Crying

Crying is another good way to express feeling, yet many times we hear people say to a crying child, "That didn't hurt. You're too big to cry." The crying may come because there have been too many failures or too much deprivation or frustration. Whatever the reason, the feeling of wanting to cry is there and needs to be accepted, not denied. No one can handle with wisdom feelings he isn't supposed to have. Words like "I know how you feel," when they are said by a person who really accepts the feeling help a good deal more than words like "You're too big to cry."

In Movements

Motor forms of expression of feeling are common forms for expression. Expressing feeling through movements or muscle activity is a common way for young children to express feeling. A young child may kick or hit or throw. Our job is to help him use motor outlets in a way which will not be damaging to others. He may even need to be put by himself so that he can act in these ways without hurting anyone. If he is older, he may be able to take a suggestion about using a punching bag to advantage. Vigorous physical activity like pounding, or throwing a ball hard against something, will serve as an outlet for feeling. If there is a warm, understanding relationship between child and adult, the child can accept many types of suggestion for draining off negative feeling. The teacher may be successful when she says, "You feel just like hitting someone, I know. Let's run as hard as we can over to that corner. That may make you feel better," and the child may be able to handle his feelings after sharing a run with an understanding, accepting teacher. Our job is to limit him so that he does not use destructive outlets. It is also our job to direct him to outlets that are possible and acceptable.

Through Creative Media

Materials which offer possibilities for creative expression can be used to drain off feelings and make them more manageable. Finger painting, painting at the easel, working with clay, playing in water, even the sandbox or a good old mud hole, will help a child relax as he expresses feelings through these media. Music offers still another possibility and is often used this way by children. Creative materials should be freely available to children because of the value they have as avenues for the expression of feeling. Adults use these same outlets. The child who has found he can turn his feelings into such creative channels has discovered an outlet which will serve him all his life. A child is more secure if he has many avenues of expression open to him. He grows as he can express himself and his feelings through art media. When he is denied self-expression in art media because patterns are set for him, he loses a valuable avenue for the relief of feeling which might help to safeguard him all his life.

Fig. 32. Confidence through motor skills and friendship.

Fig. 33. Confidence through success.

CONFIDENCE THROUGH EXPRESSION

Expression of feeling is essential if we are to feel secure and adequate. The child who says, "I'm afraid," already is less troubled by this feeling of fear. The child who says to the stranger, "Go away. I don't like you," will learn to handle his feeling more quickly than the child who says nothing and then bursts into tears when the stranger presses an acquaintanceship on him. Acting in some positive way gives us all confidence. When we do something about the way we feel, we are more confident. Psychiatrists tell us that the child who has been aggressive in his early years and whose behavior has been met with understanding has a better chance to make a good adjustment in adolescence than the submissive child, because the aggressive child has done something about his feelings and learned how to manage them.

The Timid Child May Be Reassured by Finding Even "Bad" Behavior Accepted

We will often see a timid, inhibited child swing over into unduly aggressive behavior as he begins to gain confidence in himself. This may be the first step in gaining confidence. He must first express his feelings and find acceptance for them. Then he can proceed to modify them. The child who has been inhibited may express his feelings in clumsy and inappropriate ways in the beginning. His first expression of feeling may seem exaggerated. It may seem to belong at a much younger level than his present chronological age level. But if his timidity developed in an earlier period because he was afraid of his feelings and the way people would react to them so that he was not able to express feeling, he will need to go back and act as he wanted to act earlier. With understanding guidance he will come through this stage quickly but he must "live out," for however brief a time, a period of expression at the less mature level.

Richard was an inhibited boy who found new experiences difficult to face, who for a long time could not use the toilet at nursery school and who clung to cutting with scissors as his only activity at first. He went through a short period of being very uninhibited before he built up some controls of his own. From being a timid child, dependent on the teacher, he became a child who tried out many forms of behavior which he felt were unacceptable. When he developed more confidence, he began to defy the teachers. For one trying week (for the teachers!) he kept standing on the table at mealtime and throwing food. Because he had previously been afraid to express himself in any way, the teacher accepted his behavior. She sat with him apart from the others and permitted any behavior as long as it did not interfere with mealtime for the other children. When she did restrict him, she did it without blaming or reproving him, and tried to point out what he might do that would serve the same purpose. It was about a week before he no longer seemed afraid of being "bad," before he was reassured that he would be accepted no matter what he did. Then his behavior changed. He began to act like the other children. He was able to accept the limitations ordinarily imposed in the situation without feeling helpless and inadequate. He had less need to act in unacceptable ways and in the end he became a welcomed and respected member of the group. It is worth noting, too, that Richard was probably helped by the safety he felt in knowing that the adult could and would stop him before he did anything serious as well as by the acceptance he felt for his "badness."

Children who are already sure of themselves and their acceptance by adults do not need such permissive handling as was given Richard. Confident children might even feel less sure of themselves if they found adults unwilling to limit them when they knew limits were needed. In each case handling must be based on understanding of the needs of the particular child at a particular stage.

A Child Feels More Secure When He Is Having Satisfying Experiences

The child whose needs are being met is more likely to be confident than the one whose needs are not met. This applies to his experience in the nursery school as well as at home. If the school is providing satisfying, stimulating experiences, it makes it easier for the child to be happy and secure. The whole program of the school as well as the equipment provided will contribute to the child's

Fig. 34. Confidence through real achievement.

growth in feeling more secure and more adequate. Experiences adapted to the child's level of development, equipment which fits him and makes it easy for him to solve problems, support from adults who understand what his needs are, all make it easier for a child to gain the feeling of security and adequacy that he needs.

Most important of all, in the nursery school the child is thrown with people who are on about the same level of development. He can have fun doing things with other children. Among this group of equals he does not need to feel inadequate for *he* can keep up with them. He can do things as well as many of the others. He gains strength from the feeling that he is like others, from being able to identify himself with people who are at his stage of growth. Belonging to a group of equals constitutes one of the best forms of insurance against feeling little and helpless. We will discuss this point at greater length later, but we mention it here because of the important contribution it makes to feelings of adequacy in a child.

The child needs to find teachers in the school who will accept his positive feelings, too. As teachers, we must be ready to return his smile, to take his hand when he slips it into ours, to take him into our arms when he seems to feel the need of such closeness. We must respond to his warm, friendly feelings. If it is his need and not ours that we are meeting in doing this, we can be sure that he is helped to be more independent by what we do. He will gain confidence as he feels sure of having a warm response from us when he wants it.

Good Teaching Contributes to Development of Adequate Feelings

By the techniques we use as teachers we will also help the child grow more secure and adequate. Let us take the situation of a child climbing on the jungle gym as one example, and see what it may mean.

Two-year-old Joan, just learning to climb, cautiously and awkwardly manages to get halfway up in the jungle gym and then calls for help, "Help me. I want down." An adult comes to her rescue and answers the cry by lifting her down. Joan is on the ground safe, but with all feeling of achievement lost! On another occasion a different adult comes to the rescue. She stands beside the child and says reassuringly, "I'll help you, Joan. Hang on to this bar and put your foot here," thus guiding Joan's climbing back to the ground. Safe on the ground, Joan is elated. She starts right up again and this time is successful in reaching the top. When her mother comes, she can scarcely wait to show her this new achievement.

If, when Joan starts to climb the jungle gym, her mother says in a disgusted voice, "Come on, Joan, you've had all morning to play. I'm in a hurry. You can show me tomorrow," Joan may again lose the feeling that she is a person who can achieve. But if her mother is eager to share the experience and watches her, exclaiming, "That's fine, Joan, you've learned to climb way up high," Joan takes another step in growing confident.

As teachers, we contribute to the child's feeling of security and adequacy if we tell him what he can do rather than what he can't do, if we point out what is desirable or acceptable behavior rather than what is undesirable, and if we direct his expression of feeling into channels which are not destructive and will not cause him to feel guilty. We must not hesitate to stop him when we feel that he needs to be stopped in something that he is doing, but we will be careful to do this in a way that does not make him feel ashamed. We will try to make our suggestions to him before his feeling spills over into undesirable behavior. Whenever possible, we will forestall destructive expressions of feeling although we will encourage expression. By the use of these teaching skills we will help the child develop confidence in the kind of person he is.

SUMMARY

Let us summarize briefly some of the things that we can do in the nursery school to increase a child's feeling of security and adequacy.

1. We can *accept* him as he is, his feelings and his behavior, knowing that there are reasons for the way he feels and acts. We will recognize that hitting and other forms of motor expression of feeling are normal for the young child. We will not blame or shame him for feeling as he does. If we do this, we lessen his confidence in himself as a person.

2. We can help him find acceptable *outlets* for his feelings. It is our responsibility to help him direct his expression of feeling into some channel that bears a relation to the situation but does no harm. We must be sure that feelings are expressed, however. The really destructive feelings are those that have no recognized outlets.

3. We can try to *meet the child's needs* as he indicates what his needs are, and we can leave him free to develop in accordance with

his own growth patterns at his own rate. Thus we will give him confidence and the feeling that he is an adequate person. We will refrain from "nudging" him. Instead, we will try to understand him.

4. We can *acquire skills in handling him* which will increase his confidence, making our suggestions to him in a positive way, reducing the difficulties of the situations he faces, adjusting our demands to fit his capacities, forestalling trouble when we can.

REFERENCES

1. Dybwad, Gunnar: When Children Need Comforting. National Parent-Teacher Magazine, Jan. 1956, pp. 14-16.
2. Gardner, D. E. M.: The Education of Young Children. Methuen, London, 1956, Ch. 2.
3. Wolf, Anna: Your Child's Emotional Growth. Public Affairs Pamphlet No. 264, 1958.

8

Handling Feelings of
Hostility and Aggressiveness

Hostility and Aggressiveness Are Problems for Individuals and Groups

The problem of what to do about feelings of hostility and aggressiveness is a real problem for individuals and for groups. It is not likely to be solved by avoidance or by denying the existence of these feelings. As we have pointed out, the existence of a feeling must be accepted before there is much chance that it can be handled constructively. Only when we have accepted our hostile, aggressive feelings can we discover (1) the best ways to handle them, and (2) the best ways to prevent them from multiplying.

The nursery school is a laboratory where we can study the problems of negative emotions and try to understand them. Resentment and hostility expressed aggressively are evident in the behavior of children whenever the situation is one which is not rigidly controlled by adults, whenever children are free to show us how they feel, as in the nursery school. A child who is angry may address the teacher as "You old dope," and this teacher will be the one in whom he has some confidence. He is likely to be more polite to the teacher with whom he does not feel as safe. "We don't like you," sing out two children to a third. Occasionally a chorus of "name calling" greets the visitor in the school. Some children do not reveal hostile feelings by such direct expressions, but they may have the same feelings. We can learn to recognize their less direct expressions, too. We can learn how to channel these expressions as well as how to prevent more hostility and aggressiveness from developing.

Hostility and Aggressiveness Are Tied up with Growth

In our introductory chapter we suggested that a certain amount of hostile feeling in all of us results from the growing-up process. As infants we were helpless and often our needs were not met. We felt threatened by the greater strength of the people around us. There were many frustrations and interferences for us all. Frustrations breed resentment when the frustrated person is little and helpless. The difference in the amount of our feelings lies in part in the different amount of frustration we each faced.

Some aggressiveness is necessary, for growth itself is a going-forward process which demands aggressiveness. Dr. Kubie states, "The acquisition of positive, self-assertive, commanding and demanding attitudes in the first two years of human life is an essential step in the development of every child."[*] But we now realize that much unnecessary aggressiveness as well as hostility is aroused by the traditional methods of handling children at home and at school. Healthy aggressiveness becomes unhealthy. Resentment develops which interferes with healthy growth. As we apply better methods of guiding children in the growing-up processes, we should be able to reduce the amount of hostility and unproductive aggression in the world and to do this with increasing effectiveness as our knowledge and understanding grows.

The amount of resentment and aggression as well as the amount of confusion and guilt over these feelings is perhaps greater in our culture than in some others because our training is discontinuous.

[*] Kubie, Lawrence S.: The Child's Fifth Freedom. Child Study, Summer 1948, p. 67.

In one situation the child is supposed to be submissive and obedient, as with parents at home. In another situation, as on the playground, he is expected to "stand up for himself" and come out ahead in highly competitive types of situations. The same bit of behavior is wrong in one place and right in another. These discontinuities make learning difficult for the child and may increase the number of his mistakes and the resultant guilt that he may feel. Anthropologists have pointed out the greater continuity of other cultures. In some societies where aggressiveness is valued, for example, *all* aggressive behavior is approved in the young child. The father is pleased when his little son attacks him with his fists. In other societies where generosity is valued more continuously than in ours, the parents accept the child's sharing under all circumstances and do not limit the possessions which they will permit him to share or the people with whom he may share.

Children in our culture may also carry a handicapping load of resentment because of the non-indulgent quality of our handling of them in the early years. In a study of seventy-five cultures Whiting and Child point out that Americans are "generally non-indulgent during infancy, in a hurry to start the training process (especially with respect to weaning and toilet training), and quite severe in the general socialization of their children."[*]

Since our customary methods of handling children and our patterns for conduct are likely to arouse a great deal of hostile, aggressive feeling in individuals, we are faced with a situation in which we must learn how to handle these feelings constructively as well as to avoid increasing the load which individuals carry. We have usually refused to acknowledge the extent of these feelings while we have gone on multiplying them—in children and in ourselves. The result is that they are spilling over constantly in all kinds of unsuspected ways in our personal lives as well as in our group life. Few problems are more important than the problem of facing and reducing the hostility we feel.

Children Need to Express Hostile Feelings

It is safe to say that *all* children at times feel aggressive and hostile but that not all children act out these feelings. In the past we

[*] Whiting, John, and Child, Irvin: Child Training and Personality: A Cross Cultural Study. New Haven, Yale University Press, 1953, p. 320.

Fig. 35.   Feelings are drained off in active, vigorous play.

have tended to give approval to the children who did not act out their negative feelings. From what we now know about mental hygiene, we realize that it is essential that feeling be expressed if a person is to remain mentally healthy. The problem of learning is to discover avenues of expression which are not destructive, rather than to deny expression to these feelings. The children who act out their hostile feelings probably have a better chance of achieving a healthy, mature adult life than those who are prevented from doing so. It is unlikely that we can have a peaceful world for long while the individuals in it are carrying around any great load of hostility with the added guilt that having such feelings and denying them is sure to create. We must help children face and express their hostile feelings.

It is worth quoting part of the same discussion by Dr. Kubie as follows:

. . . repeatedly in the early years of life anger must be liquidated at its birth or it will plague us to the grave. . . . If we are ever to lessen the neurotic distortions of human aggression, then it seems clear that the anger must be allowed and encouraged to express itself in early childhood, not in blindly destructive acts but in words, so as to keep it on the fullest possible level of conscious awareness. Furthermore such conscious ventilation of feelings must be encouraged in the very situations in which they have arisen, and toward those adults and children who have been either the active or the innocent sources of the feelings. Only in this way can we lessen the burden of unconscious aggression which every human being carries from infancy to the grave.[*]

Adults Must Accept Hostile Feelings in Themselves

The important job of parent and teacher then becomes as much one of encouraging expression of feeling as of diminishing the number of situations in which negative feelings are developed. Our ability to do this will depend in part on our ability to accept the existence of these feelings in ourselves as we have already pointed out. If we are to help the child, we must not deny the negative feelings which lie back of some of our own behavior. We must accept our own feelings or we will find ourselves meeting aggression by aggression and hostility by hostility. When a child calls us "You old dope," we must be able to accept the fact of his feeling of anger without getting it tangled up with our own angry feelings. This will be easier as we realize that his words offer no real threat to us as such words might have in the past or under other circumstances. We happen to be the recipient of his anger and hostility at the moment, but it has been generated by many factors in his past experiences just as our own has been.

To the extent that we were punished or shamed for the expression of our own hostile feelings, we may find it hard to accept the fact that the child needs to express such feelings. If our own defenses against such feelings are strong, if we have permitted ourselves little expression, it is likely to be difficult for us to permit expression for others. But it remains important for us to achieve this acceptance if we are to be of help to the child.

SOURCES OF HOSTILE FEELING

Let us discuss some of the common situations in which resentment is felt by children, how feelings develop in these situations, and how they may be "liquidated."

[*] Op. cit., pp. 70 and 89.

A New Baby at Home Creates a Situation
in Which Hostility Needs to Be Liquidated

One of the commonest occasions outside the nursery school in which the child will feel hostility needing "liquidation" is when a new baby arrives in his home. Parents are often afraid that the older child will be jealous and may reassure themselves that he "doesn't seem the least bit jealous." Yet it is inevitable that an older child will resent in some respects the coming of a new baby however much he may also enjoy other aspects of the changed situation. Even Julia, the well-adjusted child in one nursery school was not eager to receive a baby sister in her home. She was at school when her grandmother came with the news of the arrival of the long-awaited baby. After hearing about her and asking some questions, Julia reassured herself, "She won't come home today, will she?" and when her grandmother affirmed this, she added, "I don't want her to," and returned to her play. Julia could express her feelings.

If parents are afraid of a child's jealousy, he may have to conceal it from them. It can only come out indirectly, in his too rough hugging of the baby and some "accidental" hurting of it, and in an increased cruelty in his play with other children, as in the case of Charles, described earlier. These indirect ways are not as healthy as a direct expression for they are less understandable and actually liquidate the feeling less. There is less need to be afraid of hostile feelings themselves than of what they do to us when we try to hide them and thus lose control over them.

John's Parents Could Accept His
Real Feelings About the Coming of a Baby

Sometimes the feelings about the coming of a baby may be brought out and partly worked through even in the period before the baby arrives, as in the case of John. John's mother told him that they were going to have a new baby about six weeks before the baby was expected. John was nearly three. He had already had to adjust to his father's return after an extended absence in the armed services. He had just begun to accept his father and want to identify with him and do things "just like daddy." Now he was going to have to adjust to losing his place as the baby.

John's mother told him about the baby one afternoon after he had gotten up from his nap and they were having a pleasant little tea party together. John made no comment but a few minutes later he dropped to the floor and lay waving his arms and legs, crying, "I'll be the baby, Mummy." His mother assured him that he could be the baby, too, and nothing more was said. Nearly a week later he asked some questions when they were at the table about, "How big will the baby be?" In the next weeks he brought the subject up several times, but each time ended by declaring, "I'll be your baby," and his parents would agree each time.

His behavior became much more infantile, too. It was evident that he was struggling with a very real conflict between his need to keep his position of "baby" and his satisfaction in growing up and in relating himself to his father. Fortunately his father was gentle and accepting of him and the value of being "like daddy" steadily increased.

By the time the baby arrived John seemed to have managed his feeling about wanting to be a baby satisfactorily even though on one occasion he suddenly asked, "But when will we take it back?" He had been helped by his parents' acceptance of his feelings, and by the satisfaction he felt in identifying with his father. Incidentally, his mother planned her return from the hospital with care. She had a present for him and was not carrying the baby herself when she returned. John was eager and interested in the new arrival and there was little evidence of serious conflict in his feelings in the next weeks and months. He had managed to "liquidate" much of his resistance. He had been able to grow up.

Liquidating Hostile Feelings at the Nursery School

When there is a new baby at home, the child's feelings often spill out in his behavior at nursery school. He will act them out in the doll corner, perhaps, spanking the dolls frequently, smothering them with blankets, or throwing one on the floor and stamping on it. In this way he relieves himself by draining off some of the hostility he may be feeling, making it easier to face the real situation. A good nursery school should have some dolls that can stand this kind of treatment. A direct "draining off" of feeling in this way may be about the only means a child has of expressing the conflict he is feeling. Many parents do not understand and accept expressions of feeling at home as John's parents did.

If our interest is in sound personality development, it is not hard to see how little real value there would be in emphasizing the proper care of dolls at this point. If one did insist that dolls were not to be treated in this way, one would block for the child this avenue of expression, leaving him in an emotionally dangerous situation. There might be a good deal of trouble ahead for him in his relationship with the real baby. It is worth noting that anthropologists report that certain very gentle Indian tribes permit young children to show great cruelty to animals which, they suggest, may serve the purpose of draining off some of the hostility which children feel, and account in part for the Indians' friendly behavior with each other.

BY TOYS. Rubber dolls and other rubber toys serve as a good medium for the release of hostile aggressive feeling. They can be pinched and bitten with a good deal of satisfaction. One three-and-a-half-year old whose relationships at home had been tense and strained had felt his position in the family threatened by the return of a father who was almost a stranger to him, and then even more threatened by the arrival of a new baby. His insecurity and hostility came out in the readiness with which he attacked and bit other children in the nursery school. The teacher had to watch him constantly to prevent his attacking others. She found that she could substitute a rubber doll and that he seemed to find relief in biting it. She carried the doll in her pocket for a time so that it would be instantly available, and she gave it to him when she saw his tension mounting, saying, "I know! You feel just like biting someone. Here's the doll. It's all right to bite the doll." The least interference or the smallest suggestion of a rejection filled his already full cup of negative feeling to overflowing. He had to do something, and biting on the doll served to reduce the feeling to more manageable proportions. The teacher's acceptance and her understanding of the way he felt gave him confidence. The day came when he ran to her himself because he knew that he needed the doll to bite. He could recognize his feeling and handle it in a way that was not damaging to the other children. He began to have more success and find more satisfaction in his play. Steadily he had less hostile feeling to handle.

During this time he had been engaging in a great deal of verbal aggression against the adults in the school. When he was faced with the necessity of limiting his activity during the rest period, for example, he would lie on his bed and attack the teacher verbally, "cut her up, her legs, her head, her arms" and would sometimes "put her in the garbage can" or sometimes "put her in the toilet." His words revealed the extent to which he himself had been hurt and the anger and fear he had felt. Very slowly, with many avenues of expression open to him, he drained off some of his resentful feeling, and the acceptance and success he had in the school helped him to build other kinds of feelings. He discovered other kinds of relationships, and the warm, supporting relationships he had with his teacher left him free to find friends among the children. No child in the group was more responsive in the end to the love offered him.

Another Source of Resentment Is the Necessity for Keeping Good and Clean

Another source of resentment in children in addition to changing positions in the family lies in the demands made on them to "keep clean" and the fear and guilt they often feel when they yield to the impulse to play in dirt.

Fig. 36.   Finger painting offers an outlet for feelings.

Ruth was a child whose mother had emphasized cleanliness and proper behavior, including a strict toilet-training regimen. Ruth showed as much hostility and resentment toward adults as any child in the group at first. She refused requests or suggestions which came from an adult even though they might be ones she really wanted to carry out. Her mother characterized her behavior as "just plain stubbornness." Their life together had been a succession of issues over one habit or the other. The following incident occurred after she had been in school a year and had begun to participate in activities with confidence and was even affectionate with the teachers she knew, saying "I like you" with real feeling. Even then she still grew disturbed and anxious when faced with a little dirt.

Ruth happened to be on the playground with a student teacher. She was swinging. It was muddy and as Ruth's boots swept through the puddle under the swing, they splashed mud on her and on the teacher. Ruth looked disturbed. "What will your Dad say?" she asked the student teacher anxiously. The teacher assured her that he wouldn't say anything and that it was just an accident and couldn't be helped. But Ruth answered darkly, "Oh yes, he'll say something."

She tried swinging again but again they both got splashed. Ruth said, warmly, "I'm sorry," and then she repeated, "What will your Dad say?"

This time the teacher replied by asking Ruth what she thought he would say. Ruth answered, "He'll say you're all dirty and will have to clean up and take a bath," and then she added, "I'm going inside and stay in, if you don't mind." She went in and didn't come outside again during the morning.

Even though she expected no punishment for splashing the mud in this situation, it was a "bad" thing to her. It meant disapproval from the adults on whom this insecure little girl had to depend. Standards for behavior were high and punishment severe. Her anxiety was apparent in her words and her behavior. It was not hard to see why she had shown hostility and unfriendliness.

In this situation a more experienced teacher not only would have recognized the extent of the anxiety the child was showing by her questions, but would have tried to help her put it into words so that it might have become more understandable and manageable—so that she would not have needed to run away from it. She might have verbalized in some way as this, "Does your Dad get mad when you're dirty? Mothers and Dads often do, don't they, when children get dirty?" This might have given Ruth the help she did not find in the student's denial that *her* Dad would be mad. Ruth knew better about hers! It would have made it a common, shared experience, easier to face. The teacher might have continued, "Sometimes it is all right to get dirty because we can get cleaned up afterward just as we can now. Sometimes it's even fun to get dirty. I used to like to myself," and this might have relieved the child. She might have been able to stay outdoors and have fun. She might have been more able to trust herself.

The Clue May Be a Small One

Sometimes it is harder to identify the feeling that lies back of words or acts. The child may be afraid to express his hostility or his aggression openly. We have to find the meaning from a very small clue. Grace, for example, had always been very "good." This meant that she was not able to be very expressive or creative. In the nursery school she gradually began to find it possible to act with greater freedom. It was clear to anyone watching her that she often wanted to act differently but did not dare.

One day the teacher observed Grace carefully laying several chairs on their sides on the floor. The teacher made no comment, not understanding the meaning of this behavior. The next day Grace's mother asked anxiously about how Grace was behaving in school. She was worried because Grace had told her that the day before she had "knocked over all the chairs at nursery school." It was then clear to the teacher that this careful laying of a few chairs on their sides was in reality an aggressive act for Grace. It was as far as she dared to go in expressing her aggressive feelings and she would have liked to have made it a much bigger act than it was.

Grace needed to be helped to see that she could express aggressive feelings, that she could really be accepted as a little girl who had "bad" feelings as well as "good" ones, that there were safe limits at school, too. Her parents needed to have more understanding of the importance of accepting all of Grace's feelings.

Dick, who was very timid, showed much the same kind of need when he declared, "I'm going to make a lot of noise," and then took one block and carefully threw it on the floor. His parents approved

of quiet boys. He had few opportunities to be noisy and he was trying to show that he really dared to be the kind of person he wanted
to be.

Failure to Get Attention and Response

Failure to get attention and response will rouse resentment and
hostility in children, too, especially in insecure children who are
seeking reassurance through getting attention. Their feelings are
involved in a way that makes them sensitive to failure. Situations are
constantly arising in which children want attention from the teacher
or from other children, want to feel important and needed—and fail.
They are resentful and hostile as a result. Whenever the situation
is a competitive one, there is more chance for feeling these failures.
A child may want the attention of the teacher and, not getting it,
may attack the child whom he feels is his rival or the teacher whom
he feels is deserting him. A child like this needs to have his confidence built up so that he will see others as less of a threat to him.
He needs help in accepting and finding better outlets for his feeling.
When it is all right to admit the feeling of wanting the teacher all
to yourself, it becomes easier to work out a better solution than
attacking others.

"Nudging" and Harsh Methods of Control

Children who have been "nudged" from one stage of development
to the next, who have had high standards set for their behavior, who
have been punished frequently, feel a great deal of hostility which
they often cannot express directly. One way that these children, who
have been expected to conform to high standards of behavior and to
"mind," handle the hostility they feel is by giving attention to the
mistakes of others. They often try to identify with the enforcing
authority and impose a strict discipline on others when the teacher
is present. Identifying with the adults helps these children escape
from the feeling of being helpless. Tommy, for example, has received
a great deal of punishment from parents who have never heard of
any methods of discipline except the "good old-fashioned ones."
They punish on small provocation. Tommy was playing with Larry
and the two were building a block tower to dangerous heights. The
teacher warned, "Not so high." Tommy immediately turned to Larry

and said severely, "The teacher said no more blocks and when she says something you mind her." Thus he got rid of some of his resentment, but his "punishing" attitude makes it hard for any but the most comfortable children to play with him. Incidentally, in Tommy's behavior we got some insight into the quality of control which harshly disciplined people impose when they themselves are in power, and the need they often feel to identify with the controlling authority—the more arbitrary the better.

Sam Wanted Desperately to Feel Big

Sam is an outstanding example of a child who had been pushed around in many ways without much loving and giving on the part of the adults in return for their heavy demands. He was expected to behave like a little gentleman on every occasion when there were visitors at home and usually came to school dressed in a suit instead of play clothes like the other children. His speech was more like that of an adult—even his vocabulary of swear words. He was advanced in his development but he was also burdened with a tremendous load of hostility. It came out in the frequency and the cruelty with which he attacked younger children and animals, and in his many verbal attacks against the adults when he discovered that these would not be punished. Instead of trying to identify with authority, he fought it on every occasion.

As the group was coming in from the playground one day, he savagely attacked a friendly little boy who got in his way. The teacher separated them quickly and firmly. Sam exclaimed, "That was fun." The teacher merely said, "It wasn't fun for Jim. It hurt him," and told Sam to stay outside. As soon as the others were inside, she returned and sat down beside him. They knew each other well and she felt sure that he could accept her presence without feeling threatened by it.

"I wonder why it makes you feel good to hurt Jim and the other children," she speculated quietly, not knowing whether he could give her any clue. He immediately launched into a description of how his uncle had brought him a gun and he and his "little friend" (an imaginary friend) could use it.

Again the teacher answered, "I wonder if it makes you feel big to have a gun and it makes you feel big to hurt someone?"

With apparent relief the child answered, "Yes." They discussed how people wanted to feel big and how sometimes it wasn't fun to be little. The teacher mentioned that being friendly sometimes made people feel big. Sam stuttered as he talked and was near tears, something that almost never happened with him. He seldom dared to relax his defenses enough to cry.

At last the teacher told Sam that it was about time for them to go inside. He said, almost crying, "I could stay out here until afternoon." "Yes," she said, "you could." She busied herself picking things up and then asked, "Well, now you can either come in with me or stay outside. I wonder which you are going to do?"

He got up and said rather sadly, "I don't know." At that the teacher knelt down and put her arms around this hurt, bewildered little boy and for the first time he could accept her loving and nestled close against her, no longer "tough." She said, "I know how it is," and then suggested, "You might paint a big picture inside." He nodded and took her hand and they went inside. He went straight to the finger painting table where he knew there was a chance for him to express more of what he felt.

Sam did gain in the nursery school and became better able to play with others. He was imaginative and resourceful and found a place for himself as his hostility decreased. When he was "graduated," he was a less hostile child but still needed careful, understanding handling. There seemed little likelihood that he would continue to receive this handling. Although his mother had gained some insight into the child's problems, his father would accept none of this "sissy stuff" and continued to rely on repression and a generous use of the rod to bully his little son into "good" behavior. Sam in his turn seems destined to become a bully on the school playground someday as he continues his efforts to feel "big."

To the Child, Even Friendly Adults May Seem to Be a Threat

All children are struggling with feelings of being little and helpless to a greater or less extent, depending on the way adults have acted toward them. They show hostility toward adults because of these feelings. Even friendly adults are so much stronger and more powerful than the child that they are potentially a threat. Children handle their feelings in different ways. When they are together in groups, they are quick to blame the adult for things that happen. We may overhear remarks like these. Ricky comes out on the playground and says to Dick, "Who covered up our holes?" "Oh, some teacher probably," replies Dick. Both these boys are friends with teachers, but they recognize in them the source of many interferences and frustrations as well as the source of needed support. They are glad to identify with each other against the teacher.

Larry gives us another amusing example. He happened to throw some sand and it got into Celia's eye. Celia had to go inside and have the sand washed out of her eyes. When she came back on the playground, Larry was very sympathetic and wanted to look into her eye. He said to her comfortingly, "I should have thrown it in the teacher's eye and then it wouldn't have hurt you, Celia."

Two four-year-olds, Sandra and Jennifer, are playing in the doll corner. Jennifer has set the table. Sandra sits down, saying, "I'm the father." They go through the motions of eating soup and as they pretend to eat, they turn to the mirror hanging on the wall by the table and talk to their reflections. Sandra says, "Shut up and eat your soup."

We see thus some of the sources of the child's hostility and resistances, some of the situations out of which these feelings arise. As adults we are concerned with helping children express these feelings in ways that will not be damaging and yet will serve to reduce them or turn them into constructive channels. We must understand what possible avenues of expression there are.

RELEASING HOSTILITY AND AGGRESSION

What Are Possible Avenues for Expression of Feeling?

Motor expressions, of course, offer the simplest, most direct means of draining off feeling for children. That's why hitting, pushing, biting are common among young children. There are other more acceptable forms of expression along these lines that can be utilized instead as a direct expression of feeling. Pounding at the workbench, hitting a soft material like clay, using a punching bag, biting on a rubber toy, throwing against a backstop, even running and digging, serve as an outlet for feelings in ways that do no damage to anyone. Sue, to be described later, gave vent to her resentment at adult interferences by the hard pats she gave each piece of paper as she pasted. The skillful teacher will suggest outlets which can be used instead of hitting and bullying. She will accept the feeling: "I know. You feel like hitting him because he has the tricycle you want." But

*Fig. 37.   Children need space for large muscle activities.
(Robert Overstreet.)*

she will channel the expression in behavior. "When you feel like that, you can hit our punching bag or do some pounding at the table."

Recognition of the feeling which needs to be channeled is probably very important for the child if the feeling is really to be "liquidated at its source" as Kubie suggests. The teacher who stops a child about to hit another because this child has his favorite tricycle will say, "I know, John, you want the tricycle. It makes you cross at Bill because he has it but I can't let you hit him. When you feel cross at someone because he has what you want, you can go over and take a good whack at our punching bag. That may help you." By words like these the teacher is helping the child identify his feelings. The child needs to know what feeling he is taking out on the punching bag. He needs to be clear about the source of his feeling. Contrast the statement, "We don't hit children; we hit punching bags," which offers only a pattern, unusable many times, with no basis for understanding.

Any statement by the teacher such as "You can't hit Bill; you can hit me," is thoroughly confusing, too, because it tempts the child to be less mature than he is, to break down the controls he has just struggled to acquire. Infants hit out at adults in random protest but three- or four-year-olds are more selective. Such a statement only suggests an avenue which may make the child feel anxious and guilty. He is dependent on the adult's friendliness and the adult's ability to keep him safe from his own impulsiveness. Hitting the adult may add more anxiety than it relieves. It does not help him understand the source of his feeling.

Language Is a Valuable Outlet for Feelings

Language is another type of motor outlet. The crying child relieves himself of a lot of feeling. So does the child who hurls angry words at an offender.

They may verbally destroy the teacher in all kinds of ways and tell her "to get dead." Such verbal expression relieves their feelings. They can see that it results in no harm to the teacher. She remains their friend. It is a satisfactory way at the child's level of "liquidating" feelings which might otherwise be a source of trouble. Later, as adults, these same children may fantasy this kind of thing but without the verbal expression and be helped in relieving serious irritations as Chisholm indicates in his *Prescription for Survival.*

Children often resort to verbal defiance of the teacher when they are in groups and have some reason to resist her. She may tell them it is time to come indoors and a "gang" will shout their defiance from the top of the jungle gym. They feel strength in being together and this feeling of being strong is one of the values that group experiences hold for them.

For the teacher the problem is one of setting limits in ways that will not destroy what the child has gained in daring to be aggressive. She will recognize the child who is constantly attacking adults by verbal defiance as a child who has a great deal of hostility to drain off. She will see his behavior as a clear sign that things are not right with his world. She will give him special help.

Children may even tell us clearly what they are feeling in simple understandable language. We need to help them with their feelings

* Chisholm, Brock: Prescription for Survival. New York, Columbia University Press, 1957, p. 78.

—not reject the way they feel. Mary was four when her baby brother arrived and she found it hard to accept the changes his coming had made in her life and the interest and attention her parents gave him. She remarked to her mother one day, "When he's lying down and I feel how soft he is, I just love him; but when you hold him on your lap, I hate him."

Art and Music Are Outlets, Too

Experiences with art and music offer avenues for the expression of feeling. These avenues of expression are important because they may extend into the adult years and serve as a protection against the emotional load which adults must carry. If art experiences are to have value as a means of release for feeling, they must be free experiences in which self-expression is encouraged, in which the child uses the medium in his own way. The child who paints a certain type of picture again and again is saying something about the way

Fig. 38.   Indians make music on the auto harp.

he feels through his pictures. He may do this through his work with clay or in music, too. We need to conserve the values of art experience as an avenue of expression of feeling.

How the Teacher Meets Aggressive Behavior

Children find their own ways to drain off feelings and we need to accept these ways whenever they do no damage. When feelings have many avenues of expression, they do not pile up and become so unmanageable. The teacher encourages expression even though she may face problems in encouraging expression within the group situation. Other children must accept aggressiveness. How can the teacher meet the needs of individuals and of groups?

The Teacher Helps Children by Her Example

For one thing the teacher helps all children when she remains accepting and undisturbed herself in the face of aggressive behavior. Because of her example, the children will find it less disturbing to meet the inevitable aggressions which occur in their world. Johnny was timid and frightened by aggressive children in part because such behavior had always been labeled "very bad" in his home. His parents became very upset about it. The child who is severely disapproved of when he calls names will be the one who is most disturbed over being called a name himself. Adults have attached importance to this kind of behavior in his experience. But it is unfortunate to get upset over such experiences. Children are likely to meet some rejection and some angry responses wherever they happen to be. If their own aggressive behavior has been met casually, they will find it easier to accept unruffled the attacks they receive. They are less afraid and better able to take the world as it is. The teacher who can accept hostile, aggressive behavior will help the children in their acceptance and understanding of aggression and hostility.

The Teacher Helps When She Accepts and Interprets Behavior

The teacher may also help by interpreting to one child reasons why another child is behaving as he is. She may reassure him by saying, "Never mind. He's calling you names because he's mad. It's your turn on the swing and he wants it to be his. It makes him feel

better to call you 'dope.' You don't need to let it bother you." She
may help a child by showing him how to meet the experience of
being rejected by explaining, "They want to play by themselves. It's
all right. I'll help you find another place to play and you can look
for someone who does want to play with you."

She does not help when she blocks the children's expression and
refuses to accept their feelings. She does not help the hostile child
who has shouted at another child, "You go away," when she says,
"But you must let him play." The newcomer will not be likely to have
a successful experience with a person who feels unfriendly toward
him. It is better not to force our way where we are not wanted. The
teacher must work out a solution accepting the feelings that are
there.

There are solutions which protect the group while still respecting
the needs of individuals. If the child who is being exclusive is
monopolizing the doll corner or the sandbox or some other area, the
teacher can say, "It's all right if you want to play by yourself, but all
the children use the doll corner or sandbox. You can make a house
over in this corner and leave the rest for the children who do want
to play together."

The Teacher Gives Special
Help to Hostile and Insecure Children

Children who are hostile and insecure may need to be protected
from facing repeated failures in their group experiences. They may
need to have the difficulties of group living reduced until they can
meet these with more chance of success. The teacher may need to
help them play in small groups. She may need to help them by suggesting desirable ways of approaching others to forestall trouble for
them. Suggestions such as "He'll let you play if you'll wait for a
turn," or "You might get a block and help him build the walk," may
succeed for such a child, and bring acceptance for him where rejection would increase his resentment. The teacher often helps when
she interprets the meaning of an approach by another child as "He
wants you to help him." In this way she prevents the hostile child
from meeting an approach in an unfriendly way and ensures for him
a more favorable place in the group.

By giving hostile children a chance to assert themselves by ex-
cluding others if they need to do this, the teacher helps them feel

more secure, too. She helps them, in the end, move toward social experience. Children need protection when they are unsure and suspicious of others, not denial of the way they feel. The demands of group life are complex. Children who are hostile and lacking in social skills may not be able to play with more than one child at a time. The teacher helps when she accepts their limits and makes it possible for them to be successful at their level.

REDUCING HOSTILITY

Suitable Environment

The teacher also helps the child handle the problem of his hostility and aggressiveness by avoiding increasing these feelings needlessly. She will do this by a thoughtful planning of environment and program in the nursery school. In a physical setup which is designed for him the child will feel less hostility because he will meet fewer frustrations. He can wash his own hands, get his own coat, find the play materials he wants within reach, solve his own problems in many ways and submit to fewer limitations. The program, as well as the physical setup, can be designed to reduce, rather than increase, interferences and frustrations. If it is flexible and imposes only essential limitations, it meets individual needs in a way that minimizes hostility. Under this kind of program, teachers become people who help rather than people who interfere with the child.

Unsuitable Environment

The child who is very destructive, or even just hyperactive, is often the child who has lived in an environment which is not well adapted to meeting his needs. His behavior is only the expression of the hostility and resentment he feels, as in the case of Rex. His mother came for help because at the age of two he was already very destructive. As she described matters, "He gets into everything, pounds on the furniture, breaks his toys and has even broken a window once or twice." She reported that he climbed up on the stove or turned on the radio because he knew these things were forbidden. She had punished him severely but he persisted in spite of the punishment until she was desperate. As in many similar cases, Rex's mother had limited him severely in his early attempts to touch things; she had started toilet training when he was only a few months old; she had never played with him or "spoiled" him by giving him much attention. It was hard for her to understand now why he was wet almost constantly and demanded constant attention if he was to be kept out of mischief and destruction. Nap time, for example, was a struggle and she usually had to spank him several times before he would stay in his bed. But one could see what few satisfactions his environment offered him—how many limitations had been imposed with very little offered him in return. He was responding by expressing his resentment and hostility actively and vigorously through his destructiveness and his resistances. He was making her pay attention to him.

Punishment Adds to the Emotional Burden of the Child

When a child is destructive, we are too likely to want to punish him as this child's mother had been doing. When we do this, we add to the load of hostility the child is already feeling and make his recovery more difficult. It will often be wise to do something about his behavior, such as taking a stick away from a child who is using it for hitting, or removing a disturbed child from the group, but we do not need to do this in a punishing way. Trying to make the child feel ashamed and guilty, trying to make him say that he is "sorry," will only confuse him and add to his negative feelings instead of reducing them. The child who is blocked in expressing his hostility is handicapped in trying to handle his feelings. The child described earlier who bit the other children did this because of the tremendous load of resentment he carried. His teacher knew that she must be responsible, not only for preventing his biting, but for helping him find acceptable ways of relieving himself of the feelings. If she had punished him or rejected him because of his behavior, she could have offered him no help. The already overburdened little boy would have had to find a way out alone—or fail.

Excessive Hostility May Need to Be Reduced in a Direct and Vigorous Way

When a child is seriously burdened with hostile feelings, he may need a vigorous and direct type of release. Tim, a four-year-old, came to school each morning unable to accept or to offer any friendliness. He took every chance to interfere in the other children's play, knocking over a carefully built house of blocks, tearing some-one's picture. Whenever he could, he hurt the children through their possessions or directly by attack. Any piece of equipment became a dangerous instrument in his hands. He had been severely disciplined at home with frequent use of corporal punishment. He had not found warmth or even liking. He had been hurt and bullied with no place to turn for support and comfort. He did not know what good relationships were. It was evident from his behavior that he was filled with a tremendous amount of hostile feeling which he had to unload before he could even recognize friendliness when it was offered. Painting and music did not offer him a sufficiently direct release. He seemed to get the most satisfaction out of being vigorously destructive with materials. His teacher got a supply of orange crates and the first thing in the morning she would arrange for Tim to attack an orange crate. With hammer in hand he would demolish the box. After he had done this he seemed better able to manage his feelings with the children.

The Needs of Some Children Cannot Be Met in a Group Situation

This child's behavior indicates the strength of the hostility which can be built up by the age of four under unfavorable conditions. It also raises the question about whether such children can be handled in the group in fairness to themselves and to others. Some exceedingly hostile children may need the help of individual therapy before they are admitted to a group, and they may then only fit into a limited kind of group experience where they can have individual attention. It takes time to overcome the damage which poor handling causes, and the needs of an individual in these first steps toward recovery cannot always be reconciled to the needs of a group. This does not mean, of course, that many problems resulting from hostile feelings cannot be handled in a group situation. Most of them can be. The timid, inhibited child is greatly helped in expressing his feelings by the safety he finds within a group.

Every group will contain children who possess a great deal of hostility and some who express that hostility in aggressive ways. Most of them can be helped within the framework of the group to handle their hostile feelings in acceptable ways. Through understanding and with skill the teacher can help these children find release within the limits of the group experience even though her teaching ability will often be challenged by the problems the children present. Occasionally there will be a child whose problems are too severe to be met in the ordinary nursery school group.

Group Experience Has Special Value for the Timid Child

The value that group experience possesses for many timid children is worth attention. It provides them with an environment in which it is easier for them to accept their hostile emotions. These children will benefit greatly from the "freeing" of expression that comes in a good nursery school experience. With people of their own age who are also feeling and expressing hostility, they are no longer afraid of their feelings and behavior. They are less likely to be troubled later by repressed hostility and aggressive feelings. Not as "good" in the conventional sense, they become healthier from the mental hygiene standpoint and capable of achieving a higher degree of emotional maturity in the end.

Ben was an example of a child who grew able to express his real feelings in the nursery school. He was a quiet, timid child who remained dependent on the teacher for a long time after he entered the school. He usually found a place beside her when she sat down, and often held onto her skirt when she moved around the school. When he played, he would select the small toys and take them into a corner. He was not active and vigorous and was never aggressive toward others. Very slowly he began to join the other children in play and to identify himself with the group. He seemed pleased when they shouted names or chanted silly or "naughty" words. Finally he dared to express himself in this way, too. One day he was even a member of a group who defied the teacher from the safe height of the jungle gym.

It was about this time that some movies taken at the school happened to be shown one morning. A picture of Ben's teacher appeared on the screen. Laughing, Ben went up to the screen and slapped her image. It was probably no accident that he chose the teacher's image. That act may have symbolized the strength and the freedom to be aggressive which he was feeling. With that slap he proved that he had left his dependence behind. His relationship with the teacher was a friendly one, but he was no longer tied to her skirt as he had been in the beginning. Ben had known plenty of love at home but not much chance to express the resentments that he inevitably felt. As soon as he dared to be aggressive, to express what he felt, he became more active and social. He had no great amount of hostility to release. He was soon able to maintain and accept the limits which the teachers set for the group. Limitation was not a threat to him as a person. He developed rapidly. Tim, however, the very hostile four-year-old described above, was never able to see limitation as anything but a threat. Not having known consideration or the support of warm, loving relationships in his home, he could not find sufficient reassurance in what the teacher was able to offer him in the group to enable him to accept its limits. He continued to fight, seeing all relationships only as a threat to him.

SUMMARY

We may summarize what we have been saying about hostility and aggression by pointing out that (1) we must accept the existence of these feelings, (2) we must see that they are expressed in some acceptable way, but as directly as possible, so that the individual will be freed from the emotional load they will otherwise represent, and (3) we must learn how to handle children without creating in them unnecessary feelings of hostility and resentment which make good social adjustment difficult.

Reducing the amount of frustration a young child has to meet, building up his feelings of security and adequacy, accepting him as he is rather than "nudging" him on into being something different, will all help in the solution of the problems which these feelings present to any individual or any form of group life.

REFERENCES

1. Aggressiveness in Children. Child Study. Fall Issue 1957.
2. Body, Margaret: Patterns of Aggression in the Nursery School. Child Development, March 1955, Vol. XXVI, pp. 3-11.
3. Escalona, Sibylle: Understanding Hostility in Children. Chicago, Science Research Associates, 1954.
4. Freud, Anna: Protecting the Emotional Health of Our Children. Child Welfare League of America, 1955.
5. Greenberg, Herbert: Developing Warmth and Acceptance through Understanding Negative Feelings. Bulletin—National Association for Nursery Education, Spring 1955.
6. Isaacs, Susan: Childhood and After. New York, International Universities Press, 1949, Ch. 3.
7. Redl, Fritz, and David Wiseman: The Aggressive Child. Chicago, The Free Press, 1957.

9

Defining and
Maintaining Limits for Behavior

ᶜor Many People the Problem of Authority Is a Confusing One

"You're the boss of the whole school," remarked Susan to the teacher as they sat eating lunch together one day, and she added with deliberation, "Last year the school was all the bosses itself."

Susan had evidently been trying for some time to figure out who was "boss" at the school. She had been raised on "issues" at home and her parents were still trying to show her who was "boss" in their house. She must have been puzzled about the school situation at first until she picked the teacher as the source of authority.

For many people as for Susan the problem of authority is a confusing one and remains so all through their lives. As children these people have been made to feel that the role of boss is the most important role. When they are grown, they struggle to do some

213

bossing themselves or to resist being bossed by others. This struggle interferes with their solution of other problems. They hurt themselves and often the people they love in their efforts to boss or to resist bossing.

Discipline that leads to a struggle over who is going to be "boss" is damaging to anyone. It does not help people respect themselves or others. It is better adapted to preparing them for life in an authoritarian world rather than a democratic one. Like Susan, people who have met this kind of discipline have little concept of what it means to be a responsible member of a group. They are not ready for the self-discipline that democratic living demands.

Betsy, like Susan, had struggled against domination. The "boss" in her case was a sister two years older who interfered with almost every move the child made at home. The older sister was jealous of the attractive younger one whom the parents obviously preferred. Her defense was to try to play the dictator role with the younger sister. In the freedom of the nursery school Betsy relaxed but she was alert to resist anything which resembled domination. One day, irritated by something that had happened, she angrily threw a book on the floor. The teacher quietly said to her, "I want you to put the book back on the table." Betsy replied with feeling, "You can't always have what you want." And the teacher, recognizing the lesson which this child was trying to learn, not only that one can't always get what one wants but that one doesn't always have to be bossed, answered, "That's true. I can't always have what I want. I'll pick the book up myself and we can go outside to play."

The matter of accepting authority as well as accepting responsibility for it is more important in a democratic society than in any other. In a democracy, limits must be set and maintained by the consent of all. How can we prepare to solve the problems of authority in a democratic way?

POSITIVE VALUE OF LIMITS

We will start by reminding ourselves that the problem of authority or the setting of limits can be worked out in a way that has positive value for the individual. We sometimes think of the setting of limits as a form of interference because limitation has so frequently been experienced by us as "don'ts" and connected with punishment. In earlier chapters we have been concerned with the acceptance of behavior and permissiveness. We have tried to see the individual and his needs. We have tried to understand how to help him release and channel the creative forces within him, how to avoid blocking these forces. But to feel free one must feel safe. Limits are essential if the young child, or if any of us, is to be safe.

Because we feel confidence that cars on the cross streets will stop when the light is green for us, we are free to drive through an intersection. The child who feels confidence that his parent will stop him is likely to act with less hesitation, to explore more freely. He feels safe if he can feel sure that he will be stopped should his impulsiveness lead him in dangerous directions. If the stopping or the limiting is done with love and without humiliation, he is helped to trust himself, to develop as a spontaneous, creative person. He is left free to act because he knows he will be stopped before he harms himself or acts in a way which would make him feel guilty or remorseful. He is free because he has parents who take responsibility.

Need for a Responsible Pattern of Authority

In discussing permissiveness earlier in connection with building feelings of confidence and adequacy (page 163) we pointed out that it must be accompanied by some limits set by an adult who will take responsibility for maintaining them. The adult who cannot limit or stop the child when it becomes necessary is not offering him freedom but license which is a dangerous thing.

The young child must depend on the adult to maintain safe limits because he is often too inexperienced to judge the consequences of his actions. The toddler may be fascinated by a long flight of steps but he needs to be limited by a gate or a helping hand. Lack of limits may mean a bad fall which frightens him and makes him less ready to explore freely. The two-year-old is likely to approach another child and try to get his attention by a direct physical contact. If he's a husky child, the blow may be quite vigorous, and it will be resented and returned if the other child is somewhat older and equally sure of himself. Lack of limitation may mean in time a blocking of friendliness and outgoingness. He needs to be helped to get attention by more effective means.

The *way* he is stopped will be important. If the limiting is done in a "punishing" way, the child may feel angry and resentful or he may feel fearful and anxious. These feelings make it harder for him to exert his own controls later. He may become defiant or dependent. His confusion makes him less able to be himself.

It is worth noting that absence of limits for a child produces somewhat the same results as strict "discipline" in the sense of punishment. Both are likely to make a child defiant or dependent, unable to be himself, afraid of action. The child who is left to burn his fingers, for example, may be afraid to explore again, just as is the child who has been punished severely for touching a thing.

The setting of limits, then, is an essential part of helping a child act freely. Many of the things which have to do with safety, with health, with the rights of other people, are beyond the child's capacity to judge with wisdom. When the adult takes the responsibility for these limits, he leaves the child freer to explore and have experience. The child acts with confidence because he is protected against mistakes.

The child needs protection against the violence of his feelings, too, his anger and its expression in destructive ways. He needs to feel sure that the adult will be ready to set limits to the way he expresses feeling, or he may be frightened and feel guilty about what he does. His feelings are strong, and he reacts strongly with temper tantrums or in destructive ways. Only when he knows that the adult will help him handle his strong feelings can he throw himself wholeheartedly into experiences and be spontaneous and creative. He needs to feel sure of limits if he is to develop confidence in himself as a person.

One of the most troubled children in one group of nursery school children was a child whose mother had tried to avoid any limitation on the child's freedom. The child had found little security in her world, in part because there were no limits on which she could depend. She even put her feeling into words one day when she said to her mother, "I wish you would build a fence around my yard." Any child is more secure, freer to explore and experience when he is sure of consistent, confident handling which will set limits for his exploring and for his action.

Need for the Security of Known Limits

Children who have met inconsistent authority which sometimes sets limits at one point and sometimes at another grow almost desperate in their efforts to find some sure limitation. Behavior which is interpreted as "contrariness" may only be a seeking for the security of knowing where the limits for behavior really are. When children know what the limits are, they are reassured. They feel safer. They can accept known limits more easily—whatever these limits may be. The disturbed child will steady himself when a calm, confident adult defines the limits for his behavior clearly and enforces these limits.

Much of the defiant, "unreasonable" behavior of some children may be a result of their seeking for someone who has enough confidence to limit them and will take responsibility for limitation. These children are likely to be children who are afraid of misbehavior, their own as well as other people's misbehavior. They are children for whom a great deal of behavior has been labeled "bad." It is interesting to note, in this regard that the child who frequently goes "out of bounds" himself is often the one who is most concerned when another child misbehaves. The child who does a lot of hitting is likely to be the child most disturbed by being hit. This reaction gives us a clue as to how he looks at his own hitting and the anxiety he may feel because of it. He needs someone to keep him from doing what he regards as a serious offense.

Pam, for example, at the age of four was an extremely anxious and insecure child. Without a confident teacher to steady her she went to pieces on slight provocation. One day she was at the clay table getting acquainted with a new teacher. This teacher was rolling and patting the clay on the table top. Pam looked at her seriously; "Clay is used on boards at this school," she said. The teacher said, "But I like to use the clay on the table. It's all right on this table top." In a minute Pam said in a pleading tone, "Use it on the board." The teacher complied for she realized that Pam's self-control was so tenuous that the child felt the need for quite rigid limits. She did not feel safe with a teacher who was not maintaining limits strictly.

Children who have met inconsistent authority are especially likely to seek, not only to find the limit, but to find someone who will surely maintain this limit.

Even when people are older, they sometimes long, if unconsciously, to be free of the responsibility for limiting their own behavior. They try to return to the simpler situation where limits were set and maintained for them by others. Eric Fromm in his book *Escape from Freedom* discusses what may happen when people cannot accept the responsibility for being free. In many ways we all act out this escape in our daily living. We might mention the student who tries to put the responsibility for learning on the teacher, or the parent who tries to depend on the authority of a book. It is a real struggle for all of us to accept the responsibility for directing and limiting our behavior with wisdom and independence. It is not fair to the child to expect him to shoulder too much of this burden too soon.

DIFFICULTY IN SETTING LIMITS

Because of Our Own Experience with a "Boss" Type of Discipline

Because we know that authority can be damaging, breeding resentment, resistances and hostilities, we may have a tendency to avoid exercising it even when we realize that it is necessary. When we react in this way, however, we are ignoring the positive value that limits have for individuals and for society. Rather than avoiding limitation we should try to understand what limits are suitable and how these limits may be imposed in constructive ways.

We may find it difficult to set limits with the confidence we should have because of our own experiences in growing up. We live in a culture that is not a permissive one as far as children go. The emphasis in bringing up children is on restriction, on not-touching, on staying dry and clean, on being quiet, on the kind of things that may be damaging to individual growth. Relationships are often considered unimportant in comparison with objects. The needs of the child to assert himself and to find avenues of self-expression are not accepted. From experience we know that a handicapping loss of self-confidence may result from these patterns. As we study human behavior we become more aware of the resentment and hostility accompanying the heavy demands for conforming to standards that are customarily made on children. We become more aware of the importance of permissiveness if sound personality growth is to take place. We ourselves want to avoid the old "boss" type of discipline. But in shifting to a more permissive type of handling we must not grow uncertain about limitation. We should not feel a sense of guilt when we sometimes have to act in a way that is *not* permissive. In shifting to a more permissive type of handling it becomes all the more important to remember that limits have a positive value if they are the right limits and wisely maintained. They can give support to children. We must be ready to use them with confidence as we try in general to be more permissive in our work with children.

Because We Are Confused about Our Own Aggressive Feelings

For many of us there is another feeling which interferes with our ability to exercise authority with confidence. We face a problem because there is an element of aggressiveness in exerting authority. We ourselves may be afraid of aggressive acts. We may have tried to deny our own aggressive feelings. We may be unable to limit children wisely because we do not want to face the feelings which may come out in the act of limiting a child. In attempting to escape from being aggressive we avoid accepting ourselves as people who limit others.

Sometimes in moving toward more permissive handling we are afraid to use authority because of the hostility which the authoritarian or "boss" type has built up in us. Let us look at some of the feelings which may make it difficult for us to exercise authority.

Miss X was a teacher who was extremely "permissive." A group of children with her tended to be "wild," engaging in a great deal of destructive behavior. She was a sympathetic person with real insight and she was skillful in turning the group's energies into constructive activities in time. After overturning the furniture, for example, the children usually did some fine building. They engaged in a lot of creative, original work and a lot of group play, but some of the timid children suffered, frightened by the group behavior or by their own anxieties after they had participated in an episode of uncontrolled activity. Miss X was a person who had never been able to accept discipline herself. She had grown up as an only child in a strict household. She conformed outwardly but expressed her resistance in indirect ways. She was never on time; she never quite finished a task; she was absent-minded. As soon as she was grown, she left home. In her work with children she was determined that they should not suffer from the "boss" type of authority as she had. Because she had not experienced authority as a help, she found it hard to use it in this way with her group. She herself had had to grow in spite of limits. She carried her patterns of resistance to limitations with her. A sensitive, creative person herself, she gave her group an opportunity to be themselves but she could not meet their needs for the support of discipline.

Miss S, too, had resented bitterly the way in which she had been raised. She had experienced too often as a child a form of discipline which served only as an outlet for hostility and aggressive feeling. Her feelings against authority were very strong. She could not limit the children in her group because she would have disliked herself so much in doing it and perhaps disliked the children for making her act this way. She was unable to use discipline.

It is true that aggressive feelings often come out in the use of authority. People may punish because they wish to hurt, or in punishing they may pour out their aggressive, hostile feelings. A sensitive person feels guilt when this happens. But this is less likely to happen if we accept our own feelings. If we have faced the hostile, aggressive feelings we inevitably have, we can handle them and find safe or even constructive avenues for their expression. We can keep them where they belong. It is easier, then, for us to be clear about why we are imposing limits on the child. We can act with confidence when we impose limits if these limits are meeting the child's needs rather than serving as an outlet for our feelings.

ACCEPTABLE LIMITS

Setting Limits That Support the Child in Growth

Our problem is, therefore, to be clear about the value of limits as well as the value of permissiveness in handling children. As we untangle our own feelings in a situation, we are better able to exercise authority without feeling guilt in doing it. We can decide on the limits which will promote the most growth for each individual child at his particular stage of development. We can help the child find these limits acceptable.

Discipline, for the child, is largely a problem of accepting limits. The child discovers that there are limits to the freedom with which he can follow his impulses; there are limits to the ways in which he can express his feelings. He must accept these limits if he is to be a member of a group, and there is value to him in belonging to a group.

The child finds it easier to accept limits if they are adapted to his stage of development. The two-year-old, for example, cannot accept comfortably many limitations on his urge to touch things, while the five-year-old can comfortably accept many more. The child will also find it easier to accept necessary limits if he has confidence in the

person limiting him and if he finds satisfactions in relating himself
to the group.

How do we set limits in ways that support the child in his growth?

We Must Set Only Necessary Limits

In the first place, we will set only those limits which are essential
to protect and support the child and the group. We will avoid unnecessary limits. It is the many constantly recurring interferences
which breed resentment in the child and make it hard for him to
accept authority. Unfortunately many interferences are common in
a child's environment today. Our homes are built and furnished in
such a way that the child's activities have to be restricted constantly.
City streets are hazards and make further restriction necessary. The
child often lives under circumstances which thwart his spontaneous,
creative activity until he feels resentful. He resists or withdraws.
Wise handling will include a change of standards or of furniture
whenever possible to make these fit the child's need until he is
older and better able to meet frustrations. When we observe children who have been restricted in many ways, we observe that they
are often more intent on defying authority than in taking responsibility for limiting their own behavior—whenever outside pressure
is withdrawn. Too many limits, imposed too early, breed resistance
and lack of self-control rather than acceptance.

We Must Be Sure That the Child Understands the Limits

In the second place, the limits which are necessary should be
maintained in such a way that they are clear to the child. This
means that they must be put in simple, concrete language rather
than in general terms. Too often we assume that a child grasps a
point when he really lacks the experience and the vocabulary necessary for real understanding. We must be ready to repeat and to
define things in specific terms. We must help the child understand
what each limit means in terms of what he is expected to do.

We Must Be Consistent Without Being Inflexible or Afraid

Obviously it is easier for the child to understand a limit which is
maintained consistently. We should help the child by being consistent, but we must not confuse consistency and inflexibility. The

person who says, "I wish I hadn't said that but I can't give in to him now," is probably being inflexible rather than consistent. When we make a mistake, we should be able to shift to a position more consistent with our goals. A parent may feel that her child is ready to stay at nursery school without her, for example, but when she leaves him there, she finds that he is not ready to stay by himself. She will help him most by continuing to stay with him. If she feels that staying with him is "giving in," she is taking a stand that is inconsistent with mental hygiene principles. She is being inflexible. Phil's mother, mentioned earlier, helped him grow more independent when she really accepted his need and stayed with him at nursery school.

Resistance may be the beginning of a better attitude on the part of the child toward authority. The child may gain in some cases because a usual limit is not maintained but is disregarded. For example, Peter was a quiet, passive child who spent most of his time watching. He listened to records and joined the story group but engaged in few activities. He was concerned about "bad" behavior, calling the teacher's attention to things other children did which he thought they shouldn't be doing. For many weeks he remained outside the group, engaging in only a few safe activities like playing records or wheeling a doll buggy and watching others. One day he took a ball and carefully, deliberately threw it over the fence. The teacher observed this and felt that it might represent a step in overcoming his fear of misbehaving. She smiled and said, "You threw it over the fence. Do you suppose I can get it?" She went outside and threw the ball back to him. After she returned, he threw it out again. She went out and returned it, throwing it very high to his delight. This was repeated several times and another child joined and they began playing with the ball together and the teacher left. Peter seemed far less afraid of risking himself in play after this incident.

Just as obviously we do not help a child when we shift to a different position because we may be afraid or unwilling to handle the consequences of our stand. John, for example, may scream and kick when he is thwarted, but if the adult sees him about to take a tricycle from a child who cannot defend himself, she is responsible for stopping John even if he does scream and kick. She may stop him in different ways, some of them more skillful than others. She may step between the children before John has the chance to take the tricycle and direct him to another one, or she may have to restrain him; but she will be ready to accept his emotional outburst even though she is always careful not to add to it by blaming him or reproving him. When she restrains him, she is accepting her responsibility and need feel no hesitation. She is helping him face a necessary limit which is consistent with his goals for growth as a person. For the same reason the child who runs out into the street or out into the rain without a coat must be brought back. Only when the adult is unafraid to take this responsibility will the child be safe and secure. The child is helped when these limits are clearly defined and consistently maintained.

Giving a clear definition of what is expected should never be confused with making a threat. The child who is being noisy at the table may be told that noisy behavior at the table makes it hard for others to attend to eating. If he wants to be noisy, he can move into another room where it will be all right to make all the noise he wants. This child would not be helped to control his own behavior if the choice were presented to him as a threat. "If you can't be quiet, you'll have to eat in another room." This kind of statement is a threat used to control behavior rather than a definition of limits to help the child manage himself.

We Must Feel Comfortable about a Child's "Testing Out" Limits

We must feel comfortable about a child's need to "test out" the limits we set. The tremendous urge to be independent and to show initiative which Erikson considers the important developmental task of the nursery school years means that the healthy child will not conform passively to our demands. If he is to acquire the ego strength he needs, he must assert his difference from others. He must disagree. "I don't like that." He must reject. "Get out of here." He must defy. "I'm not going to." The fact of his resistance is healthy. We can accept his right to resist but we will not feel threatened by it. We will not be afraid to maintain our position.

In many situations we cannot allow the child to act out his resistance. When it's time to go home from school, for example, he has to leave. But we can maintain this necessary limit with full respect for his right not to *want* to leave. We can value his strength in asserting himself as a person even though we must help him leave. In maintaining the limit, in this case the necessity for leaving, we

Fig. 39. It may be hard to leave play.

can act in such a way that he does not feel blamed for his defiance or any less loved because of it. When we respect his urge to assert himself, we make it easier for him to accept himself along with the necessary patterns of authority. We make it easier for him to see authority as a constructive force, easier for him to be responsible for exercising it in his own behalf and for the sake of others some day. Resistance is healthy in a child but accepting his need to resist does not make us any less responsible for sound discipline.

It is, of course, only avoidance of responsibility on our part if we accept the three-year-old's refusal to put on boots and let him go out and get wet feet. This kind of "permissiveness" is misleading and unfortunate.

We Must Adapt Our Limits to the Needs of the Individual

The limits we set must be adapted to the need of the individual as he is at the moment if they are to contribute to his growth. We have mentioned the difference that a variation in age levels makes in what can be expected of children. But even the same child can be expected to accept demands differently at different times. If he is tired or ill, he will be less ready to face limits than at other times. His readiness to accept limits will depend on the circumstances he finds himself in as well as his physical condition. In a situation where he is unsure of himself, he may be unable to accept a limit which he could face easily under familiar circumstances. The child who feels confident and adequate can accept many more limits without suffering damage to his growth than the child who is insecure.

We will keep adjusting the limits we set to make them fit the needs of the child. A child who is just beginning to feel strong enough to assert himself may need to be quite free of restrictions for a time. Richard was given a great deal of freedom in asserting himself at the table until he was reassured about being accepted by the teacher. For Jean, who was already secure, such permissiveness would have been unnecessary and undesirable.

We Must Give the Child Time

When we set limits, we must give the child time to accept them. We should avoid forcing them or imposing them on him. If we say to a child, "You need to put your boots on before you go outdoors," we do *not* need to see that he marches right over to get his boots on. He may have to protest a bit until he convinces himself that there is a limit which will be maintained. We can stop him if he starts to go out without his boots but we can also give him time to decide to accept the limit. We help him in making the decision if our attitude is friendly and accepting. We may add, "I'll be glad to help you with your boots." We must respect his feelings as he struggles with the conflict between the urge to assert himself and the necessity of conforming to an adult demand. He doesn't realize that little boys sometimes catch cold with wet feet. The occasional child whose need to assert himself is very great may decide that he won't go outdoors if he has to wear boots. He should be helped to feel comfortable staying inside, so that he may feel really satisfied about asserting himself and gain strength from the experience. The key to helping a child is often just to give him *time* to accept what has to be accepted. Our own uncertainty or our own need to control only too often makes us want to push the child into an unwilling acceptance.

We Must Respect the Child's Feelings

We must impose limits in a way which will respect the child's feelings. Shaming him, blaming him, frightening him, all show him that we do not respect the way he feels. When we use these methods, we make it harder for him to accept the limitations. Let us take a simple situation in which there is a necessary limit, such as the necessity of leaving school at the end of the morning, and observe the different ways in which this limit can be imposed. Here are some examples which are typical of those constantly occurring in any school.

Lee is a roly-poly somewhat immature little boy. His father comes in and says to him, "Are you ready to go?" "No," says Lee sturdily. His father answers, "Well, even if you're not, you're going anyway. Put your things away and come along." His smile relieves his words but the words suggest a reason why Lee remains immature. He is treated as such a little boy. One senses that he feels helpless.

Dick says to his mother when he sees her, "I don't want to go home." His mother answers with a smile, "I know. I'm glad you like it here and want to stay, but we have to go now. We'll be back in the morning." Her words show that she accepts his feeling and it isn't hard for Dick to leave.

In any situation limiting can be done in a way that shows respect and consideration for the child or it can be imposed without consideration for the child's feelings. Even the baby who cries because he cannot touch something and wants to do so can be given something else to handle. It is the satisfied child, rather than the resentful, frustrated one, who learns to accept authority.

Acceptance of Limitations Depends on Interpersonal Relationships

Last, and among the more important considerations in setting limits, is the relationship which exists between the child and the person doing the limiting. If the child has confidence in the adult, if he feels accepted by him, he in turn can accept limitation by this adult.

It is well worth taking time to build a relationship in which there is confidence before we act in a limiting way toward a child. If it is possible to wait until a child has had time to develop confidence in us before we limit him, we avoid creating unnecessary fear and resentment in the child. Our goal is to help the child accept and assume responsibility for limits. We make this difficult to achieve if we assert authority before there is a foundation of understanding. In the situation described earlier the teacher would not have handled Sam in the way she did if she had not felt sure that he understood that she accepted him. She could not have helped this angry, hostile four-year-old with his feelings as she did, except on the basis of the relationship they already had established.

We set different limits at different times, and do this in different ways because the ability of children to accept limitation from us varies with the relationships we have with them. The familiar teacher in whom the child has confidence can step into a situation and help an emotionally disturbed child limit his behavior in a way that a person unfamiliar to him cannot expect to do. An unfamiliar person may use the same methods with the child, but she may only increase his resistance and his difficulties. Because relationships are so important, we will want to consider the effect of what we do as we work with children on the friendliness and confidence it builds between us and them. Good relationships make the acceptance of authority easy—and lack of good relationships makes it difficult.

Good relationships are never built on methods of control which depend on fear, especially fear of loss of love. "Mother won't love you if you act like that," or "I'll have to go off and leave you if you don't hurry," may be effective in getting immediate results but such words are disastrous in their effect on the child as a person and on his relationships with adults. They deprive him of confidence in them. He is dependent and helpless and he resents being controlled through this feeling.

Exploiting a feeling does not build a sound relationship, either. A parent once commented on how much her child liked milk, saying, "In fact she likes it so much that we can make her eat other things by threatening to take her milk away from her." Psychologically as well as nutritionally such a course has nothing to commend it. About the only defense a child has in such a case is to keep himself from liking anything very much so that he will have no vulnerable points. But he will resent this kind of control.

Unintentional Limiting and Interference

We have enumerated some considerations which make limiting a constructive rather than a damaging experience for the child. It is also important for us to be aware of how many interferences a child may be meeting in the course of a day. Many times our limiting is unintentional. We do not realize what is happening. We need to be able to identify what we do—to recognize the number of limits which are actually occurring in the child's experience. Let us take a series of situations which occurred in one laboratory nursery school in less than an hour and consider what two children met in the way of interference from adults. The following situation is typical of those that occur wherever children are exposed to adults.

The Experiences of Sue and Sally Illustrate This Difficulty

Sue and Sally are painting, one on one side of the easel and one on the other. The two girls are friends, with that close relationship which often develops between two children who need support and find it in each other's company. The differences between the two girls are apparent as they paint. Sue uses lots of paint in a rather sloppy way, putting it all over the paper. Sally makes a few careful strokes with her brush. She leaves much of her paper blank.

When they finish their paintings, the student teacher steps in and helps Sue as she starts to take her paper off the easel. Sue accepts her help but she turns to Sally who has just started to lift her painting off. "Let me help you," she says eagerly to her. Sally smiles and Sue puts Sally's picture up to dry while the teacher is putting Sue's up (Interference number one with Sue's move to take care of her picture independently. In return Sue waits on Sally.)

"Let's paint some more," says Sally and Sue replies, "Let's get back to our paint."

They scamper back to the easel and laugh as they paint, calling each other's attention to the way they are using different colors. Then they settle down, growing more absorbed in the painting, although the situation remains a social one for them. They continue their talking. When they have finished these pictures, Sue says, "Let's paint some more." Sally replies, "No." (She usually has the longer attention span.) Sue persists, "Oh yes, let's paint once more."

Sally acquiesces and asks the teacher for more paper. The teacher replies, "Oh, you've painted two pictures already. Don't you want to work with clay now?" The two girls look at each other. The teacher makes no move to get paper for them so they start toward the table where the clay is. (Interference number two with the children's purposes by the adult. She directs them into an activity in which they have shown no indication of a spontaneous interest. They are helpless to continue their painting in the face of her blocking.)

As they move away, the teacher says, "Take off your aprons first." (Adult direction again.) Sally points out that they will need aprons at the clay table, but the teacher does not accept the child's reasoning and answers, "You can put on clean aprons over there." (Another interference which is apparently an attempt by the teacher to justify her first and probably thoughtlessly made request about removing aprons. The same kind of aprons are used at the easel and the clay table.)

The student teacher helps them off with their aprons, Sally looking a little disturbed. Just as they sit down at the clay table another adult approaches and reminds them that they will need aprons on there. She offers them aprons with a pleasant smile. (Adult direction again.) Sally refuses to put an apron on. Is it any wonder? The adult insists firmly, "You'll need an apron. You'll get your hands dirty." To her, Sally is acting "unreasonably."

Still being logical Sally holds up her hands, "My hands *are* dirty," she says. Sue says nothing, leaving the battle to Sally but waiting patiently for the outcome. There is a deadlock.

A third adult approaches, apparently trying to avoid an unpleasant issue, and suggests helpfully, "Maybe you girls would like to paste. You could wash your hands first." (Adult direction to still another activity.)

Sally seems to seize on this suggestion as a way of escape. She will not put on an apron. Sue joins her and they go into the washroom where they giggle and laugh as they wash their hands. They are supported in meeting these interferences by their sense of being friends. It doesn't matter too much to them whether they paint or use clay or even paste, as long as they are together.

They are very gay as they return and sit down at the table with the paper and paste. In a few seconds they start throwing papers around. It isn't hard to suspect a connection between the way they have been pushed around, gently, but nevertheless pushed, and their present behavior which may afford some release for their feelings. As they relieve themselves by tossing the papers, their dominant feeling just the same seems to be merry and friendly in spite of the "bad" behavior. Pasting wasn't their idea, anyway.

A teacher quickly arrives on the scene and says pleasantly, "You'll have to pick these up. I'll help you." (Adult interference again.) She starts picking up the papers. Silently they join her. After the papers are all in the box again, the children start pasting, humming together and making unverbalized noises which they seem to enjoy for they stop and laugh occasionally. They turn the box of papers upside down on the table and select pieces from the pile.

At this point the teacher sits down at the table beside them. "How come you want to sit with us?" inquires Sue. Is she right that there is another interference in the offing?

The teacher makes no direct reply but she says, "You have so many pieces of paper out. I'll put them back." She puts all the pieces of paper back in the box and when she finishes, she says, "Now you can take just one piece out of the box at a time." (Adult interference again.)

The girls say nothing to this but Sally gives her paper some hard pats as she pastes. Then she says, "Susie, let's paint some more." About seven minutes have elapsed since they left the easel. Sue makes no reply and they go on pasting. Sally begins to giggle in a "silly" way. Just then they appear to notice a group playing with the turtle. They leave to join this group. Their interest in pasting is not sustained.

A few minutes later finger paints are made ready. A student teacher who evidently hopes to interest some of the children in painting approaches Sue. "Would you like to paint?" she asks her. (Another adult interference.)

"Yes," says Sue who never refuses anyone anything. She puts on an apron and starts painting. Sally notices this and runs over to join her. She seems excited. Sue is more relaxed; she makes big, sweeping movements covering the whole page. She finishes five pictures quickly. As she did at the easel, Sally covers only a small part of the paper. She seems to be making an effort to finish quickly as though to keep up with Sue. Just at this point the teacher glances at Sue and calls her attention to some paint spilled on her leg. Sue looks down and discovers, to her distress, that the paint is also on her dress. "Oh, oh," she whimpers. (The adult is responsible for this distraction.)

Sally gets up, looks at Sue's dress and is sympathetic. She says to her, "See, I have some, too," holding up her dress. Her remark gives us some insight into the supporting quality of the relationship between the two.

Sue is relieved immediately and when Sally says, "Let's wash it off," they run to the washroom again. They laugh as they scrub the hems of their dresses. Again, we see the comfort and reassurance children give each other against disturbing adult standards and the crime of paint-on-dresses.

As we look over a record of events like these we are aware of the many direct as well as indirect interferences that children meet in a short period of time. It is likely that no one of the adults in the situations just described thought of her contact with the children as an interference. All of the adults acted pleasantly, but their actions were typical of inexperienced people. They did not intend to handicap the children. They interfered because they thought the standards they were maintaining were important standards, such as the proper use of aprons and a neat pasting table. They seemed to feel that variety in activity was desirable, that one could paint "enough." They were largely unaware of the real values in the situation for the children, of their real needs, and, in some of the cases, unaware of their adult need to be dominant, controlling people. The children gained from the situations because they were together as friends. They gained largely in spite of and not because of the adults.

Children receive more of this kind of limitation than we may be aware of. They are subjected to frequent, petty interferences which are often unintentional or are for some "reasonable" purpose, but the sum total of these restrictions is large. In children who were less friendly than Sally and Sue, the interferences in the situations described might have culminated in "unreasonable" resistance on their part. Sally resisted putting on an apron; she gave her paper hard pats; she became rather silly and aimless at the paste table. These were her ways of reacting to the piling up of adult interference. Sue was more undiscriminating and cheerful. Perhaps the kind of adjustment she makes to adult demands explains her distractability and irresponsibility.

Such an observation indicates the need for a thoughtful analysis of the kinds and amount of pressure that children are receiving if they are to find the important values in the experiences they have. Less control rather than more may help the child.

A Child's Behavior Changes When Patterns of Authority Change

A special problem is likely to arise when children find themselves faced with a pattern of authority which is different from the one to which they are accustomed. This kind of situation may arise when a child enters nursery school and finds that the patterns there differ from those in his home.

The environment of the nursery school is set up so that there will be fewer adult interferences than in many other environments. The child is free to do what he likes most of the time. He does not meet many frustrations in his physical environment or many interferences, relatively speaking, from adults. Toys are available on low shelves; there are hooks and washbasins within his reach; adults are generally permissive. After their initial adjustment to the new experience, children who come from homes that are less permissive and more limiting often go through a period of being resistant to limits or authority of any kind. In school they change from being "good" and "easy" to manage, to being negativistic and resistant. At home they are more defiant than they have ever been. They are impudent and uncooperative. They try out all the "bad" words and deeds they have heard and seen at the nursery school.

Home and School Need to
Understand the Significance of These Changes

It is no wonder that parents, and sometimes teachers, may question whether the nursery school is desirable for these children. Only if the meaning of this behavior is clear, can adults accept it and handle it in such a way that the child really gains from the experience. If we can accept the fact that the resentment which accompanies many limitations must be expressed before healthy growth takes place, if we can accept the fact that these feelings must be expressed when they exist, then we will not be disturbed by the child's behavior even if he appears to be going backwards. If we can see this behavior as a sign of the growth in self-confidence that follows a sudden increase in freedom, then we can meet it wisely.

Expression of feeling in speech or action safeguards mental health; the capacity to act when one feels something leads to creativity, and gives self-confidence. These are things that we want to achieve. We must pay a price for them. The child who has been unnecessarily and unwisely limited may need time to unload negative feelings and acquire confidence. When he suddenly discovers he can express himself, he must be given time to gain assurance by doing this. Then, without sacrificing the valuable elements in the child's responses, we can help him feel responsible for his behavior and the way it affects others. We can help him accept reasonable limits and substitute self-direction within these limits for imposed direction. All this takes time. But it is important that we take this time so that the child will feel accepted as he is. It is important that we neither blame nor frighten him, but help him in positive ways to understand what the limits for his behavior are. It is really by his "misbehavior" that the child shows us that he is working through a change in his concept of the part he can play in a group. It is through this behavior that we have the chance to help him become a more responsible, self-directing person.

The period during which the child asserts himself and expresses his resentment is not an easy one, particularly for parents. By "cracking down" on a child at this point they may increase his problem and make it very difficult for him to work out any sound adjustment to the problem of authority in a democracy. Home and school need to understand what is happening to the child and to work together.

Our Goal Is Self-Control

The problem of authority is not simple. It is tied up with a child's total development pattern. In one child defiance may be a constructive step forward. In another it may indicate distressing confusion and conflict. In both children it calls for understanding on the part of the adult.

Our goal is self-control, the only sound control. But self-control can be sound only when there is a stable mature self. Our responsibility is to help the child develop this maturity through giving him the security of limits maintained by responsible adults while he is growing.

REFERENCES

1. Auerback, Aline, and Larsen, Faith: The Why and How of Discipline. New York, Child Study Assn. of America, 1957.
2. Baruch, Dorothy: How to Discipline Your Child. Public Affairs pamphlet, No. 154, 1949.
3. Bettelheim, Bruno: Don't Deny Them Discipline. National Parent-Teacher Magazine, March 1955.
4. Fraiberg, Selma: The Magic Years, Ch. 8. New York, Scribners, 1959.
5. Frank, Lawrence, and Frank, Mary: How Much Freedom for the Preschool Child? Child Study, Fall 1954.
6. Hymes, James L.: Discipline. Bureau of Publications, Teachers College, Columbia University, 1949.
7. Read, Katherine H.: Discipline in the Nursery School. Childhood Education, March 1956.

10

Developing
Relationships in Groups

Group Relationships Deserve Our Study

The child's first sustained group experience outside the family is likely to be that which occurs in the nursery school. His experience at nursery school differs from his experience in the family because the school group is made up of contemporaries whose interests and capacities are on about the same level as his own. Living with a group of equals is a significantly different experience for a child from that of being a member of a family group. As students in the nursery school laboratory we can add to our understanding of what relationships mean to people as we observe the children in their group living.

Difficulties exist in working out relationships with equals and in accepting the limitations that are necessary in a group. One observes these difficulties in any nursery school or on any playground

235

where children come together. Some children withdraw, some are defensive or aggressive, some are friendly and seem to expect friendliness from others. But out of these relationships with equals may come some of the deepest satisfactions in life. In spite of the conflicts and problems which occur, it is important that all children find success in relationships with people of their own age. Group relationships in the nursery school are worth our study.

VALUES OF GROUP RELATIONSHIPS

A More Realistic Concept of Self

What does the young child gain from being with a group of other children?

One of the most significant values for the child in being a member of a group of equals lies in the fact that he has a chance to find out more about what kind of person he really is through this experience. He has an opportunity to build a more realistic concept of himself as a person apart from his membership in a family.

In the family group each of us is valued, or should be valued, because we belong to that particular family, regardless of what we may be or do. We do not need to prove our worth in order to belong to the family group. When the family situation is a favorable one, each member can count on receiving attention and affection freely.

In a group of contemporaries, on the other hand, the place each one of us holds depends more on our skill and what we have to offer the group. We must demonstrate our worth. We must measure ourselves against others who are like us, finding our strengths and facing our weaknesses, winning some acceptance and meeting some rejection. When we experience success, it is based on achievement to a great extent. The limitations we face are likely to be real rather than arbitrarily imposed. A favorable family situation helps us feel secure, but experiences with our own age group help develop an awareness of ourselves and of social reality which family experience alone cannot give. Both family and outside group experience are necessary for complete social development.

Self-confidence

Besides seeing himself in a more realistic light, the child can gain self-confidence from membership in a group of his own age. The nursery school child feels himself like others in the nursery school. He can identify with them with less strain than when he tries to identify with adults. He finds strength and safety through group membership. This feeling of belonging in a group has special value for the less confident child. As a member of the group he will often feel strong enough to act in ways that he would not have had the courage to act if he were alone.

Children gain from realizing that they like each other and can value each other as children. Such feelings are evident in the following incident. Six children had gathered at a table and were doing puzzles, talking and helping each other. The teacher sat near by. Suddenly Nancy remarked, "I like you, Andy," and Andy replied, "I like you." Nancy went on, "And I like Jane and Larry and Linda and Debby." The others began naming each other as people they liked. Then Nancy began again. "But we don't like her, do we?" pointing to the teacher. "We only like little children." Andy agreed with her, "We only like little children." Everyone laughed and seemed very pleased.

Fig. 40. Friends enjoy just being together.

Fig. 41. Sharing a worm.

Overcoming Feelings of Being Helpless

Children may need to identify with equals as a defense against the strength of adults. It is hard for a child to feel a measure of self-sufficiency when he is with adults all the time. As a member of a group of other children, he dares to act with more confidence. The fact that their acts are often directed against adults and their authority suggests that it may be fear of the powerful adult and a sense of helplessness that keep some children from developing confidence. They lose some of this fear and helplessness in a group. Lester, described at the end of the chapter, found a friend and gained confidence when he was with him. He began to defy adults. He refused to conform and attacked them verbally with "You dummy" or "You stinkpot." His behavior, like that of other timid, fearful children, suggests that he had feared adults. When he belonged to the group, he felt less fear and helplessness.

Children who have confidence and do not feel helpless have less need to fight against adults. They can accept adults without feeling threatened by them. Jean, as a secure, confident child, seldom felt the need to be defiant or resistant with adults. Lester was ready to accept their limitations when he developed more self-confidence. Some children, on the other hand, never develop sufficient confidence to defy adults but remained anxious and dependent on them, "good" children but not happy or emotionally healthy children.

Resistance May Be Expressed Indirectly

Jimmy was a child who kept urging other children to do things which he wanted to do but did not dare. At four he was the oldest of three children and seemed afraid to displease adults openly. He would encourage another child, "Hit him, Steve," or "Pour your milk on the floor." Too often the teacher in this case, concerned with handling the child who hit or spilled at Jimmy's suggestion, overlooked Jimmy. Such a child needs help in accepting himself and not being afraid of his own impulses. He needs a teacher who will act quickly to keep the other child from following the suggestion, but who will give him reassurance with words like "Do you feel like hitting him? We all feel like that sometimes. I can't let you hit him but you can do some pounding at the workbench," or "Do you want to pour milk on the floor? It's fun to pour. You can pour all you want in the wash basin or the sandbox but I can't let anyone pour milk out." Such a child usually needs reassurance, too, that he is important and valued, but most of all he needs help in facing and not being afraid of his own impulses. Using other children to "try out" what he does not dare do directly is at least a first step in doing something.

The child who expresses feeling even more indirectly may be piling up much more hostility. John was a passive, "good" boy. At juice time Steve pushed him off a chair and took it from him. John quietly moved to another chair at the other side of the table. A few minutes later he spilled his juice. "I spilled my juice, I'm very sorry," he said to the teacher but later he spilled his second glass. Already John had turned away from direct expression of feeling to an "accident proneness" and perhaps an unconscious attack on the teacher who had failed to protect him when he could not protect himself. John needed help from her before he could find strength in experiences with groups.

We Need to Value Children's Resistance

For many parents and teachers, as we mentioned earlier, the phase in a child's social development in which he is resistant and defiant is a disturbing one. It takes experience and confidence to see the value in behavior which is usually considered unacceptable. When a quiet little girl, for example, begins to "talk back" and resist suggestions, her parents may question the value of experiences which seem to produce this kind of behavior. They are likely to raise a question because the child's need to resist may have arisen out of their own need to control and dominate her. It takes insight to perceive that resistant behavior may mean growth for the child as a person. It takes insight both into the child's behavior and into our own behavior. It takes skill, too, to guide a child through this stage so that its values are retained and at the same time safe limits and a respect for them are maintained.

We will try to achieve some of this insight and some of the needed skill as we study children's behavior and participate in the nursery school laboratory. We will remind ourselves that resistant behavior may mean growth.

As in other situations, understanding children who are in this phase of development means understanding our own feelings. Because most of us have many areas of insecurity, we find it hard not to feel threatened by resistance. The adult who meets children's attack with "I won't have that" or "You can't get away with that" reveals himself as an adult who is defending himself against feelings of being helpless rather than as one who is helping the group.

We are apt to handle resistance on the basis of our own feelings. If we find ourselves wanting to punish the child, the strength of our need to punish is likely to be in direct ratio to the helplessness we have felt in our past. It becomes important for us to realize that we are no longer helpless, that we can be strong enough to accept the child's behavior without feeling threatened by it and that we can do something about his behavior without acting for the purpose of relieving our own feelings. It is important for us to realize that we can even afford to let the child assert himself if he can gain needed strength and confidence through doing this. We have discussed this point in Chapter 9, Defining and Maintaining Limits for Behavior.

hildren Find That They Can Like Teachers

Children in groups respond to adults in other ways than by assert-
ng themselves against the adult. They want the adult's attention
nd must share it with each other. As we have mentioned earlier,
haring the teacher's attention with others is less difficult than shar-
ng the attention of one's mother. If the teacher gives her attention
reely and generously when children ask for it, she helps them feel
hat there is enough for all. They are less likely to feel deprived at
he times when they cannot have attention. They are more likely to
)e satisfied. It may be easier to learn this lesson in a nursery school
group than at home.

Children may also take a step in learning that it is all right to like
nany people, adults as well as children, as their relationships with
he teachers develop. A child usually finds a teacher on whom he
lepends as he enters the group. He may want this teacher and no
)ther to help him and share experiences with him. He may seek her
)ut when he comes to school. But as he grows more sure of himself,
ie has less need to depend on her. He begins to reach out to others
ind it is important for him to feel that this is a good step to take.
The following incident shows us something of how a child feels
ibout the relationship.

Anita is building with blocks and talking with a teacher sitting
near by. She happens to glance up and sees Miss Smith with another
child. Miss Smith has been her favorite teacher, the one on whom
she depended at first. She pauses a minute and then says to the
teacher with her, "Sometimes people like teachers to sit by them
even if they like Miss Smith best. I still like Miss Smith, but you can
sit here."

The teacher asked, "Do you wish that Miss Smith was sitting
here?"

Anita answered, "No, you can sit here, but if you have something
you need to do, you can go and do it and come back."

The teacher said, "I like to sit here beside you."

Anita smiled and said, "O.K."

Children gain from living in groups by asserting themselves in
many ways, not only by resistance but by accepting their right to
like and be liked.

READINESS FOR GROUP EXPERIENCE

Group Experience Has Value if the Child Is Ready

Some of the values of group experience for the child, then, lie in the confidence he gains from feeling like others, from identifying with them and freeing himself from some of his fear of the powerful adult. Besides confidence he builds a more realistic picture of the kind of person he really is.

These are values that the child will find if he is ready for the experience of belonging to a group of other children. His readiness to enter the group will depend on two factors. The most important factor is the preparation he has had within his own family. The second is the nature of the group he enters and the help available to him there in making the adjustments.

Fig. 42. A new child joins the group by supplying water.

Readiness for the Group Depends on the Preparation of the Child in His Family

The kind of life which the child has lived within the family will determine the adjustments which are possible for him outside the family. By a seeming contradiction which often holds in the field of mental hygiene, the child is apt to be prepared for life in outside groups to the extent that he has felt sure of his worth and his acceptance in the family, rather than to the extent to which the family situation resembles the situation with contemporaries. If he has felt secure in possessing a love which has never been withheld, he will have confidence in undertaking the different experiences of entering a group in which he must win acceptance. He seems to need to be valued in the home without proof in order that he may have the courage to prove his value outside.

The question of "spoiling" a child may be raised again at this point. Does giving a child what he wants prepare him to meet situations in which he cannot have what he wants? Does offering him love no matter how he behaves prepare him to meet situations in which he cannot expect unconditional love? Is not this "spoiling" a child?

The so-called "spoiled" child is obviously handicapped in social relationships. He is far removed from reality in the value that he tries to place on himself. But if we understand his situation, we will usually observe that this child has not been truly accepted by his parents. He is likely to have been a child who has been showered with the things that his parents wanted him to have, or indulged because it was the easiest way for them to escape effort and responsibility. His own real needs have not been met, but only the needs that they wanted to meet. When a child is without a real feeling that he is loved and valued, he becomes very demanding and may never be satisfied. He continues to seek attention no matter how much he may have, and he turns away from reality. Other insecurities may make a child demanding, too, but lack of an accepting love leads to the deepest insecurity and results in selfishness and unending demands for attention in the vain search for satisfaction of this deepest need. Children whose needs have been met are not "spoiled" children.

It may be well to remember that the term "spoiled" is often used

loosely. Some people use it to refer to any child who does not behave in a way that pleases the adult. If the adult happens to be a
self-centered person, ignorant of child behavior, he may apply the
term "spoiled" to behavior which is far more healthy for the child
than behavior of which he approves. We will do well to avoid use
of a term so heavily loaded with popular misconceptions.

Readiness to Enter the Group
Depends on What the Group Is Like

The child's readiness to enter a group will also depend on the
group itself and the help that he receives there in making the step
from home to school.

If the child is to be successful, the group must be one in which he
has a good chance for a satisfying experience. He must be able to
identify with it rather than feel overwhelmed by it. He is likely to
be helped in feeling that he can belong if the group is not large and
if the age range is not wide. He is often helped if he knows that he
can depend on one adult. It is usually desirable to limit the time that
the child spends with the group at first and to plan his beginning
experiences carefully as we discussed in Chapter 4. All these are
factors in making group experiences more satisfying.

Some of the advantages of group experience in a nursery school
over that in an unsupervised neighborhood group lie in the greater
likelihood that the needs of each child are being met. In this situation, experiences can be modified for individuals while preserving
the values of initiative and resourcefulness which a free group offers.
The unsupervised group may be a good experience for some children, but it may be a poor experience for others. There is little protection for all the individuals to an equal extent in it. Absence of
conflict may simply mean that the weaker children have accepted
the domination of a bullying child. There may not be much growth
for anyone in this type of situation.

TEACHER GUIDANCE

The Teacher Helps the Child by Her Acceptance of Him in the Group

When the child leaves home and enters the group, he finds the
support which the teacher offers in a good nursery school serving as

transition in the step from home to school. The teacher stands ready to act as "mother substitute" as long as the child needs support of this kind. He is helped by his relationship with her just as we are all helped when we know there is someone to whom we can turn when the need arises. If the child can feel that the teacher is completely accepting of him, if he can turn to her when he meets failure with the children, he will not be as likely to retreat within himself or to fight blindly when he runs into trouble.

Just as important, if the child feels accepted, he will later be able to turn away from his dependency on the teacher when he has finally found enough strength through identifying with the group. In turning away from his dependence on her he need not feel the sense of loss or the guilt that he might feel in turning away from his mother. Ben, described earlier, grew out of his dependence on the teacher to the point where he could slap her image in the screen but feel sure of her acceptance of him at the same time. He could safely take this important step in emancipating himself—the goal of individual growth. For any child a good relationship with the teacher is important in helping him grow as a person outside his family.

Fig. 43. Together they enjoy singing with the auto harp.

The Teacher Helps by Promoting Sound Feelings

The teacher will also help the child by promoting the kinds of feelings in him which are an essential basis for social skills. As we know, sound social skills grow out of feelings of security and confidence and freedom from any large amount of hostility. The teacher's best efforts will go into helping children feel more secure and more adequate in the experiences they face and thus better able to like other people. Children with these feelings find it easier to acquire social skill. Jean, for example, was secure and confident. She possessed a high degree of skill in getting along with others; while Charles who had not found much acceptance at home wanted to play with other children but managed his relationships with them poorly.

The "forms" of getting along with others are of little use when they are imposed on a background of insecurity and distrust of others. A common mistake of teachers and parents is to attack the lack of skill, the inability to take turns, or the tendency to exclude others, and to try to correct these things without first changing the feelings which have brought about this behavior. Such treatment may in fact actually increase the child's problem instead of reducing it. It's as useless as trying to keep the furniture dusted while dust continues to swirl through the open windows. When we try to help a child get along with others, we must first help him feel sufficiently secure, adequate and free of hostility, so that he can really like others and not act defensively toward them. Then he will be ready for techniques, and can enlarge the horizons of his satisfactions with people.

In Chapter 5 we mentioned the importance to the child of feeling that his parent would give him attention freely. This same quality of giving freely is important also in group relationships. If the child experiences a generous giving by the teacher, he will be more likely to give freely to others himself. When the adult is niggardly in her giving of attention or of materials, she does not help the child feel like giving freely in his turn. For example, Bill asked the teacher to give him the box of nails which was up on the high shelf. Bill was working on an airplane. The teacher refused and gave him a few nails. Bill took them and returned to his work but he guarded the nails closely and was careful not to let anyone else use them. While it may not have been desirable to let Bill have the whole box of nails, t might have been possible to give him a different feeling about "givingness." Group relations are different in an atmosphere where giving is done freely and generously and where even withholding is based on generous feelings.

The Teacher Helps with Techniques for Getting Along with Others

When there is a foundation of positive feeling, the child's progress in group relationships will be facilitated by our suggestions of techniques, such as ways of approaching others. As the child meets success in using desirable techniques, he will tend to use them oftener and will be accepted better by others. A child learns these things from experiences that are within the level of his comprehension, from situations whose reality he can understand.

What are some of the techniques that we can suggest to a child who is ready for our help? What social skills will be useful to him?

We can help children by suggesting good ways of approaching others or by helping them understand the feelings which lie behind the approaches of other people—however clumsy these approaches may be. If we are to do this, we must understand what methods of approach are most likely to be successful in the situations in which children find themselves. We do this best if we observe what actually happens when children play together, for we must not be content to rely on suggesting adult forms of getting along. What works at the adult level does not necessarily work at the nursery school level.

An approach is usually more successful if the approaching child has some suggestion about what he might be or do, or if he makes some contribution to the play in progress. A straight request "May I play with you?" is often doomed to fail even if it is accompanied by the adult word "please." In helping a child the adult offers more help if she can suggest something specific to the child that he might be or do. Another advantage in this technique is that if one is rejected in one role, one can always find another role or a different activity to suggest. This way there is more protection against failure.

Children are often very realistic—and successful. Terry calls to Tommy, "Say, Tommy, you'd better let Doug play with us because he won't let me have the rope unless he plays and I want it."

Possessing something desired by others is as much of a social advantage at three as at thirty-three. A wise teacher may utilize this fact in helping the shy child. Letting the child introduce a new piece of equipment, or bring something from home for the group to use. may help him feel more accepted and give him added confidence. Obviously such a technique should not be depended on too heavily or for too long, but it can sometimes be the basis for a social start

Offering something in return for something else one wants is a successful device. Some children have amazing skill in making a second object appear desirable when they want the first. Even secondary roles can be made attractive by an imaginative child.

Regan, for example, wanted to join the group who were playing "policeman" mounted on tricycles, but there were no more tricycles. Terry encouraged her to join anyway, saying, "You can be a walking policeman, Regan. They have walking policemen. You can play if you are a walking policeman," and he made it sound worth while, for Regan became a "walking policeman."

Cindy and Larry are riding tricycles. Debby wants to ride with them but there is only a small tricycle left which she doesn't want to use. She is unhappy and tries to take the tricycle from Larry. Cindy settles the matter by saying, "If there's not any big ones, then you can't ride one now. But if you will wait then Larry will get tired and then you can ride with me." Debby appears convinced and lets go of Larry's tricycle.

Adjustments like these are likely to be reached only when the children involved *like* each other. When they have had pleasant experiences together in the past, they can make compromises more easily to ensure their getting along in present situations.

Terry is already a past master at working out compromises. On another occasion he was busily building with blocks when Regan wanted him to play house with her again. He satisfied her by saying, "I'll live over there with you but I'll work here, and I'm working now," and he went on with his building. Terry has had many successful experiences of getting along with others. He has confidence and his confidence shows in the way he meets his problems.

The same situation has different meaning for each child and he responds to it as it looks to him. Patty and Lois, who had been playing house together, took their babies out for a walk. Lois, looking back, saw two boys in their play house. "Someone's getting into our house," she exclaimed anxiously. Patty turned around, too. "Oh, we have company," she cried joyfully and hurried back to welcome the boys.

As we listen to children in their play and try to understand what techniques are adapted to their level, we find that they approach others in friendly ways far more frequently than we may have been aware. We may not have noticed their consideration for each other because our attention is more likely to be directed to the times when they hit or grab. We will find, too, that there is more friendly behavior in a group where the children are receiving courtesy and consideration from the adults. They adopt the patterns of those around them.

The Teacher Helps by Being Careful Not to Interfere

Good guidance sometimes consists in being able to stay out of situations so that children may work out their own relationships. Here is a situation. Let us look at what happens in it.

Eric and Chip, two three-year-olds, are swinging side by side. Eric, who is the taller of the two, swings himself, going quite high. A teacher is pushing Chip in the swing.

Chip:	One day I used to go to college.
Eric:	I go to the big college.
Teacher:	You visited, didn't you? You didn't really go.
Chip:	You're my friend, aren't you, Eric? You're my friend. (and he starts singing)
Teacher:	That's a good song to sing in the swing.
Chip:	(to Bobby who passes by) Eric is my friend. You're not Bobby's friend, are you, Eric?
Eric:	Yes, I am.
Chip:	Oh! I thought you weren't Bobby's friend. But Donnie isn't your friend, is he? (He paused) I don't hear any birds around here.
Eric:	I can tell if it's spring now. No one ever told me. I just know it.
Chip:	When I was home, I heard them say "peep peep."
Teacher:	Oh! Baby birds do say "peep peep."
Chip:	Baby chickens say "peep peep" too.
Teacher:	Do you think baby ducks say "peep"?
Chip:	No, they say "quack."
Eric:	I'm getting a little tired here. One time David and I swinged until juice time.
Chip:	One time I swinged until juice time.
Eric:	That wasn't you, just David and me.
Teacher:	Chip's probably done it, too, Eric.
Eric:	Ya, after we did.
Chip:	It takes a long time to swing. I hear a whistle. Maybe it's for the college boys to go in.

Eric: Chippie, you don't know everything I know.
Chip: You don't know about baby horses and my Mommy and Daddy do.
Teacher: Would you like to stop and have some juice now, Chip? Let's stop
            for juice.

Eric jumps out of his swing and Chip gets out of his. Both boys go
to have their morning juice.

One gets the impression that the teacher, for some reason, is
identifying strongly with Chip, the smaller child whom she is pushing. She does not accept Eric's comments, countering them with,
"You didn't really go," and "Chip's probably done it, too." She com-
pliments Chip with, "That's a good song . . . ," and sings with him.
She seeks his attention by comments on his remarks, "baby birds do
say 'peep peep' and asking him questions, "Do you think baby ducks
say 'peep'?" She suggests that he have juice but does not include
Eric.

Both boys are quite ready to end the experience. In fact, Eric says
earlier, "I'm getting a little tired here," a remark which may not
apply entirely to the effort of swinging. What the boys appear to
want is to test themselves out in a relationship with each other. Chip
wants to be sure of a place with the bigger, more capable child,
saying, "You're my friend, aren't you, Eric?" Eric is willing although
he will not exclude others as Chip would like to have him. Chip
introduces the subject of birds which Eric picks up to relate to spring
and his own sense of being adequate. The teacher does not give
Chip much chance to continue for she introduces her questions here.
Eric goes on to remember a previous experience in swinging with
David—which may have been free of interruptions! Chip continues
to try to interest Eric with his mention of the "whistle" and the
"college boys," but he is losing out. Eric's answer is "You don't know
everything I know," and Chip falls back on bringing his mother and
father into the conversation. He knows they are bigger than Eric
and they like him. Both boys stood up for themselves well but they
were handicapped in their relationship by the teacher's interference.

CONCEPTS TO BE LEARNED

Children in Groups Learn about Property Rights and Taking Turns

An area in which children often need help from the adults is in
learning about property rights and "taking turns." Living in a group

of equals provides many opportunities for learning in this area and the child's concepts develop from his experiences in the group.

Since property rights are considered very important in our society, the child must begin early to learn about possession. In his home he discovers that some things are not his to touch. The wise parent helps him accept this fact by giving him something that is his when she takes away something that he cannot have. She teaches him that some things are his, and she does not insist that he share the things that are his until he is willing and ready to share. Pushing him into sharing before he is ready will only confuse him and may prevent sound learning. She will find that he can share first with people he knows and likes, and then slowly he can broaden his ability to share in most situations.

The nursery school provides an excellent place for the child to continue his learning about sharing, taking turns, and possessions. Equipment at the school does not belong to individuals but to the group as a whole. No child feels as threatened by a sense of loss when he shares things like this as he might in sharing things that belong to him personally. Two simple principles can be established

Fig. 44. Friends often have conflicts. (H. Armstrong Roberts)

to cover most of the situations. First, when a person is through using a piece of equipment like a tricycle or swing, it "belongs" to the next person who may wish to use it. One does not continue to claim a thing one is no longer using. Second, after one has used a piece of equipment for a time one may have to let someone else use it even though one is not through, but one can expect to get it back again.

If these principles can be translated into very specific terms, they will be easier for the child to understand, as "After he rides around the circle once, you may have a turn. You can ride around the circle once and then give it to him." Words like these are easier for the child to understand than "you must take turns with him." A group at the slide will be helped more when the teacher says, "First you go down and then Jim and then Lucy." They may not understand when she merely says, "You must all take turns at the slide."

The teacher often needs to interpret situations to inexperienced children to prevent misunderstanding. Bill was pulling a wagon when he observed Rickey on the tricycle he had been riding earlier. Rickey was new in the group and uncertain. Bill approached him aggressively; "I was riding that," he said. Rickey just smiled, and the teacher replied, "You are pulling the wagon now, Bill." "Yes, I am," said Bill, half surprised but satisfied. In a few minutes both boys were playing together on the jungle gym.

It is interesting to observe the children themselves discovering the general aspects of specific situations. Jill, for example, was playing with a stick and some wooden rings. Kay came past, watched her, and then touched the rings. Jill hit Kay as if in protest at her inter- ference. Kay turned to the teacher nearby for help. The teacher helped by interpreting Kay's action to Jill. "Jill, Kay wants to use the rings when you're through." Jill nodded assent, and Kay climbed into the teacher's lap to wait. Jill quickly finished putting the rings together and handed them to Kay. Then she took Kay's place in the teacher's lap. Kay used the rings, handed them back to Jill and took her place again in the lap of the teacher. The two girls continued this play, reversing their positions six or eight times. Kay suddenly exclaimed, "We're taking turns."

It is probable, in this situation, that if the teacher had reproved Jill for hitting in the first place, their friendly play together might never have developed. Jill would have felt resentful and Kay abused. With feelings like these they would not have been ready to move into a game together and discover "turns" for themselves.

When we try to teach children about "turns," we must be sure to follow through in the situations. If a child gives up a swing so that another child may have a turn, we must see that the first child gets it back afterward if he still wants it. Even if he isn't standing there waiting, it may be wise to say, "Johnny, Jane has had her turn now and you can have the swing back again if you wish." This clarifies the concept and prevents the child from feeling that taking turns really means losing something.

Special Cases Arise Under This Concept of Property Rights

An interesting situation is sometimes created by the children themselves. An aggressive child may prefer a certain piece of equipment. Almost before the teacher is fully aware of what is happening, he may establish that it is "his" and the other children, fearing his attack, may prefer to leave it for him and give up their turn with this piece of equipment. The teacher must be alert to such situations and protect the other children in their right to use all equipment equally. She must see that they suffer no retaliation later. Charles, whose aggressiveness was making him unpopular, preferred a red tricycle. With his usual lack of awareness of the needs and feelings of others, he proceeded to take it when he could. It became important for the teacher to accept responsibility for maintaining the right of others to use the coveted red tricycle. It was important because Charles needed to have other children feel friendly toward him. No one in the group was more eager to be liked. The fact that there were occasions when he possessed the red tricycle legitimately made it easier for him to bear the limitation of not having it every time. It was also important for the teacher to watch this situation because the other children needed to be successful in standing up for themselves in the face of the threat Charles offered them.

A slightly different situation exists when a timid child may depend on a particular piece of equipment for a feeling of security. He may cling to a tricycle or a doll because he feels safer with it. It may happen to be the first thing he played with, or the toy with which he had his most satisfying experience. It is important for him to have the teacher protect him in his possession of this piece of equipment until he has found other areas of security. The teacher must suspend the rules in his case, interpreting to the other children with "We'll let him keep the doll because he's new in our school and still feels strange. Remember when you were new? When he knows that we're his friends, he can take turns with us." In doing this the teacher helps other children understand and accept differences, too.

Bill, for example, was a quiet, thin child who held aloof from the children and the teachers. One day he discovered the large red wagon. It may have been like one he had at home. Whatever the reason, he began to play with it almost exclusively and could not bear to share it with another child. The teacher felt that it was important to protect Bill in his use of the wagon for a time. She helped the more secure children find a substitute whenever possible and allowed Bill time to grow more sure of himself at school before she expected him to take turns with the wagon.

The time comes, of course, when a child like this should be ready to accept the standards of the group. The teacher must watch for this readiness and, for the sake of his relationships with others, not prolong needlessly the child's dependence on one piece of equipment.

ADJUSTING TO THE GROUP

Children Find Their Place in the Group Step by Step

In finding their places in a group, children usually go through certain steps in adjustment. After they have been able to relate themselves to an adult in the school and feel safe with her, they move on to relationships with individual children. There are many ways in which the adult can help the child move on into play with other children. If she sits at the table with the child, she can make sure that there is a place for another child to join them. She can encourage a second child to join the activity and then quietly withdraw herself, not absorbing the child's attention longer than necessary. Friendships with contemporaries in nursery school are more important than friendships with adults, and the adult must give children every encouragement to move on into having experience with other children.

Some children, lacking aggressiveness, appear content to depend on adults as long as adult support is available. They find contacts with adults easier to maintain and sufficiently satisfying so that they make little effort to move on to the more difficult and more rewarding area of building up relationships with other children. The children who depend on adults are usually "good" children from the conventional standpoint, and adults are sometimes tempted to keep them dependent unless they analyze the child's problem thoughtfully.

In the nursery school most children have relationships with other children that are temporary or shifting. Two children may play together for a morning or for a few days, drawn by a mutual interest in digging a hole, or playing firemen, or setting up housekeeping somewhere. Then each will have an equally close but short-lasting friendship with someone else. But even in these shifting relationships there are likely to be certain children who are rather consistently antagonistic to each other or attracted for reasons we may not fully understand. We can help children better if we are aware of their feelings of liking and not liking, so that we can be careful to use the one wisely and not to add to the other.

Close Friendships Are Often a Source of Strength

A timid child often gains from a close friendship with one child in the beginning and the new child, too, may be helped by contacts with individuals before he is ready to enter groups. Both the timid child and the one who is new may need to gain confidence in simple social situations before they are ready to solve the more complex problems which arise when several children play together. The teacher may need to see that their contacts are largely with individuals at first. It is safer to like individuals before one tries to like groups. It may even be dangerous to try to love humanity without loving individuals!

Sometimes children discover one particular friend and from this close friendship they develop confidence and assurance. There is nothing much better at any age level than having a special friend. The confidence and assurance that comes from feeling that one is liked by an equal, sought after, depended on, makes possible a great deal of development. Such friendships are worth encouraging even though at one stage they may mean that the pair exclude others. The friendship is likely to lead later on to a growth in friendliness.

Close friends often have conflicts with one another, especially if they are beginning to play more with other children. They may quarrel frequently and call each other all the current names, "dummy," "mashed potato head," and separate with "I won't play with you any more." But they are still best friends, quick to defend each other against outsiders.

While close friendships offer real support to children, the teacher needs to be alert to offer help at the point at which one of the pair may be ready for new contacts. Janice and Jerry had both developed confidence after they began playing together. It was several weeks before Jerry began to assert himself. One morning he announced, "I'm going out." Janice had previously decided she didn't want to go out. Janice complained, "Jerry shouldn't go out when I don't go out." The teacher pointed out to her, "But you could go out." Jerry persisted, "But I want to go out. I'm going out with Timmy." Janice protested again and Jerry finally went out. Neither child was very happy. A wiser teacher might have recognized the real problem which the situation presented for the two children. Instead of pointing out to Janice that she, too, could go out, she might have said, "You like to have Jerry with you, don't you? He's going out now but he'll be back. You and he will play together again." She would then have tried to help Janice have fun away from Jerry, so that the two children might find satisfaction in greater independence while still remaining friends.

Lester Developed After He Found a Friend

Let us take Lester as an example of a child who developed rapidly after he found a friend, because he is typical of many rather quiet children who find it easier to work through the conflicts they feel when they have the support of a good friend.

Lester was the only boy in a family with three girls. He had received a great deal of anxious attention from his parents and steady dictation from his three sisters. It had been hard for him to be a person in his own way. When he entered nursery school he was defensive and self-conscious, holding back from activities. He watched the other children, often trying to belittle what they were doing. Tears came into his eyes if anyone made a disparaging remark about him or his efforts. He risked very little action anywhere. Even at the table he seemed to feel that he might spill something or do the wrong thing, and be subject to teasing or criticism. He sat without eating much of anything but toast. On the playground he would lean against a post, half hidden, unhappiness showing on his tight little face.

Lester had been in nursery school several weeks before he became friends with Albert. Albert was timid and unsure of himself, too, but he did not seem to be as sensitive to his problems as Lester. No one entirely understood what brought them together, but it might have been their interest in imaginative things.

Whatever may have brought them together, the two boys began to play with each other almost exclusively. The first one to arrive at school would wait around the door until the other one appeared and they would literally fall into each other's arms. It was as though no other children existed for them. The change in Lester's behavior was remarkable. He seemed to come alive and was purposeful, active. It was clearly an important experience for him to find someone who depended on him and who offered no threat to him. Soon the two began to challenge other children and to exclude others actively from their play where previously they had merely ignored others. Their passive behavior was replaced by defiance of the teacher and her suggestions. Instead of sitting in front of his food, Lester was noisy and sociable at the table—if Albert were there. It was as though from this friendship he found the security he needed to enable him to defend himself in a world that had previously overwhelmed him.

When the two boys left nursery school at the end of the year, they had began to accept others and were playing successfully in the group although they were still bosom friends. Lester had become a person and a most engaging person, who found fun in many situations. Out of the friendship with Albert which was close, and for a time exclusive, he had gained confidence. He became able to face and accept the demands of group living.

Some Children Never Find Close Friends

Not all children seem able to find this release and stimulus to growth through finding a close friend. Charles who was in nursery school as long never found any close friend. The aggressiveness he displayed undoubtedly handicapped him, but does not completely explain his lack of close relationships. Children who are not aggressive may still fail to find close friends. Beth was like Charles in being without friends but she was not at all aggressive. In fact, she sought affection from children and adults. She would run after any teacher saying, "Lady, I love you." She wanted children to play with her, but even in the shifting relations characteristic of preschool groups she seldom had much of a place. In spite of Beth's words her relationships with people were superficial and lacked warmth. What makes such differences?

One explanation lies in the quality of the relationships each child had experienced earlier. Lester, with all his handicaps, had still known a loving, warm relationship with his busy mother; while neither Charles nor Beth had found much warmth and acceptance in any of the adults with whom they had lived. Beth had even experienced a surprising amount of neglect in a home where some of the standards seemed high. Again we see how the relationships which the child has experienced in his home influence and limit the kind of relationship he is able to establish outside his home. Sometimes a teacher can supply the child with a relationship sufficiently warm to make up the deficit when there is one, so that he can achieve an adequate measure of social satisfaction as in the case of the boy who used the rubber doll for biting. But this is only likely to happen when some measure of warmth and affection has been experienced earlier by the child.

Our Goal Is to Help Children Like Each Other

If we were to sum up our goals as we work with children in groups, we might say that they all lead in the direction of helping the children like each other more rather than less because of what we do. We might use this as a yardstick. Will the children like each other better if we do this?

As teachers we may have to redirect children as they try to unload hostility onto other children. Louise and Stevie were washing their hands side by side. Louise was a child who carried a heavy load of hostile feeling and was always attacking others in a critical way. She said, "Stevie's a bad boy." The teacher replied casually, "Oh, he's my friend and you're my friend. Isn't it nice that I have two friends?" Stevie beamed and Louise picked up the idea with, "And Anne's your friend and Mike and Jim." "Yes," said the teacher, "there are lots of friends here."

Isolation Does not Usually Help

Following the example of some adults children may be overly concerned with "bad" behavior. Giving undue attention to a child's undesirable behavior may make it hard for that child to find his place again in the group. We sometimes see a parent or teacher isolating a child as punishment for not getting along with others. We have come far enough in our discussion to be aware of the fact that punishment may be undesirable because of the load of resentment and hostility that may accompany it. While the child may not repeat a particular act after being punished, he is not likely to feel more friendly toward others or to get along better with them because of it. Isolation deprives him of the chance to have other, and perhaps better, experiences. It also labels him as "bad" in the eyes of the group and thus adds to his difficulties in getting along with others.

Isolation may be desirable when it is used with a child whose difficulties are the result of over-stimulation and fatigue because of too many experiences. In this case the teacher may accept the child's need of a simpler environment. She will try to achieve it without giving him a feeling that isolation is a form of punishment. She may suggest a story alone or a walk or she may put him in a room with his favorite toy for a rest, explaining that he will get along better with the others after a rest. She may remove a child who is disturbing other children and put him where he can be free to do as he wishes, but she will not do it as punishment for his failure.

A Child Gains from Being Given Help in the Group

Usually a child gains more from being helped in a situation than from being taken out of it, because most of the child's learning about how to live in a social group comes from the responses of other children to him. As he faces, in the reaction of others, the consequences of what he does, he learns what is acceptable and what is not. We may need to temper these consequences for him, but for the most part we can leave the child free to find his own way if the group is one of equals. We help him most when we help him discover that being with other people is fun. Then he will want to modify his behavior to fit the pattern of the group in order to belong.

When the situation is too difficult for the child, he will show us by his behavior that he needs help. Aggressive, attacking behavior is often a sign that the child feels helpless and is seeking a way out of the situation. The teacher needs to step in with the words, "I'll help you." A child will stop hitting if he sees some real hope of getting help. He can wait while the adult helps work out a solution. But he cannot be expected to trust the adult if she blames him for the diffi-culty. He must have confidence in her acceptance of him and her willingness to help. Confidence is based on past experience, and we must remember that the present experience will itself become a past experience, helping or hindering the child the next time. To con-demn a child, to blame him for his social inadequacies, will only lessen his chances of success and our chances of offering help that he can accept. He will like being with people less if we act in these ways when he is having difficulties.

Rivalry Creates Problems

One of the least helpful things that the teacher can do is to en-courage direct competition among children. Competitive situations breed ill will. Comparing children, holding one up as an example to others, is unfair to all because of the hostility it arouses. "See who will finish first," or "See how much faster Jane is dressing," or "See how quiet John is," all these comments are likely to make children like each other less rather than more. They make others appear to be rivals or competitors rather than friends.

The teacher must be aware that young children, in part because of their dependency, will be competing for her attention. Comparisons increase the rivalry they feel. She should be very careful to do nothing to increase jealous feelings. These feelings can cause real unhappiness. Often a child will misbehave at rest or at the table be-cause he wants the attention which the teacher is giving another child. His teacher must be ready to reassure him by a word or a smile that she cares about him, too.

In Spite of Conflicts Children Belong Together

Conflicts will keep arising when children are in groups because it is difficult to solve all the problems that exist when people actively play and work together. Because children are in the process of learning, they meet many situations which are beyond their limited skills to handle constructively. Even Terry could say "Let's talk it over" only when he was with children whom he knew very well. It is the teacher's responsibility to help the children understand others and themselves better, so that they can meet their own problems.

As we observe children in the nursery school, we are aware that the satisfaction they find in all activity is enhanced by the fact that other children are sharing it, just as we ourselves enjoy experiences that we can share with others. Whether children play cooperatively or merely side by side, they show us that each experience has more meaning for them because it is a group experience. Children belong together.

Kay expressed in her own way what should be our goal in group relationships. She and another child were on a walk with their teacher when they met a stranger who stopped to inquire whether the girls were sisters. "No," replied the teacher, "just friends." Kay smiled at him. "We make friends out of people at nursery school," she said.

REFERENCES

1. Gardner, D. E. M.: The Education of Young Children. Methuen, London, 1956, Ch. 2.
2. Rudolph, Marguerita: Living and Learning in Nursery School. New York, Harper & Bros., 1954, Ch. 2.
3. Stott, Leland, and Ball, Rachel Stutsman: Consistency and Change in Ascendance-Submission in the Social Interaction of Children. Child Development, Vol. XXVIII, Sept. 1957, pp. 259-272.

IV

Observing Individual Growth and Guiding It

11

In Dramatic Play

Dramatic Play Is Like Frosting on a Cake

The dramatic play which we observe taking place in nursery school has significant values for the study of human relationships. It affords us another important avenue by which we can increase our insight into what children are feeling and into how they are interpreting the situations they meet. It affords the children themselves a means of reliving and clarifying experiences and thus reducing anxiety. It is a source of fun and pleasure for them as well, like frosting on a cake!

ENCOURAGING DRAMATIC PLAY

With time, with properties, with freedom from interference, the children act out what is important to them. Because of all its values the good nursery school encourages dramatic play by careful planning.

265

Fig. 45. Sharing experiences in dramatic play. (Earl Dible)

In planning it is important that the program be flexible, so that there is a chance for dramatic play to continue once it has started. The group may be absorbed in housekeeping, in playing firemen, or in moving, over most of a morning or over most of a week or more. They need the chance for sustained play when they develop such an interest, so that they may work through all that they are thinking and feeling about the subject. Uninterrupted time is needed by children for developing their dramas—not just bits of time between scheduled activities. Supervision that is casual and unobtrusive is important, too, if the play is to have meaning to the children. They often need help but they do not need direction.

Heading the list of desirable properties which encourage dramatic play are materials for homemaking play. Dolls, doll carriages, beds, tables, chairs, dishes, an iron and ironing board and telephone are among the things which will be used. The doll family should be large and should include several "babies." In one group, the most popular doll was a baby doll with eyes painted shut as though she were sleeping. Group play is often promoted by having at least two things of a kind—two beds, two telephones, two or more doll buggies, and plenty of dishes and chairs for company. All the equipment should be simple in construction and substantial so that it can take hard usage without the need for limits to save the equipment and perhaps lessen the value of the play for the children.

The realistic quality of the play is increased if the equipment is strong enough for the children themselves to take the roles rather than relying always on the use of dolls. If a bed is strong enough to hold a child, he can use it to act out the part sometimes, and thus enter more directly into the play and gain more from it.

Variety results from the introduction of materials which can serve many purposes, such as boxes and boards. These things can be used by a resourceful group in many ways. Barrels, large and small, have many uses and even cardboard cartons will serve for a morning of play in endless ways. One group delighted in using the barrel to roll in, like the little pig in the story. A ladder and a short piece of

Fig. 46.   The home making corner. (H. Armstrong Roberts)

hose may suggest a whole fire department and all its activities. A bicycle-tire pump may be the beginning of a "gas station" where wagons and tricycles are serviced by eager attendants. Empty cereal boxes, butter cartons, cans with smooth edges, paper and string may transform a house into a store with the wagons turning into delivery trucks. "Raw materials" such as squares of bright-colored cloth for costumes bring variety into the play. The resourceful nursery school teacher will provide materials which suggest uses limited only by the imagination of the children themselves.

The Meaning of Dramatic Play

The dramatic play at nursery school centers around episodes and relationships that seem significant to the children. Through play they reveal themselves and their concepts of the world to us.

Family dramas are the ones most frequently re-enacted. Relationships of mothers and children and fathers and mothers are an almost universal theme. In their play children re-create and thus strive to clarify for themselves the grown-up world. Cooking, setting the table, washing, ironing, caring for a baby, going to the store, carrying on telephone conversations, entertaining friends, dressing up, going to the doctor, are activities which reappear day after day. Fireman, gas station man, garage man, milkman or any other occupation with which the children may be familiar are also included. These are activities which have an absorbing interest for children.

What meaning does such often repeated play have for children?

Dramatic Play Is One Way to
Handle the Problem of Being "Little"

We can be sure that children want to understand what it is like to be grown up and do grown-up things. In their play they are preparing themselves for these roles someday. Play is also one way to handle their own special problem of being "little" in a world of big people. In play they have a chance to be the big mother or father, or the important workman. They can escape from being little through identifying themselves with the "big" roles. Doing this has real value in lessening some of the inevitable frustrations of growth. Notice which child wears the holster and gun or the biggest cowboy hat.

It is likely to be a small child or a child who is unsure of his place or a child for whom being little seems especially handicapping. These appendages help him pretend that things are different.

It is usually difficult to find anyone willing to take the role of the "baby" in homemaking play unless being this baby is the only way to be accepted by sought-after playmates or unless the child's dependency needs have not been adequately met in earlier relationships. Being little usually stands for deprivation. "You can't because you're too little." Lois, who loves the pet goat at school and wishes she had one at home, says sadly, "I've never had a goat. I'm only a very little girl." Ruth looks at the clock and says, "It's eight o'clock. That's grown-up time." When someone wants to join her play she pauses, then asks, "How old are you?" The child answers, "Three," and she replies, "Only kids that are four can play here." Ruth has had her fourth birthday.

Few children are as able to accept their size as Damon is. Damon is small for his age. When Donald taunts him with "You're little. You're as little as my brother. You're only four," Damon defends himself, "I know I'm little but I'm going to have a birthday and I'll be five. You can be little and five, too." One imagines that Damon's parents had not used the phrase "You're too little to do that." Instead they had helped him feel comfortable about being just his size.

Play Makes Children Feel Less Helpless

Taking adult roles in play also gives the child the chance to feel in control of situations. He can make things come out as he would like in his dramatic play. He can be the one to put the baby to bed, to do the scolding and spanking, to make the decisions. Doing all this probably serves to relieve the sense of helplessness which sometimes overwhelms him. Things become more manageable because he can escape at times into play. He finds it easier to face the reality of his age and size, to accept being put to bed, being disciplined. Toilet training had been successfully completed for John mentioned later in this chapter. But some of the feelings built up on the process remained and came out in his dramatic play. There he was the one to impose restrictions, reprove and finally forgive.

In dramatic play the child also has a chance to drain off feeling

Fig. 47.   An engineering project.

and work through anxieties. It is significant to note how many times children play out being sick, going to the doctor, having "shots."

Play which is repeated by individuals and by groups is almost sure to have meaning for them. We need to try to understand what its meaning is if we are to offer sound help. It is probably neither accident nor perversity that makes a child knock over things or throw them down. We must remember that he himself has tumbled many times. He has been startled, and perhaps hurt, by falling in the course of learning to walk. He may recover some assurance by making other things fall, and thus reduce the threat which falls have offered to him. We know that children are frightened by sudden, loud noises and yet as soon as they are able, they pound and bang, making all the noise they can. In this way they may be better able to handle the fear they have felt. Because they can make noises themselves, they are less disturbed by noise. The child who lives with adults who disapprove of noisemaking on his part, or who consider knocking over block towers as destructive and useless play, may carry a heavy burden of unresolved fear and anxiety.

Disturbing Experiences Are Often Acted Out

Dramatic play is often an acting out of experiences which have been more disturbing or frightening to the child than anyone realizes.

Sam, for example, was withdrawn and inarticulate. He did not find it easy to enter into group play with the other children and seemed suspicious of adults. One day he was building with blocks near a group. Suddenly he turned and kicked at the tower the others were building. He was disturbed when they kicked at his in return. The teacher sat down between Sam and the group, and quietly turned the attention of the others back to their building. Sam went on with his play. Later he kicked at his own building, saying to the teacher, "Betty does this." Betty was his sister.

The teacher began to understand what his behavior meant. She interpreted for him, "You mean that when you build things, Betty sometimes knocks them down?"

"Yes," he said; "she kicks my blocks when I build." He was able to put his trouble into words.

The source of much of Sam's difficulty lay in his relationship with his young sister. He was confused and resentful about what was happening, and his conflict stood in the way of his establishing successful relationships with the group. As he acted out these feelings, he found that the adult could help him, and that other kinds of relationships were possible. He was not considered "bad" because he felt and acted this way, so that he became less troubled by the problems in his sibling relationship. He was freer to understand what play with other children might mean.

A striking illustration of the need of a group to act out an experience which had caused fear occurred in one group of four-year-olds. A piano being moved on the floor above caused a section of plaster to fall off the ceiling into their playroom. Fortunately no one was hurt, but many of the children were frightened. After this experience one of their favorite games was that of climbing up on something and throwing blocks to the floor. They called it "making the ceiling fall." They continued to play it almost daily for weeks. It was noisy and appeared "unconstructive," but their teacher realized that it was very important for them to repeat the situation again and again in play if they were to recover from the damaging effects of the actual experience. By making the ceiling fall in their play, they gradually recovered from the fear the real experience had caused them. The game disappeared, but only after weeks of play.

Play Offers an Opportunity to Drain off Negative Feelings

In their play children often act out aggressive, destructive feelings. These are the kind of feelings which create anxiety and need to be drained off. It is important to accept them in play, being sure only that the children are safe and that the impulses are under control and kept on the "pretend" level. An adult may need to remain near to "steady" a group which is acting out negative feeling as in a war game, or a fire play. It is important to the children to know that they can stop or that they will be stopped before they do real harm. Without this help the play may not serve the purpose of draining off hostility and keeping it within manageable proportion. It may only increase the anxiety of some children about their ability to handle their impulses. As adults we should have no hesitation

Fig. 48. Dramatic play is an avenue for the expression of feeling.

about making a suggestion, redirecting or limiting play which we can see is going "out of bounds."

In doing this, of course, we do not want to deny expression to negative feeling. We must avoid what is a tendency to want only "good" behavior. Here is an example. Ruth, Marilyn and Gordon are playing they are lions. Marilyn, who is an inhibited child, says, "I'm a good lion." Gordon says, "Don't eat me up." Lions fascinate him because of their dangerous possibilities. Marilyn changes her role. It's safer. "Don't eat me up," she says. Ruth boldly says, "I'm a mean lion," and chases Gordon. Then she stops and asks him, "Are you a mean lion?" When he answers "Yes," Marilyn feels braver and says, "I am, too." "Pretend you can't get us," says Ruth. Gordon answers with, "I'm going to eat you up," and at this point a teacher steps in and tells them to be "good lions" and they drop the lion play. It no longer serves a purpose for them. Marilyn, who has conformed to high standards of good behavior and has paid a price in loss of creativity, had just reached the point of joining Ruth and Gordon in daring to be a "mean" lion. The teacher's words close this avenue of escape from adult demands for Marilyn. It is interesting to get further insight into what Marilyn is seeking by watching her subsequent play. A few minutes later she climbs up high in the jungle gym and says, "This is dangerous."

Many Kinds of Feelings Are Revealed in Play

Unable to bring out feelings directly, children sometimes hide them under what they feel is the safer guise of pretending to make a joke just as adults often do, or they may pretend that they are acting a part. A three-year-old, who had been hurt and frightened repeatedly by what had happened in his world until he could not bear to face reality, used to deny that he was "Bill" and insisted that he was an "elephant." As an elephant he felt free to trample over the other children's materials, to resist the adults, and to escape from being the poor, frightened little boy that he really was. In time he grew to feel more secure with one of the teachers and sure of her support. This brought him confidence. He began to drop the role of an elephant and dare to be Bill, and take some responsibility for his own behavior.

It is always interesting to note what children consider funny, for understanding humor is one clue in understanding the kind of ad-

Fig. 49.   Properties for dressing-up include old nylon stockings.

justment a person is making. Children's dramatic play often has a humorous quality, but underneath the humor may lie disguised meanings. We must be aware that feelings of many kinds are likely to be expressed under the acceptable guise of a joke.

One child tickles another with a leaf that he is carrying. They both laugh for his gesture expressed friendliness. Another child tickles a companion with a leaf and the child objects. He senses the attacking quality which exists under the apparent playfulness of the gesture and he resents it.

It has been clearly established that dramatic play has therapeutic values for children. We need to recognize and accept this fact. Such acceptance does not imply that nursery school teachers are in a position to undertake play therapy in the more technical sense of the term. But in the nursery school we need to see that children have plenty of opportunity to play out feelings, try out roles, clarify concepts through their own spontaneous dramatizations. We can make sure that children have a chance to benefit from the therapeutic values of dramatic play.

Television is having an effect on the dramatic play of young children. Patterns appear in the child's play which are a reflection of what he has seen on the screen. In some of the portrayals of aggressive behavior on TV shows, children seem to find patterns for playing out their own aggressive feelings. While we are not sure what the effect of television may be on young children, we can be sure that it is desirable for the child to re-enact what he sees on TV shows. In this way he is doing something about what he sees, trying to understand it better and make it less frightening.

Examples of Dramatic Play and the Teacher's Role

Some dramatic play takes place when children are alone. They may talk to themselves as they play with a small family of dolls, as they build with blocks, play in the housekeeping corner or play with water.

Fig. 50. Servicing the car. (H. Armstrong Roberts)

David is playing with some small doll figures and furniture, while the teacher sits near. He talks to himself as he plays. A comfortable, happy child, his words nevertheless reveal something of the conflict all children feel because of the process of socialization. He puts the littlest doll in a bed saying, "She has to stay right in her bed. If she makes a noise I'm going to spank her little bottom—spank her little bottom—spank her little bottom." He turns to the teacher. "She's a nasty little girl because she got up and made a noise, didn't she? She's a nasty little girl. She has to go sound to sleep." He turns back to the doll and continues as if two people were talking together. "Quit doing that. I'm just going to stay downstairs all day. Shut up. It's not daytime. It's still nighttime. I want to stay up all day. Do you want to peepee or not? You're not going to peepee. Stay right in your bed." In this play David is handling some of his feelings about the training issues he has faced. He is probably reassured by the teacher's presence although she makes no comments. He feels her acceptance but she is there to steady him if the play should become too disturbing.

Here is an example of the play of two boys which seems influenced by television in the beginning but turns into a familiar picnic situation in the end.

Kevin and Michael were playing together in the housekeeping corner. After rearranging the furniture, they picked up the suitcases. Michael opened his. It was full of clothes and articles. Kevin opened his and seemed disappointed because it was empty. Michael poured some of the contents of his suitcase into Kevin's. He then proceeded to put on some dark glasses and picked up the suitcase and left. Kevin called good-by to him.

Michael came back into the housekeeping corner, saying to Kevin who was playing with a string of beads, "We're robbers. Come on, robber."

"They'll be here in seven minutes. Call the police," Kevin answered him.

Michael picked up the phone and pretended he was calling the police.

"They're coming right away," said Michael.

"Call the cowboys," said Kevin. "Come on, let's hurry; go on outside and I'll be there in a minute before the cowboys come. Go on outside, don't walk on the lawn. I'll be with you in a moment." Michael went outside the housekeeping corner.

"Come on back in; we'll eat a light supper first," Kevin said. "Hurry up, now, hurry up. If you don't want to set the table, I will," he added. (All this time Kevin was separating the plastic beads as he talked.)

Kevin told Michael to get some more silverware and put it in the suitcase. Michael made a sound like a siren.

Kevin said, "Put more silverware in the suitcase."

"Let's take the plates, too," Michael replied. He got the cups, more plates and silverware. They worked together to shut the suitcase.

"Now let's go," said Kevin and they ran out of the housekeeping corner into the adjoining room and unpacked the suitcase.

"We're having a picnic," said Kevin. Kevin filled the sugar and creamer with water. They set out the dishes. Michael had previously put a phone in the suitcase, so he took it out. They pretended to eat. Michael picked up the phone and made a call. "Let's drink some more tea," said Kevin and they did.

"Would you help me snap these beads together, Michael?" asked Kevin. "You'd better."

So Michael started putting the beads together. "You make you a string and I'll add onto mine," Kevin said.

Michael replied, "Leave a lot for me. Here I'll put some more in a cup for you and some for me." They put the beads together working very hard.

Kim came in and Michael popped up and said, "We're playing house and you can't come in."

Kevin repeated this.

Kim stood at one side watching. Kevin and Michael then packed everything in the suitcase and returned to the other room.

These boys are friends. Each makes suggestions which the other accepts. They try to fit ideas together. Although Kevin is perhaps the leader, he does not dominate. He says, "If you don't want to set the table, I will." They start with concepts which may have come from a television show and go on to what they know about, picnics and playing house. Kevin continues his interest in the beads and draws Michael in finally. They enjoy being together but they do not accept another child, Kim. Instead, they move back to where they began. One feels that they are ready to end this experience. They have participated as friends who understood and accepted each other.

The Beginnings of Group Games Develop Out of Dramatic Play

In addition to revealing feelings, dramatic play sometimes shows us how children can share experiences with each other. We see the beginnings of group games developing in their spontaneous play— forerunners of the more organized games which they will enjoy later.

When Kay and Jill played with the rings and discovered that they were "taking turns," they were developing a game with a clearly repetitive element. Group chants and play with word sounds are a form of dramatic play which comes with group consciousness. As we observe, we will see many examples of "games" appearing at the four-year level which have an "acting out" quality, characteristic of the growing ability of four-year-olds to be objective about experiences.

Here is an example of play which developed into a game and was possible because both children were secure and friendly and not defensive. They had a degree of social maturity which some four-year-olds are already beginning to achieve.

Regan was sitting in a rocking chair looking at a book. When she left to get another book, Larry came along and sat in the rocking chair. Regan returned to find him there. Without any change in her expression she walked over and sat in his lap as though it were the chair she was sitting in, and opened her book. After a second's hesitation Larry pushed her off. She took the nearest chair and smiled at him. He smiled and got up from the rocker. As she moved to take it, he rushed back and sat down in it again. She said to him, "You should let me sit in your lap." Larry smiled and half rising from the rocker said, "Now you get the chair." When Regan made a move to take it, he sat down in it again and they both laughed. They repeated this "puss in the corner" game many times. Larry would pretend to leave the chair and Regan would make a playful effort to recover it, until something else caught their attention and they left together. They seemed to have appreciated the way this "game" brought them together.

The more mature four-year-olds enjoy very simple activities in groups. Four or five children and a teacher may join hands in a circle on the grass in "ring around the rosy and we all fall down" with appropriate action. Marching becomes a group activity with a variety of instruments in the band. We need to guard against too much patterning or we may lose the spontaneous development of group feeling which holds much value for children. We should be ready to accept the non-conformists with their individual variations or the play may lose some of its meaning for the children.

As students in the nursery school laboratory, our task is to observe and interpret the meaning of the dramatic play which brings children so much satisfaction and through which they express so many of their feelings.

REFERENCES

1. Frank, Lawrence K.: Play in Personality Development. American Journal of Orthopsychiatry, Vol. XXV, July 1955, pp. 576-590.
2. Gardner, D. E. M.: Education of Young Children. Methuen, London, 1956, Ch. 4.
3. Hartley, Ruth; Frank, Lawrence, and Goldenson, Robert: Understanding Children's Play. New York, Columbia University Press, 1952, Chs. 2, 3, 4 and 5.
4. Read, Katherine H., and Wiggenhorn, M. W.: How Essential Is Play? Journal of Nursery Education, Fall 1958, Vol. 14, No. 1, pp. 4-8.

12

Through Creative Expression

Why are we interested in creative expression? What are the values in expressing ourselves creatively when so few of us are artists?

We are interested in using the nursery school laboratory to study creative expression, for one reason, because such expression can serve as a safety valve, draining off feelings which might otherwise pile up to disturb us in unrecognized ways. Doing what we feel like doing in an art form may be far less dangerous than acting that way on the highway or in a social situation. In earlier chapters we have pointed to the fact that feelings will come out, if not in one way then in another, if not in recognized forms then in unrecognized ones. It becomes important, as strains and tensions mount, for people to have avenues for draining off the feelings which might otherwise be destructive to them or to others. Art media offer an important avenue for the expression of feeling.

Fig. 51. The sight of colors and forms appearing on paper as one paints.

We are interested, too, in creative expression through art because of the satisfactions which this kind of expression may bring. These satisfactions have therapeutic values for us. There is fulfillment in expression. We are happier when we are creative. All of us have within us warm, loving feelings, a responsiveness to beauty, to laughter, and all the richness of life itself. As we find avenues for the expression of these positive feelings, we find that our expression releases the expression of these same feelings in others. These are feelings that need expression, and through expression we grow as people, or develop personality. Art is an important avenue for this kind of growth. When expression through art is blocked, the blocking limits personality growth as well, taking away the protection that comes from having a safe means of release of feeling.

Because of these values, it is essential that children have opportunities for creative expression through art media and that we recognize and protect the spontaneity of their expressions. By keeping many avenues of expression open in language, in movement, in the arts, we leave the child freer to grow as a person. We protect him against the effects of blocking and inhibitions which result when few avenues of expression are open. We help him find the satisfactions which come from expressing himself freely as a person, without fear and with confidence.

As we watch children in the nursery school, we may become more aware of the avenues of expression through art which are open to us as adults. In the nursery school we see children expressing a feeling through an art medium. But the need for expression and the values of expression may be as great for us as adults. The kind of adjustments that we are making may depend in part on whether avenues for creative expression have been blocked for us or kept open. We may need to seek ways in which we can express ourselves creatively.

Here we will only suggest some of the ways in which children express themselves in language, in music, and rhythm, in the graphic and plastic arts.

LANGUAGE

Ruth Expresses Her Feeling Through Language

Ruth is a delightfully verbal four-year-old whose spontaneity seems a gift from two accepting parents who have been able to limit her without considering her naughty. Ruth welcomes approaches by others as gestures of friendliness. She disarms the most aggressive children by her own friendliness. She expresses her feelings freely in language which it is fun to listen to.

"Wouldn't it be funny if I were an egg, or I were a tomato and someone picked me in the garden?" she laughs as the group is returning from a trip to the farm.

She feels a part of whatever she sees and identifies closely with the world around her. "I'd like to have a comb like that," she says as she looks at the rooster. Patting the setting hen she exclaims, "I'd like to be a chicken and have someone pat me like this!"

Her imagination seizes on many things and weaves them into fascinating patterns. In the spring the nursery school had two ducks and a white rabbit. Ruth gave this version of the Easter legend when she came to school one morning. "When this bunny and the ducks grow up, we can teach them to paint eggs, can't we? The ducks will have the eggs, and the bunny will paint them, and when we come to nursery school there will be painted eggs all over, won't there?"

Ruth's feelings tumble out in words, and she finds these feelings easy to handle as she creates pictures of her world through language.

Language Is More Than an Avenue of Communication

Not all children use language as freely as Ruth, but for most children language is an important avenue of self-expression, not just an avenue of communication. They use it to express the delight they feel as well as the anger and resentment. They use it without regard to any listener. A young child will chatter to himself as he plays, or he will accompany his more rhythmic activities with singing.

Cindy is swinging and she talks to herself. "I'm going to ride a horsey, a horsey, a horsey. It's going to be a real big one. I'll be big, too, 'cause I ate my breakfast this morning."

When a group of children are happy and satisfied, they talk and sing as they play even though they are not communicating with each other. Sometimes their singing is in the form of a chant, repeating sounds or words together in a rhythmic pattern. Sometimes their chanting is an expression of their delight in companionship as well as in sounds. Often these chants have an element of humor, as when Terry sang to the group, "Would you like to eat a hammer?" and the three other children replied together "No." He continued the song with "Would you like to eat a tongue?" and they chorused, "No," and so on through a long list of nonsensical questions with the group replying "No" in great delight. This is not only language expression but it is a form of group game which is beginning to make its appearance with four-year-olds as we have noted earlier.

Teachers or parents should jot down these language expressions for the light they throw on the feelings or ideas and concepts of the child, as well as for their literary interest.

Connie, for example, is playing in the sand and as she plays she talks, half to herself and half to the teacher who is sitting near. She associates many things.

"See that path? Well that's what it is. Making a dead end road. We digged it up. This is a deep road. Know what it is? A swimming pool. This is the park and here is where the cars park. I make a jumping off place. This is where they put the swimming pool. There's a little bench. The daddy and mommy and everyone can leave their swimming clothes and change clothes here. [She rubs sand on the board.] It sounds like crying. Those children cry 'cause they don't have no mommy or daddy and they can't go to bed without any supper."

Linda climbs high on the jungle gym and says: "I can climb right up here. Now look what I can do. I'm higher than mommy now. She can't catch me. Now she can, now she can't."

She expresses her delight in being up high, out of her mother's reach but not really out of reach!

Children who use language as an avenue of self-expression are not likely to be children who have been taught to recite the words of poems or songs. As in any art experience, especially in the early stages, self-expression is blocked by "patterning." The young child who speaks "pieces" may never discover the creative possibilities of speech. He may continue to depend on learning the words of others and never perceive the possibilities which language may hold as an avenue for expressing his own feelings.

Self-expression Through the Use of Language Can Be Encouraged

There are ways in which we can encourage self-expression through language, on the other hand, by giving children many opportunities to hear language which expresses thoughts and feelings that are within the level of their comprehension. Simple, well-written stories about everyday experiences with which they are familiar, and imaginative stories later such as they themselves might create, bring the medium of language expression within their grasp and yet leave them free to find their own way. Gone are the days when the frightening folk tale and the moralistic, unreal story were considered good literary fare for preschool children. Romney Gay's small books about Toby and Sue and their adventures are examples of modern books which tell of a world that the youngest children can recognize. Understanding and enjoying these stories, children are more ready to tell their own stories which grow from similar experiences. Careful selection and a generous number of books with stories and poems available for children encourage a growing interest in language expression.

Equally important in encouraging this form of expression is the fact that the teacher must be ready to listen to what the children say. She must listen, and she must show that she appreciates the children's expressions. Sometimes a child comes with a "story" to tell and finds his teacher's attention divided, with more of it going to her work of straightening up the equipment than to listening to his words. He realizes that his story has no great value for the busy teacher. He does not bring another one to her. If we are to encourage the use of language as a means of self-expression, we must listen to what the children create, and value it.

Baruch outlines some steps to take in encouraging language expression in the chapter "When Children's Words Make Poems" in her book *Parents and Children Go to School.* She points out that jotting down the expressions one hears and later reading them back to the child help him grow aware of the possibilities of creating with words. The bits of poetry or story can be read when the child asks for a story and he will gain a sense that he, too, can create things that have value. Baruch warns against requesting the child to "tell a story," for then we are likely to get products aimed to please us rather than true expression of self.

When they find a real interest shown in language expression, many children enjoy creating more and more frequently. It may be surprising how many lovely and interesting things can be recorded in any group when one listens. Children whose expression of feeling may be blocked in other ways sometimes can express themselves in words. They gain confidence in themselves through using this avenue until they gradually become free enough to use other avenues of expression, too. The more avenues for expressing feeling that an individual has, the more he will be protected against having to deal with his feelings in the dark. For some timid children, success in language expression may be an excellent way of gaining confidence and building feelings of greater adequacy which enable them to participate in more active play, as in the case of Lester described in Chapter 10.

There will be more language expression in groups where the children can participate freely in many activities. Large-muscle activities which are rhythmic, such as swinging and bouncing, stimulate language. In fact, almost any satisfying experience may find expression in language. The dramatic play which centers around housekeeping materials is often rich in its output of song and story. The teacher who sits quietly near this area with pencil and paper will record much interesting material which will give her an insight into what the children are feeling, as well as how they are using language as a means of expression.

Children are conscious of word sounds, too, and enjoy using them. As Connie uses the crayons, she talks. Holding up a red crayon, she says to Judy, "Red, red, wet your bed." They both repeat this several times, giggling together. Then Connie adds, "Rain, rain, what's your name?" They repeat this several times with obvious pleasure. Judy leaves and Connie continues, "Know what this is? A baby bat on his back!" She goes on, "Know what this is? Camel with a hammer in his hand. I saw a camel at the zoo. Camel, pamel." Connie likes words and the way they sound.

Children are also helped by putting experiences into words when the experiences have an element of fear or of discomfort. When Kay saw a girl skating as the group went on a walk, she said, "I have skates. I fall and that's all." She repeated this again and again, enjoying the words and seeming to gain reassurance from thus making the experience more objective. Perhaps next time she won't mind the "fall" as much!

Lynn, aged 4 years, 9 months, reminisces pleasantly, as he is swinging, about an experience which was not entirely pleasant.

> Last night my Daddy got a needle,
> A needle, needle, needle, needle,
> He took the sliver out of my hand,
> And it didn't hurt one bit,
> And it didn't hurt one bit,
> And I didn't cry at all.
> It didn't hurt at all.
> Last night my Daddy got a needle,
> And he stuck it in my hand
> Took the sliver out,
> And it didn't hurt one bit,
> And I didn't cry one bit,
> No, I didn't, cause it didn't hurt,
> Because he did it with a needle.
> Needle, needle, needle, needle.

When we encourage the use of language as a means of self-expression we help keep open for the child an important avenue through which he can drain off feeling, or share it with others, or find creative delight for himself. We also have for ourselves a valuable means of gaining insight into what experiences mean to the child as we listen to what he expresses through his words.

MUSIC

Music offers another avenue of expression to children which is closely related to that of language. It is an avenue which is used by children everywhere. There is significance back of the concept of a mother as a person who rocks and sings to her child. The sound of a mother's voice, the feeling tones expressed in it, the rhythm of rocking are important to a child very early in his life.

The Tones of the Human Voice Tell Us a Great Deal

The child in nursery school will respond to the tone of the teacher's voice as much as to the words she uses. He will be reassured if her tone is confident and friendly, without regard to what she says. The "music" of the voice is an important medium for communicating feeling. As teachers and parents we need to be aware of the effect that the tones of our voices have on children. We need to use with effectiveness the important tool of voice quality as we work with children.

Just as the child senses meanings through the tone quality of adult voices, so we can be alert to what the child is communicating through the tones of his voice. The high-pitched tight, rapid speech of one child, the low, only half-articulated speech of another, the strong full tones of a third, tell us a great deal about each of these children and what they are feeling. We can learn to identify more and more accurately what the voices of children reveal as we listen and observe.

Satisfying Activities Stimulate Singing

When children are happy and content, when they are engaged in satisfying activities, especially rhythmic activities, they will sing. We can encourage musical expression when we help them find satisfactions and see that they have plenty of opportunity for the kinds of rhythmic activities that they enjoy. These activities are such things as swinging, bouncing, pounding, running or pedaling a tricycle. Two swings side by side make possible companionship under simple circumstances, so that the joy of having a friend may find expression along with the joy of movement through space. Swinging and singing go together, and even a two-year-old can swing in a three-point suspension swing without needing to depend on an adult to push him. One school used a large truck inner tube for many rhythmic activities. Two or three children would sit on it and bounce, or the group would use it for a drum, pounding on it with their hands as they listened to music or set their own rhythmic patterns. When a long board is placed between two low sawhorses, bouncing may take a rhythmic pattern, too. In fact there are endless ways in which rhythm can be introduced into the experiences of children, bringing singing with it.

Dancing as well as singing will occur in many areas when children are free to act spontaneously. Running in the wind through the falling leaves, or crunching the dry leaves underfoot in a marching rhythm, rolling down a grassy slope on the first warm spring day when space and the sunshine seem to make everything burst into song and movement, imitating the movements of the swimmers seen in the pool and their splashing, these may all be experiences in movement and dance for children.

Fig. 52. Expression through song: "This is the way we wash our face."

The teacher who can sing "on the spot" and move freely to music will encourage spontaneous responses in the children. Parents may be glad to bring musical instruments they can play to nursery school, so that children will have a chance to see and hear wind, string and percussion instruments. Music belongs with activity. Singing around the piano may be fun, but it does not take the place of singing in connection with activities. There should be plenty of singing by the children and the teachers on the playground and through all the areas of play activity in the nursery school. There should be the opportunity for dancing wherever there is space and music.

Setting Patterns Should Be Avoided

We must keep in mind through all these experiences that the values that we seek are those which come with creativity. Music and dance have their greatest value for young children as avenues of self-expression. Children will use them in this way unless adults block them by offering patterns or defining limits for their use.

Setting patterns for musical expression will serve to block the use of music as a means of self-expression. If the teacher sets a pattern for a rhythmic activity by directing, "This is the way we'll play we're leaves blown in the wind" or "big tall elephants" or anything else, she is seriously interfering with the creative possibilities of the experience for the child. If, in marching, she endeavors to show the child how to keep time, to fit his response into the pattern of the music she is playing, she is blocking him in the expression of his own feeling in response to the time. The skillful teacher will, instead, adapt the music to the child's own rhythm. She will fit the music to what he is expressing, playing a running rhythm when he is running, for example. She will not say "This is music for running." She will give the children many opportunities to respond to music, but she will not attempt to dictate what their responses will be.

The Ability to Keep Time
Improves with Maturity Rather than Practice

There is evidence that ability to keep time is not improved by practice but that it depends on maturity and innate ability. At four, a child keeps more accurate time than he did at three—whether he has had training or not. One four-year-old will keep better time than another, regardless of experience, because of innate differences in ability. But if a child has been subjected to pressure to "keep time with the music," he may find less enjoyment in music experience than he might, and he may feel less adequate in this area. There are individual differences in the rate at which a child develops a sense of time, but all children enjoy rhythmic experiences—if this enjoyment has not been interfered with. The more opportunity they have to move freely, either with music or without it, the more pleasure they will find and the more release for their feelings in this form of expression.

The Ability to Sing Improves with Practice

Ability to "carry a tune" responds to training, according to what we know at present. Singing with the teacher gives a child practice, but the teacher must value singing as a means of self-expression rather than as a skill, especially with the young child. She can help him enjoy this avenue of self-expression, by bringing songs within the measure of his ability to sing them, rather than setting him difficult patterns. Children's singing voices are not high-pitched as a rule. Children usually pitch their own songs below rather than above middle A, for example. Many of their own songs are sung in a minor key, quite different from the songs that we often give them to sing. Simple, childlike songs, used in connection with activities, build skill and enjoyment of singing in the children.

The teacher with a musical background can encourage creative expression in singing in the children by jotting down the songs that the children themselves sing in their play, and playing and singing these songs back to them later, in the same way that she encourages their stories and poems. Her interest will heighten their awareness of the creative possibilities of music.

Listening Is Important

Another important experience that the nursery school can offer is that of listening to good music through victrola records or music played on the piano, the violin, the flute or any other instrument. If the teacher herself is not a musician, she can often find someone who likes children and will enjoy sharing music with them. This adds to the variety of the children's experiences with music and increases their interest. Not all children may wish to listen each time such a music experience is offered. There should be no compulsion about listening, for this does not build desirable attitudes toward music. The child who does not wish to listen can respect the needs of the listening group for quiet by playing at the other end of the room himself or playing outside. Many times curiosity about a new instrument will bring even a non-listener into the group for a time.

When a record player is used, it needs to be placed where children can listen undisturbed by others. Some children will want to listen far more often than others, and they should be free to listen without interfering with the play of other children or being interfered with themselves as they listen. With the proper physical setup, listening to music may form a large part of the curriculum at nursery school for some children at some period. There should be a place for listening, as well as for responding to music, in the program of the school.

Sometimes we find a child who spends a great deal of time listening to music—or listening to stories. He may be doing this as a form of escape from facing difficulties, such as attempting to adjust to other children in play situations. The teacher needs to recognize this situation and to take steps to encourage the child to extend his interests, giving him more support in his group relations and building up his confidence, when she meets such a case. It is important that the total pattern of the child's adjustment be understood. Music should *not* serve only as an escape.

Children Enjoy Using Many Instruments

Most children love to play the piano and many of them will go often to the piano to play and sing there, turning the pages of a favorite song book, perhaps with a friend beside them. With very little supervision children can use and enjoy the piano by themselves. Drums of all kinds and bells are fun, too. They should be freely available. Wind instruments may have only restricted use because children cannot be expected to keep from passing them from mouth to mouth. But every nursery school should have plenty of all types of sound instruments, and the children should experiment with sound freely both indoors and outdoors.

Children Find Rhythm Experiences Everywhere

Elaborate settings are not necessary for rhythm and music. In one of the wartime child care centers a group of two-year-olds was playing in the limited area available to them. They had little in the way of play materials and less in the way of stable, continued contacts with reassuring adults. Their long day at school was followed by a home experience that offered little security to most of them. In the tiny court where they played, the wind was blowing one day. It picked up some stray pieces of toilet tissue (used to wipe drippy noses) and swirled them round and round in the corner of the cement courtyard. Observing this, one of the two-year-olds suddenly began turning and whirling with the bits of paper. Several children joined her, and in that bleak corner they did a graceful dance with the bits of tissue in the wind for a few brief minutes, and then ran off, laughing.

Children who are in groups where there is plenty of expression through music have less need to drain off feeling in undesirable ways. They are likely to have fewer difficulties in working out relationships as they play together. When teachers are aware of the values which music and rhythm offer and the dangers of patterning these expressions, they can offer many experiences in these areas to children, limited only by their own talent and resourcefulness and the limits imposed by the physical environment. The children will welcome these opportunities and profit from them. They will use them in creative ways.

ART

The Process Rather than the Product Is Important

Experiences in the graphic and plastic arts offer another avenue through which individuals release their feelings and find satisfactions. It is another avenue of expression which may serve as an outlet throughout the life of the individual. Too many of us have had this avenue blocked for us by the teaching we have received at home or at school. We are convinced that we can't draw a straight line, and we probably are right. Nothing that we are likely to do will ever rate as a "work of art." But we probably could have drawn much better than we think and, more important, we could have found pleasure and emotional release in the process if we had

Fig. 53.   The feel of paint through one's fingers.

had sound teaching, or at least had been left alone. The anxious attention on the product rather than the process, the coloring books and other "patterns" which were imposed on us, have all served pretty effectively to prevent most of us from expressing ourselves through art. Few of us as adults are fortunate enough to enjoy painting and to feel better for doing it. Yet art is an important means of expression and of draining off feeling as well as a means of finding satisfaction. No avenue could be less likely to do damage to others.

As we ourselves work with children, we must try to safeguard their use of art media as a means of self-expression. For every child, art can serve as an outlet for feeling if the process is emphasized more than the product. It does not matter that there are differences in ability just as there are in music. Given an easel, paper and paint and no directions, every child will paint. For some children painting will remain an important avenue through which they can express feeling all through their lives.

How Do We Avoid Patterning?

How do we keep open the avenue of individual, creative expression?

In the first place, as we have said before, we must avoid making or setting models to be copied. We must never say, "Do it this way" or "Do it that way." Even the drip from a full brush can make fascinating patterns on the paper. Some methodical children will wipe their brushes carefully because that is the way they want to make their pictures—no drips. Others may slop on the paint, expressing their own overflowing and as yet less well-controlled feeling; while others may drip the paint deliberately on the paper as they explore the possibilities of the medium. They do not all use the paint in the same way.

Bruce puts on green paint in one big spot. Then he adds blue, then orange and then red, smearing the red up to the top of the paper. He paints so that the colors overlap with only some of the pure color showing. He puts yellow in the middle of the red and then smears black over the yellow and part of the red. He paints in a serious, intent way and covers the whole paper before he is through.

Betty picks up the brush from the jar with red paint and draws a circle. She puts red lines and dots inside the circle then smears red paint in a few places outside the circle. "All done with this one," she says. On a fresh piece of paper she begins with paint from the orange jar and dabs the bright color on the paper in one spot then uses broad, brisk strokes to paint with orange across the paper. She picks up the red brush and makes a few more strokes across the paper, covering very little of her previous work. She dabs a small amount of yellow in one spot near the corner of the paper and says again, "All done with this one."

Kay was a child for whom painting became a favorite medium for expression. When she first entered nursery school, she explored all the possible experiences with paint. The teacher watched her as she approached the easel with evident satisfaction on that first day. She painted on the paper with full strokes of brush, using all the colors. Then she touched the tip of the brush to her tongue, and stood relishing its taste. Next, she brushed it under her nose, getting its smell. Afterward she carefully painted the palm of her hand. She found out what paint felt like. She had enjoyed all the sensory

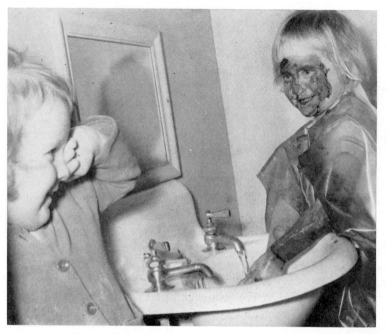

Fig. 54.   Paint feels wonderful.

experiences that paint offered, and she used it often during the time she attended nursery school.

Ginny was a child who delighted in the feel of paint on her skin. She usually ended a session at the easel by carefully painting her hands, arms and face and then, just as carefully, washing off the paint, enjoying the sight of herself in the mirror all the while.

Large sheets of paper, an easel or wall board of suitable height, large brushes and rich colors, a location relatively free from distraction, with perhaps an oilcloth on the floor to take care of the drips, give the child what he needs. For the rest we can show our interest and appreciation when the child wants these things, and refrain from asking questions about what he is painting.

The youngest nursery school children usually do not intend to represent anything when they use paints. They are using art as a means of expressing themselves, and paint as a medium whose possibilities they are beginning to explore. By the time they are three or four, they may name and describe what they are doing as they work; but we should be careful to avoid pushing them into naming their picture by asking questions. Again it is Kay who gives us a clue as she laughingly said when she put her painting away, "What is it? What is it?" The teacher asked her, "Is that what you think your mother will say when she sees your painting?" "Yes," replied Kay with a smile.

Left alone, children put down many of their experiences on paper even though they may not add titles for our benefit. A large barn burned near one nursery school in a spectacular night fire witnessed by some of the children and described vividly to the others. Following that, there were many paintings of "barns burning." Most of them were splotches of dark paint covered by red color. These pictures appeared again and again, and many of the children were probably helped to drain off the fear which the experience had roused, by expressing it in an art form and thus turning it into a more pleasant and manageable experience.

When we leave children free to use art media as avenues of self-expression, we gain a great deal of insight into what they are feeling as we observe what they paint and how they paint. It is worth reading some of the studies published in this area in order to understand better what we observe.

Finger Paints Are Valuable

Finger painting is another form of painting which allows for a great deal of valuable, spontaneous expression. The pressure to keep clean may be less damaging to a child if he has this acceptable outlet for sensory experience and for messiness. Being messy with finger paints should reduce the need he feels to be messy in other places and times, and lessen the damage he may suffer from having to limit himself at these places and times.

We learn something about the kinds of control that a child has built up as we watch him approach the new experience of using finger paints. Is his response wholehearted and immediate? Does he hesitate and withhold himself, finding participation difficult? In what ways does he enjoy the experience, by patting or squeezing or just poking the paint? Does he use a small bit of paint or a whole lot? Does he touch it with only one finger as though afraid of the sensation, or does he use his whole hand or even his arm?

Changes in the child's behavior at the finger painting table will give us clues as to changes taking place in behavior in other areas,

Fig. 55.   The fascinating possibilities of water.

too. Finger painting may help to free children for more creative activities in other areas. It offers a valuable avenue of release to children who have had too little chance for play with mud pies or for messy play at other times.

Crayons Versus Paints

For reasons of convenience many preschool children are limited to crayons in their art experiences at home. Crayons are a much "tighter" medium than paints and are used with more cramped movements. They are in fact more suited to the level of representation which belongs at a later stage in development. All this makes it especially important to supply children at nursery school with a good setup for painting. When this is done, they usually turn to crayons for expression only occasionally. The child who continues to use crayons in preference to paints is often a tense, tight child. Richard, for example, had a very difficult time adjusting to nursery school, and during this period he used crayons frequently. After he had relaxed and become more comfortable, he turned to the easel where he painted freely, seldom touching crayons again.

Clay Is Another Desirable Medium

Clay is another medium which may have many of the same values for children as finger painting. It offers a direct, sensory experience.

Children who have felt conflict over toilet training are especially likely to use it for release of feeling. The squeezing, the patting and pounding which they do with clay, serves to drain off some of the resentment at interferences which they may have been unable to express in other ways. We often see a child make something out of clay and then destroy it by flattening it on the table. It is all right to smash clay, and one can get rid of hostile feelings in this way. It is a way of "acting out" feeling which does no harm and may have much value.

Because the sensory experiences offered by clay are important, it

Fig. 56. Play which offers sensory satisfactions.

is wise to encourage handling it with the fingers rather than to introduce tools of any kind. We are less interested in products than in the process, and fingers are the best tools to achieve what we want. By making the clay wetter and thus messier, we may increase its value for some children. Some inhibited children, on the other hand, may be unable to touch clay at first if it is too wet and sticky. These children need to have clay that is only soft and moist until the barriers they have built up against messiness in any form are relaxed. The older preschool child who produces something that he values may find satisfaction in letting it dry, and later painting it. It may even be possible to fire the product to give it added value for the older child.

There is no art medium which seems more likely than clay to tempt the inexperienced adult into model making. The idea that one can play with clay, rolling it, patting it, feeling it without making anything, seems hard for even a well-intentioned adult to act on. Shades of past experiences in which it was necessary to "make" something operate against one's being content to play with the medium. We all need to be on our guard, or we will find ourselves making models that the children are only too prone to follow. Then we may have deprived them of the creative values in using clay.

Children need the "messy play" types of experiences which clay and finger painting offer. These experiences help to lessen the burden imposed on children by the effort to be clean. Because they are sensory experiences, they are deeply satisfying to children. As teachers we must look at our own attitude toward the sensory satisfaction of messy play. We may have suffered from training experiences in our own childhood so that it is hard for us to see children delighting in using sticky clay or gobs of finger paint. Unless we can accept our own feelings, we may find ourselves avoiding the use of clay or finger paint, preferring dough or plasticene. We may find ourselves depriving the child of a satisfying experience or, on the other hand, being unable to set limits when limitation is necessary because we are afraid of being too restrictive. We may need to take steps to handle our own feelings before we can offer help to the children here.

It is probably important to mention here that mud and sand and water offer many of the same values to the child as clay. We might even consider clay and finger paints as sophisticated substitutes for the mud hole or mud puddle that have brought joy to the hearts—

Fig. 57. The smell and feel of the daisies.

and fingers—of many healthy children. Children who have been denied access to mud and water have more need of experiences with clay and finger paints if they are to satisfy the desire for sensory experience which is strong in all young children. But children who use clay and finger paints will have a richer experience if they also know the feel of sand, both dry and wet, through their fingers and have dabbled in mud, and explored the possibilities of water play. A good nursery school will supply these "down to earth" experiences for they, too, are avenues of self-expression and among the most direct and satisfying open to a child.

REFERENCES

1. Andrews, Gladys: Creative Rhythmic Movement for Children. New York, Prentice-Hall, Inc., 1954.
2. Bland, Jane Cooper: Art of the Young Child: Three to Five Years. Museum of Modern Art, New York, Doubleday & Co., 1957.
3. Jones, Betty: What Is Music for Young Children? National Association for Nursery Education Publication, 1958.

4. Landick, Beatrice: Time for Music, a Guide to Parents. Public Affairs Pamphlet, No. 260, 1958.

5. Lowenfield, Viktor: Your Child and His Art. New York, Macmillan Co., 1954.

6. McVickor, Polly: The Creative Process in Young Children. Journal of Nursery Education, Vol. 14, No. 3, Spring 1959, pp. 11-16.

7. Rudolph, Marguerita: Living and Learning in Nursery School. New York, Harper & Bros., 1954, Ch. 5.

8. Sheehy, Emma: Children Discover Music and Dance. New York, Holt Dryden Co., 1959.

9. Siks, Geraldine B.: Creative Dramatics: An Art for Children. New York, Harper & Bros., 1958.

10. Sundberg, Norman: The Conditions of Creativity. Journal of Nursery Education, Vol. 14, No. 3, Spring 1959, pp. 4-10.

11. Water, Sand and Mud as Play Materials, National Association for Nursery Education Publication, 1959.

13

Working with Parents

We Need to Understand the Parent-Child Relationship

In our study of human relationships with the nursery school as our laboratory we have centered our attention on children. We have tried to understand people better through understanding the behavior of children as we see them in situations similar to those we have all experienced.

We can learn, however, not only from the behavior of children but from that of parents as we see them with their children. All of us know something about parents because we have had parents. We know that parents are people with past experiences of their own, some of which are favorable and some unfavorable to the business of building sound relationships with children. We are interested in the problems which parents must face and try to solve. We need some understanding of the parent-child relationship if we are to understand people, or if we are to be adults who can guide children with wisdom.

We Get Acquainted with Parents as They Come with Their Children

What do we see as we observe parents bringing children to nursery school? Here are some examples.

Jean and Her Mother

On their first day in nursery school Jean and her mother are obviously enjoying themselves. Jean has discovered the easel and uses the paints freely and systematically, one color after another in solid masses. She shows delight in the experience and calls her mother over to see. Her mother comes readily, interrupting her own exploration of the book corner where she has been looking over the books. She shows pleasure in Jean's painting and they smile at each other. One gets the impression of two independent people, respecting each other and confident of the bond of love between them.

Jean's mother watches the other children, appears interested in the activities that are being carried on and comments or questions the teachers as things occur to her. She is dressed comfortably in a simple dress which will not be hurt by fingers covered with paint or wet sand. She does not direct Jean's attention to objects or children. She does not attempt to tell her what to do. On one occasion when Jean is hit by another child, her mother appears to take it in a matter-of-fact way, neither approving or disapproving of the behavior. Later when Jean pushes a child down, her mother shows no special concern. She leaves matters up to the teacher. She is friendly and outgoing. In her handling of Jean's vigorous protest at leaving, she is casual, "It has been fun, hasn't it! Of course you don't want to leave but we're going now and we'll be coming back tomorrow." Jean relaxes and smiles at the teacher as they go out.

After a couple of days of visiting she and the teachers agree that Jean is ready to stay without her. Before the end of the week Jean has stayed through the whole morning and had her lunch there. In the following weeks Jean's mother often stays for a few minutes to watch. She greets the staff and the other children warmly and often shares incidents from home with the teachers. She reported with appreciation one morning that Jean had remarked, "Mother, you do have such nice kids," adding, "You know, she's right." Often she comes in slacks and sometimes she has to hurry off and does. She has a good deal to manage in a home with four children but one feels that she respects herself and doesn't expect the impossible of herself.

Beth and Her Mother

Things are different with Beth and her mother. They come on the first morning, both dressed carefully in clothes that are more for spectator than active play. The impression is confirmed when Beth starts toward the pail of water standing by the sandbox and her mother hastily removes her and leads her to another part of the playground. She calls the child's attention to specific materials and the mother's choices appear to be puzzles, books and the record player. Perhaps she might have directed the child's attention to the dolls if the housekeeping corner had not been occupied by two children who were washing dishes, and dripping water on the table and floor.

The materials which Beth's mother encourages the child to use tend to be of an intellectual type and reflect her interest in seeing the child achieve something more nearly like that which an adult might. One gets the impression that childlike behavior bothers this mother in some way. She is trying to push the child toward more grown-up things. Her expectations for the child are high. Beth keeps escaping from her mother and returning to spots where active and often messy play is occurring. She is eager and interested and seems to be asserting herself with a quiet persistence which indicates strength on her part. Her mother speaks to her without harshness and they both seem to feel real affection for one another. But there is an uneasiness in the relationship. What they each want is different and they are often in opposition even though there is no open conflict.

It takes longer for Beth to feel at home with the teachers and the children than it did for Jean. Her mother has to stay with her for more than a week and Beth does not stay for lunch until two weeks have passed. It is not really difficult for her, however, although one can sense the mother's relief when Beth is successful in staying through a complete morning. It may seem to her mother that the child has taken a long time to meet this expectation.

Tommy and His Mother

Tommy and his mother arrive on the first morning with anxiety showing plainly on their faces. They had met the teacher, visited the school on an afternoon previously, but still they do not feel at all sure of what it will be like. Tommy's mother sits down on the chair the teacher indicates is for her. When Tommy finally leaves her to explore some trucks and calls for help, she only goes to him after she asks the teacher, "Is it all right for me to help him?"

She watches him closely and only occasionally appears to notice what other children do. She quickly turns away when she observes a dispute or children coming to blows. Once another child grabbed the small truck Tommy was using. He burst into tears and rushed to his mother who holds him tightly and does not conceal her concern. One feels her disapproval of much that goes on and her uncertainty. She does not seem comfortable with the teachers and volunteers few comments. When she told about an incident, she added, "I know what I did was wrong." She seems to be passing judgment on herself and others and expects the same from them. Perhaps a school situation makes her feel this way even more than usual because childhood experiences of feeling failure and distance between herself and teachers are being revived.

For Tommy and his mother the process of adjusting to nursery school is a slow, difficult one. It is a long time before Tommy feels sufficiently at home to stay alone comfortably. He continues to get upset when something unpleasant happens and to need his mother again. She shows anxiety over what is happening and continues to need the teacher's reassurance.

These are some of the parents one sees. These are some of the parents one must learn to understand. There are many others, responding in somewhat different ways, just as each of us would have a characteristic way of meeting the situation if we were accompanying a child to nursery school.

Most Parents Look Forward to the Child's First School Experience

As we can see, the experience of having a child enter nursery school means different things to each parent. The school will offer each parent something different. The wise teacher needs to understand that the parent's feelings toward the school and the experience of having a child there may be somewhat mixed.

In bringing a child to nursery school, as we pointed out earlier, each parent is undertaking what is for her a significant experience. She is taking a step which will bring changes in an important relationship, her relationship with a child who has only recently been a baby and completely dependent on her. Now this child will quickly develop much more independence than he has had. He will have experiences in which she does not share. He will have, if he develops well, satisfying relationships with other children and also with his teachers.

Most parents look forward to the child's entry into nursery school. It opens a new period in his growth. They will, of course, need to get acquainted with the teacher and see what goes on in nursery school before they are really able to give the child the feeling that it is all right to have this experience. But after their initial uncertainty about what it will be like, they enjoy watching the spurt in growth which usually occurs. All kinds of changes appear in the child's language, his social skills, his ideas about himself and what he can do. He is no longer a baby and he now appears more sure of this. As one mother remarked, she found herself enjoying her child much more after he started attending nursery school. He seemed more like a person to her. Most parents have a real appreciation for what the nursery school accomplishes.

We Need to Help Parents Feel Comfortable at School

In the first contacts parents have with the school it is important to consider carefully what we do to make parents feel at home. Do we have a comfortable place for them to sit? Is the teacher really glad to have the parent there? Does she make a point of doing things which will make the parent feel welcome, as in stopping to point out something which may be interesting or reporting an incident which involved the child? Does she help the mother feel comfortable by making clear to her just what is expected of her—the time for coming or for leaving, which decisions are hers to make and which the teacher herself will make? Does she listen for what may be behind the question the mother may ask?

In many small but significant ways the teacher conveys a great deal to a mother in the atmosphere she creates in the school and through the informal contacts they have there. These are important because they occur so many times and also because they involve

Fig. 58. Parents may assist the teacher with groups. (Robert Overstreet)

first-hand experiences in which mother and child are participating. The parent is ready to learn when she trusts the teacher.

Some Parents Find It Difficult to Enter a Child in Nursery School

Some few parents, whose own growing-up experiences have been filled with too many conflicts, may find it hard to share with the teacher responsibility for the child and what happens to him. They may not find it easy to let the child feel that it is all right to enjoy nursery school. They may have more mixed feelings about taking a child to nursery school than most parents do. The teacher needs to be aware of the parents' feelings.

If it has been unduly important to a mother to have the child dependent on her, she may find it difficult to accept the change, difficult to accept his liking for nursery school and his readiness to leave her. It is interesting to note in this connection that it is often the father who is more in favor of sending a child to nursery school than the mother. He has less of an emotional adjustment to make than the mother. A mother's reluctance to have a child start school is easily understood and can be handled once it is accepted by both mother and teacher.

If a mother has found the care of a young child more than ordinarily difficult, she, too, may be reluctant to put him in a nursery school. She may be afraid of her own feeling of wanting to escape from the care of her child. A relative or neighbor may even remark, "People who put their children in nursery school only want to get rid of them so that they will have more time to gad about." This kind of remark reinforces what the mother fears may be true of her. She finds it hard to face her real need to have some time free from the demands that every young child makes. It is a reasonable need for parents and one for which they should make some provision. Nursery schools are a way of meeting this need while they are also meeting the child's need for independence and companionship with other children. A parent who faces and understands her feeling can accept what the school has to offer.

The difficulty a child may have in entering nursery school is likely to be directly related to the difficulty that the parent has in leaving him free to enter. Children who have had brothers or sisters in school previously usually enter more easily than those who have not, less because they themselves are familiar with the school than because their parents feel at home there. If the parent has accepted school experience for the child, the child is likely to find it easy to do the same.

Teachers Need to Be Aware of the Feelings of Parents

The parent-child relationship is one which is loaded with strong feelings. The teacher needs to be aware of these feelings. A parent's own childhood experience will condition the way he or she reacts to what happens to the child at nursery school. One parent may feel very strongly about a child's hitting or spitting and another about manners at the table or keeping clean. Another may be concerned about health matters. There are reasons for the way a parent feels and it is important for the teacher to recognize and accept the parent's feelings. The mother who wants something done immediately about a child who hits or spits may have known strict discipline herself in respect to this behavior when she was a child or at least have been taught to regard it as very naughty, and so remains afraid of it. Only gradually can she change her attitude as she gains confidence in the teacher and the school. She will be helped if the teacher can listen and can understand her attitude toward the situation. The teacher's acceptance may free the parent so that she can look at the present and judge its meaning without being as entangled by emotions from the past.

Most parents will feel strongly about matters pertaining to health, also. Frequently teachers are less alert than parents to adjusting a child's wraps to changes in temperature or activities or to avoiding drafts. They may be less concerned about wet feet or wet sleeves. Teachers are not the ones who are up at night with the sick child. They do not have the same heavy emotional investment in the child as the parent. Good parent-teacher relations are based on understanding on the part of each as to how a thing looks to the other. The inexperienced teacher must train herself to be very careful in matters involving wraps, rubbers, etc. With experience she will come to appreciate the parent's viewpoint. If she is careful, she relieves the parent of a source of anxiety and makes better relationships possible.

Lack of experience with children and lack of knowledge about them make most parents feel inadequate and unsure of themselves as parents. They are anxious about the behavior of their children. Because they feel this way they are often defensive. They expect the teacher to criticize what they do. They may react as if she had criticized them even when she says nothing. They are in need of reassurance before they can really learn to look at children as they are and learn more about children's behavior.

Parents are sometimes especially defensive when they come into a school situation. Their childhood experiences with schools may make them expect to be judged or graded, and perhaps even fail to pass the test!

Parents who are older than the average parent of a preschool child, or parents who have a background of professional experience, especially people who have been teachers of older children, are likely to feel anxiety about the behavior of their children. They have valued achievement in other areas and they now wish to achieve as parents. They may have had little in their background to help them understand and have confidence in the growth impulses of young children. They are likely to see failure for themselves in the childlike behavior of their offspring. They need reassurance from a teacher who accepts children as they are.

In all her contacts with parents the wise teacher will remember that the relationship between a parent and a child is heavily loaded with feeling, and she will respect this feeling. She will do all she can to reassure the parents and help her feel accepted in the situation of being a parent in the nursery school, just as she helps the child in the new situation. Her most important goal will be to reassure parents and give them a chance to develop more confidence in themselves and their children.

Parents' Interest in Learning Is Very Great

For parents as for children the nursery school can offer rich opportunities for learning. Parents, like children, are ready to learn at this point. They are interested in what happens to their child in his first school experience. As they come with their children, they watch the teachers and other children and parents. They see rapid changes taking place in children. They have many questions.

They have many reasons for wanting to learn. Not all the changes taking place will seem like desirable ones to a parent. Growth seldom proceeds smoothly or in one direction. They may find a quiet, docile child becoming more aggressive and defiant after he has been in nursery school for a while. He may not share his toys as willingly as he did earlier. His vocabulary may be increasing rapidly, but it may contain words which the parents find quite unacceptable. Many of the changes taking place need to be interpreted to parents. Parents and teachers need to work together, if the changes are to be integrated into a framework that can be understood by the child as well as by the parents and teachers.

LEARNING MEANS CHANGING.
WHAT IS IT LIKE TO CHANGE?

Learning involves changing, and making changes in attitudes or ways of behaving is not easy. How does it come about? How can the school help parents learn? What is it like to change an attitude or a way of behaving when you are no longer a child? One doesn't necessarily have to keep the same attitudes and ways of behaving one learned as a child.

We can understand what it is like to change if we try to think of what it has been like for us. Perhaps as we have been studying about children, we have changed in the way we feel about seeing a child playing with his food or covering his hands with paint or even hitting another child.

How did this come about? It may have happened because we had the chance to watch a skillful, understanding teacher whom we respect and like as she responds to children. We understand how she feels in these situations and suddenly we experience a change in our feelings. We have identified with her because somehow she has built a bridge for us out of the warmth and acceptance which she has communicated. This positive feeling has given us enough confidence to risk the uncertainties of change. Her example has provided the new pattern. Perhaps, also, in learning we have had some satisfying first-hand experiences with a child. We have come to care about him and this caring has enabled us to see in situations the meanings they hold for him rather than to see our previously accepted meanings. Suddenly we find that a situation looks different because we are seeing it through his eyes.

Such changes in our attitudes take place as a result of first-hand experiences, involving meaningful relationships with someone we feel cares and can give us a feeling of confidence and self-respect. People fail to change when they feel too unsure of themselves to risk the uncertainty which change brings and can find no help in a supporting kind of relationship with someone.

People who are motivated to change are helped to gain the confidence they need if they feel they have the respect of someone who is important to them. The teacher may be this kind of person. Teachers who are critical of a parent and who blame him for a child's difficulties are not going to help this parent make much change in his way of living with the child. Attitudes come out in many ways, usually unverbalized but quite easily identified by the person. Parents have a tremendous job and do it remarkably well on the whole. They usually receive little appreciation outside of their homes and little help. They resolve many difficult problems against almost overwhelming odds at times. They try to be good parents but they face many obstacles because of the demand of other jobs, community responsibilities, health, housing conditions and many other factors.

Most parents will have achieved a warm supporting relationship with their children and are able to give them help although some will have established relationships in which a great deal of fear and anxiety is apparent. These parents are in need of special help from the teacher before they can help their child as much as they themselves may want to.

Resistance to Changing Will Be Expressed in a Variety of Ways

Even when the teacher is friendly, parents are likely to show resistance to what occurs at the nursery school if it involves their acceptance of new attitudes or ways of behaving. Resistance is part of a response to changing. It is present in learning experiences and must be met and overcome or at least reduced if change is to occur.

The resistance that parents feel may be evident in unreasonable demands they make on the teacher or the school, such as bringing the child at inconvenient hours. It may be evident in their criticism of unimportant details such as a torn mitten, or in their disregard of requests from the school such as filling out a form. It may even lie back of uncritical acceptance of anything a teacher says, for in this way the parent can hold the teacher responsible. It may be shown through the indirect attacks a parent may make on what is done at school. In all these ways parents show they are resisting learning and changing. Their resistances must be faced if change is to occur. The teacher may need to say, "I have the impression there are things you don't like about what's happening." These things must be discussed.

Sometimes parents bring up criticisms directly. These criticisms should be considered carefully to see whether situations should be handled differently as well as to understand what may lie behind the criticism or complaint. It usually represents a step in growth when a criticism is expressed by the parent and accepted by the teacher and a mutual understanding reached. The teacher needs to remember that parents will have ambivalent feelings toward the school and the teacher and toward learning. Negative feelings will appear but can be changed by frank discussion and cleared away so that they do not block the growth of more positive attitudes. Resistance is an important part of learning.

What Are Our Goals as We Try to Help Parents Learn?

Our primary goal is to help parents gain more confidence in themselves as parents. With more confidence in themselves they can work out their problems in better ways.

Helping parents learn more about what children are like is another goal. With more knowledge their expectations for the child are more reasonable. They benefit from knowledge also because of the greater interest it gives them in an individual child's development. They can watch growth patterns as they unfold, reassuringly similar to those of all children yet unique and different in wonderful ways. They can treasure the individuality of their child because of increased knowledge.

Giving parents opportunities to meet and learn through sharing their concerns with other parents is another goal in working with parents. Parents gain from sharing their concerns. It is often a relief to them to know that they are not alone in facing problems. They gain this relief as well as get specific help in problem-solving by talking together. A mother in today's home is likely to be rather isolated as she cares for her children. She needs contacts with other adults who are interested in children. She finds these contacts at school, with the teacher and other parents. The cooperative type of nursery school where parents participate directly in some phase of the school's program may be of great value because of what it offers in this respect.

The Teacher Offers a Professional Relationship to the Parents

What part does the teacher play? The teacher helps the parent largely because of the kind of person she is. Her friendliness, her genuine interest in the child and his family, in all that is important to them, her acceptance of them as they are, the way in which she refrains from passing judgment on what the parent says or does mean that she is offering a relationship in which the parent can feel secure and safe to be himself or herself.

The relationship between a teacher and parent differs from the personal relationship between friends. Just as a child learns the possibilities of a new relationship when he starts to school and finds that the relationship with his teacher differs from that which he has with his mother, so the parent and teacher should discover and explore the possibilities of the professional relationship. Some teachers are unaware of these possibilities and seek only to make friends with the parents. In these cases, the teacher's own need for friendship and for closeness to people may stand in her way of developing a different type of relationship.

The teacher who can offer a professional relationship to parents must have a real understanding of herself. She must be able to recognize her own needs and feelings and the part they play in her relationship with others. She must have ways of handling these needs and feelings which leave her free to offer her interest and skill as a professionally trained person. She must be able to offer what she has in response to the parents' needs, and not to satisfy her own personal needs. She accepts the parents, but she herself does not depend on feeling accepted by the parents.

The inexperienced teacher will need to guard against becoming entangled in personal relationships with parents of the children in her group. She will want to know them as people and be a person herself with them, but she will not seek to satisfy her own need for close, personal relationships through these contacts. She will be careful never to discuss the problems of parents with others outside the professional staff. She will try to understand and learn to use wisely the professional relationship, so that she may be able to offer real help to parents.

Parents and Teachers Work Together Through—

Individual Conferences

Individual conferences represent one of the most profitable ways in which teachers and parents can share their experience. The nursery school teacher and the parent will hold many informal conferences at the beginning or end of the school day. Planned conferences will also be held where there is time to raise questions at leisure and think through problems that have arisen, when both parent and teacher can become more aware of how each may be of help to the other.

Often the first contact will be one made by telephone. Initial contacts are important even if they take place over a telephone. The parent always hangs up the receiver with some kind of feeling which will influence her attitude toward the school and will somehow be conveyed to the child.

The next contact will probably be a conference between the teacher and parents. In most cases the first conference takes place without the child. It is very desirable but not always possible to have the conference with both mother and father. The parents have a chance to become acquainted with the teacher and she has a chance to begin to know them. She will explain the general policies of the school, its regulations such as those in regard to health or to fees, the steps to be taken in entering school. She gives them a chance to raise questions and encourages them to talk about the child. Together they try to understand what the experience may mean to him and the roles they each will play in it. She will try in this first conference to create an atmosphere in which communication is easy so that future conferences will come as a matter of course.

If the teacher is to understand the child, she will need more than one conference. The parents, too, are almost sure to need additional conferences before their uncertainties are cleared up and they are confident of what the school may achieve for them and their child. In these conferences the teacher keeps in mind her goals for working with parents, those of helping the parent gain assurance and self-confidence. Problems will come up for discussion. The teacher helps the parent approach problems, not by giving an answer, but by pointing out possible factors involved and perhaps suggesting several possible solutions. The parent may select a solution from those suggested by the teacher, but it will only work in the end if he makes it his own. He knows the child, the situation and what he himself can do.

The responsibility for solving a problem belongs to the parent, and the teacher should not attempt to take it over, any more than she should solve the child's problems for him. She only tries to help the parent to solve his own problem through listening to him, asking questions to clarify a point or suggesting factors which may be related. She may point out the possible meaning of a course of action and share experiences of others or of her own which are similar.

But the experienced teacher does not offer advice or pass judgment. If she is wise, she knows that there is no one "right" answer. Her interest and sympathetic understanding help the parent. The parent is also helped if the teacher is not anxious, but seems to feel sure that there is a solution even if it takes time to find it.

Every teacher is helped if she has had some training in conference methods. She also needs the opportunity, especially as a beginning teacher, to discuss the conferences she has with a professional person, such as a supervisor or a consultant. She learns from analyzing her actual experience and identifying the meanings in both her responses and those of the parents. In-service training is needed here. Only a beginning can be made in learning as a student.

At intervals while the child is in school and certainly before he leaves, the parents and teacher will want to confer and evaluate his progress. As they look at what is happening, and pool their thinking about him, they may see new significance in what he does and find new suggestions for helping him as well as gain new appreciation for what he is like. Such evaluation is well worthwhile.

Home Visits

Home visits present another avenue for working with parents. The teacher gains a great deal from being in the child's home and observing the relationship of the child at home with his mother and father. It deepens her understanding of him and of his parents. What is the atmosphere of the home? Does she feel relaxed in it? Or is she uncomfortable? Is the mother able to let the child participate in activities? Are her expectations for him reasonable? Is there a difference between the demands the mother and the father make on the child? Finding some answers to questions like these will help the teacher understand the child better.

For the child the visit of his teacher is very important. She is giving him a special experience, showing she values him and his home. The visit of the teacher has some of the same meaning for the parents. It shows them that the teacher cares enough to come to their home. Even though a parent may feel somewhat anxious and strained, she may still appreciate the visit and her relationship with the teacher should be a more comfortable one after a visit. It should be easier for her to bring up important questions and for the teacher to understand what these questions mean to the parent.

Observation at School

Another important avenue for learning for parents is the opportunity they have to observe in the nursery school. Parents often gain reassurance from spending time in observation at the nursery school. They see the child as more like others instead of different, as they perhaps feared. They see children under favorable circumstances.

They find suggestions for kinds of play materials, ways of handling situations. Often they will need interpretation by the teacher of some of the things that they observe, explanations as to why a situation was handled one way instead of another and what one bit of behavior may mean. With interpretation, the parent who is facing and accepting her job as a parent will deepen her insight and grow more successful and satisfied. Observation at the nursery school makes many things that children do seem more acceptable and less annoying.

The teacher should encourage parents to observe and give them a chance to talk with her about what they see. She can help by interpreting what happens. If the school provides adequate observation space, such as a booth with or even without a one-way vision screen, parents will find observation easier.

Parent Meetings

One of the important contributions which the nursery school makes in its work with parents is the opportunities it gives them as parents to have contacts with other parents. These contacts are not the same as those in clubs or at social events. At the nursery school they meet as parents. They are there because they all have children. Their concern is with children. Talking about children and their common problems is not just an aside but the main purpose in getting together. Moreover, as a group they have children at the same stage of development. They are all concerned with nursery education. Each has taken a step in the process of giving a child more independence. With the support of other parents a parent may find it easier to let the child be free. Since many adults live far from their own childhood families, they cannot turn to their parents and may be relatively alone in facing uncertainties which they hesitate to share with friends. They are in need of the "extended family experience" which the nursery school offers. It lightens some of the drudgery which is part of caring for children if experiences can be shared in conversations with people who have the same interests.

Group experiences may be of many kinds. Most schools have general group meetings. Held in the evening, they are for mothers and fathers. The more chance for parent participation, the more the individual parent will gain. Techniques can be used to bring about participation even when groups are large.

If there is a speaker, his talk can be followed by a question period or the group may break up into "buzz" sessions so that everyone has a chance to raise questions. There are many films which present good material on child development and family life. Discussion can follow the film showing. Reading one of the plays* written to bring out points relating to family problems is an excellent basis for discussion. The parents who read the play or act in it will usually gain a good deal. Spontaneous acting-out of incidents as a way of presenting a situation for discussion is another device which may stimulate thinking and sharing, especially if after the problem is presented, groups try out different solutions in this practice situation to see how they seem to work.

The whole matter of planning a series of programs for the year should be done in such a way as to bring out the real interests of the group and provide for participation. If the parents share responsibility with the staff for making plans or take on the responsibility themselves, the experiences are likely to come closer to what parents really want and thus be more valuable for them.

Sometimes parents bring up particular situations for discussion. It is only natural that parents will wish to discuss the particular problem of their own child but the discussion leader will need to keep relating the specific example to general principles or group interests. "Is this a problem which occurs frequently?" "Have some of you met this problem in other types of situation?" "Shall we look at reasons why this behavior appears in children just at this point in their growth?" Parents may be encouraged to bring in *typical* situations for discussion at a meeting.

It may be helpful to have some agreement before discussion starts on the length of time any one person should talk and what the group wishes to do about handling questions on personal problems. It is seldom wise to have a discussion of more than an hour and a half. Frequently small groups will stay to talk more informally about points which have been raised and this is a valuable part of the experience for them.

Other types of meetings include discussion groups held when the children are in school. These may be informal "coffee hours" with discussion led by someone on the staff at which parents bring up questions, or they may be planned to cover some definite subject.

* American Theatre Wing Community Plays, distributed by the National Association for Mental Health.

There are also "work meetings" in which parents and teachers repair equipment and talk as they work.

A lending library with books and pamphlets is useful to parents as is a bulletin board where teacher and parents can share things which have stimulated their thinking.

Parent Participation in the School

Parents will learn a good deal by participating in the program of the nursery school itself. They may help by providing transportation on trips. They may help by enriching the children's experiences through things they may bring—a picture, a bird's nest found on the way to school, or by their skills as in playing an instrument like a violin or flute or saxophone. Fathers especially are welcomed for what they can bring or do. Seeing the variety of responses children give broadens the parent's experience and makes him more sensitive to the responses of his own child, and often more appreciative of him. He picks up ideas, not only for equipment and activities but for ways of guiding interests.

Many parents are participating as assistants to the teacher in nursery schools, especially those which are operated as parent-cooperative schools. In doing this they have rich opportunities for learning provided the situation is a good one. To ensure its being a good situation parents need to have a general knowledge of principles of child development and of nursery school philosophy. They also need an adequate orientation in the procedures of the program as it is carried on in the particular school where they will be sharing responsibilities with a trained teacher. They need to attend regular meetings in which there is discussion of current problems, review and planning experiences for the children and a chance to bring up questions, especially those about their own uncertainties or resistances. In other words they need the same opportunities the professionally trained staff members need if the experience is to be a learning experience.

In addition to the problems faced by teachers ordinarily, parents face the added problem, and perhaps the added motivation for learning, of protecting and strengthening the relationship with their own child while they are with him in the nursery school situation. They must function in the role of a parent while also filling the role of teacher. This may be a formidable task and in many cases the parent faces it without realizing what is involved and without professional help readily available. Since both the need to learn about children and provide them with sound group experience and the interest in learning on the part of parents is great, we may hope that better programs for parent participation will develop steadily. Perhaps a much more imaginative approach is called for than any we have yet tried.

As Chisholm has written, "The role of the parent in relation to the upbringing of a child is perhaps the most important thing that happens in our culture."[*] He adds that we have implemented as yet very little of the knowledge we have about child growth and development and that one of the greatest dangers the young child faces is the danger of "running into the certainties or rigidities of his parents, but there is plenty of danger in that for most children."[†] Someday nursery schools may provide far more effective ways of helping parents carry on a role which has so much significance culturally and personally.

What Would Any One of Us Want to Find in a Nursery School to Help Us Learn?

Perhaps a good way to think about these opportunities is to ask ourselves, "What would we like to find in a nursery school in the way of help with our task of being parents?"

There is an increasing emphasis on education for parenthood today as we recognize the tremendous importance of the parent-child relationship in personality development. Rabinovitch has suggested that family life centers may develop around nursery schools with teaching being done there for parents and professional workers.

The nursery school teacher is in a key position to help parents with the problems they face. She can often reassure parents and give them a better chance to develop confidence in themselves and their children. She can help the parent value what the child does and is. She can help the parent see the relation between a single bit of behavior and the total growth pattern. In this way she may help the parent gain a perspective and yet keep a sense of closeness to his

[*] Chisholm, Brock: Prescription for Survival. New York, Columbia University Press, 1957, p. 26.

[†] Ibid.: p. 40.

child. She will not stress techniques, or ways of doing things with children. Techniques are not enough, however good they may seem to be. They may even interfere with spontaneous relationships. Behavior expresses feeling and a technique is good only when it is a genuine expression of a favorable feeling. It isn't so much what people do as how they feel about what they do that is important.

As the teacher works with different parents, she will strive to understand the differences in their feelings. She will gain much in working with them which will help her in her own understanding of the children. She in turn may help increase their acceptance of their children, so that both parents and teacher can move toward practices which will make possible the optimum health of the child, physically, socially and emotionally. Working together, parents and teachers will be helped to find the satisfactions which come with confidence, skill and understanding.

REFERENCES

1. Behrens, M. L., and Ackerman, N. W.: The Home Visit as an Aid to Diagnosis and Therapy. Social Casework, Vol. 37, 1956, pp. 11-19.
2. Beyer, Evelyn: Sharing—a New Level in Teacher-Parent Relationships. National Association for Nursery Education Bulletin, 1954.
3. Clark, Eileen: A Nursery School Procedure. New York, The Dalton Schools, 1949, Part 2.
4. English, O. Spurgeon, and Foster, Constance J.: A Guide to Sucessful Fatherhood. Chicago, Science Research Associates, Inc., 1954.
5. Fraiberg, Selma: Counseling for the Parents of the Very Young Child. Social Casework, Feb. 1954.
6. Freud, Anna: Safeguarding the Emotional Health of Our Children: An Inquiry into the Rejecting Mother. Child Welfare League of America, New York, 1955.
7. Gardner, D. E. M.: Education of Young Children. Muthuen, London, 1956, Ch. 5.
8. Hymes, James L.: Effective Home-School Relations. New York, Prentice-Hall, Inc., 1953.
9. Kahn, Robert L., and Connell, Charles F.: The Dynamics of Interviewing: Theory, Technique, and Cases. New York, John Wiley & Sons, Inc., 1957.
10. Knowles, Malcolm: Role Playing at Home. Adult Leadership, Nov. 1953.
11. Langdon, Grace, and Stout, Irving: Teacher-Parent Interviews. New York, Prentice-Hall, Inc., 1954.
12. Leonard, Edith; Vandeman, Dorothy, and Miles, Lillian E.: Counseling with Parents. New York, The Macmillan Co., 1954, Chs. 3-8.
13. Moore, Sallie Beth, and Richards, Phyllis: Teaching in the Nursery School. New York, Harper & Bros., 1959, Part 3.
14. Pearson, Gerald J. J.: The Most Effective Help a Psychiatrist Can Give to the Teacher. Orthopsychiatry and the School, edited by Morris Krugman. New York, American Orthopsychiatric Association, Inc., 1958, pp. 3-22.

15. Slavson, S. R.: Child-Centred Group Guidance of Parents. New York, International Universities Press, Inc., 1958.
16. Strauss, Bert, and Strauss, Frances: New Ways to Better Meetings. New York, The Viking Press, 1955.
17. Winnicott, D. W.: Mother and Child: A Primer of First Relationships. New Yolk, Basic Books, Inc., 1957.

14

Accepting
Our Responsibility

All through this book we have been looking for ways to increase our understanding of children. We have discovered that observing them will teach us a great deal about human behavior. We have discovered that if we are to handle children wisely we must understand something about ourselves. The kind of people we are influences what we do for children.

The longer we study, the more we appreciate the complexities of human behavior—the more we hesitate to propose ready-made formulas for solving problems or set standards as to what a child ought or ought not to do in a situation. We realize that as yet we know only a little of all that we need to know about people.

We have taken a big step forward when we have learned to *observe* children, to recognize the *uniqueness* of each individual, to search for the *meaning* back of an act, *to accept the child as he is* and *to have confidence in his growth impulses.* We have taken a big step when we have learned to make our contribution to the child through reducing the difficulty of the problems he must face, through enriching the experiences he has and through helping him find avenues for creative satisfactions, rather than by depending on admonition and interference. We have also taken a big step when we can assume responsibility for defining and maintaining limits for the child's behavior with confidence because we understand his developmental needs and his level of readiness.

We need all the preparation for parenthood that is available to us. It is perhaps the most important profession that any of us will undertake. As one writer says, "The single most important thing in human cultural behavior is literally and specifically the way we bring up our children."* It is important because the kind of human beings we bring up will determine the kind of world we have. Perhaps one of the hopeful things is that we are now sure that we can change so-called "character structure." We cannot honestly shrug our shoulders and put the blame for what happens in the world on "human nature." The responsibility belongs to those of us who bring up children.

As students and teachers and parents we must accept the challenge put by Chisholm, "Dare any of us say that he or she can do nothing about the desperate need of the world for better human relations?"†

REFERENCES

1. Chisholm, Brock: Prescription for Survival. New York, Columbia University Press, 1957.

APPENDIX

Some Recent Books in the Field of Nursery Education

1. Barnouw, Elsa, and Swan, Arthur: Adventures with Children in Nursery School and Kindergarten. Thomas Y. Crowell Co., 1959.
2. Fraiberg, Selma: The Magic Years. New York, Scribners, 1959.

* LaBarre, Weston: Wanted: A Pattern for Modern Man. Reprinted from Mental Hygiene, April, 1949, by National Committee for Mental Hygiene (20 cents).

† Chisholm, Brock: Social Responsibility. Science (Jan.) 1949, p. 43.

3. Gardner, D. E. M.: The Education of Young Children. Methuen, London, 1956.
4. Hymes, James L.: Before the Child Reads. Evanston, Illinois, Row, Peterson & Co., 1958.
5. Lambert, Hazel: Teaching the Kindergarten Child. New York, Harcourt, Brace & Co., 1958.
6. Leavitt, Jerome E.: Nursery-Kindergarten Education. New York, McGraw-Hill Book Co., 1958.
7. Moore, Sallie Beth, and Richards, Phyllis: Teaching in the Nursery School, New York, Harper & Bros., 1959.
8. Moustakas, C. E., and Berson, M. P.: The Young Child In School. New York, William Morrow & Co., 1956.
9. Rudolph, Marguerita: Living and Learning in Nursery School. New York, Harper & Bros., 1954.
10. Sheehy, Emma: The Fives And Sixes Go to School. New York, Henry Holt & Co., 1954.
11. Stone, Dena C.: Children and Their Teachers. New York, Twayne Publishing Co., 1957.
12. Taylor, Katherine W.: Parent Cooperative Nursery Schools. New York, Bureau of Publishers, Columbia University, 1954.
13. UNESCO: Publication No. 9 (1953), Problems in Education—"Mental Hygiene in the Nursery School."
14. Wolffheim, Nelly: Psychology in the Nursery School. (Translated by Charles L. Hannam) New York, Philosophical Library, 1953.

Some Recent Books in the Field of Child Development

1. Almy, Millie: Child Development. New York, Henry Holt & Co., 1955.
2. Breckenridge, Marian, and Murphy, Margaret: Rand, Sweeny and Vincent's Growth and Development of the Young Child (6th edition). Philadelphia, W. B. Saunders Co., 1958.
3. Hurlock, Elizabeth: Child Development. New York, McGraw-Hill Book Co., 1956.
4. Josselyn, Irene: The Happy Child: A Psychoanalytic Guide to Emotional and Social Growth. New York, Random House, 1955.
5. Murphy, Lois B.: Personality in Young Children. (2 vols.) New York, Basic Books, Inc., 1956.
6. Mussen, Paul H., and Conger, John: Child Development and Personality. New York, Harper & Bros., 1956.
7. Stone, L. Joseph, and Church, Joseph: Childhood And Adolescence. New York, Random House, 1957.
8. Strang, Ruth: An Introduction to Child Study (4th edition). New York, The Macmillan Co., 1959.
9. Watson, Robert: Psychology of the Child: Personal, Social and Disturbed Child Development. New York, John Wiley & Sons, 1959.

Other Books About Young Children

1. Brody, Sylvia: Patterns of Mothering. New York, International Universities Press, 1956.

2. Robertson, J.: Young Children in Hospitals. New York, Basic Books, Inc., 1958.
3. Sears, Robert R.; Maccoby, Eleanor E., and Levin, Harry: Patterns of Child Rearing. Evanston, Illinois, Row, Peterson & Co., 1957.
4. Soddy, Kenneth: Mental Health—Infant Development. (Proceedings of the International Seminar held by the World Federation for Mental Health at Chichester, England). New Yolk, Basic Books, Inc., 1956.
5. Winnicott, D. W.: Mother and Child: A Primer of First Relationships. New York, Basic Books, Inc., 1957.
6. Winnicott, D. W.: The Outer World of Childhood, New York, Basic Books, Inc., 1957.

Index

329